331·872

RN 6747

6644

below.

Shopfloor Politics and Job Controls

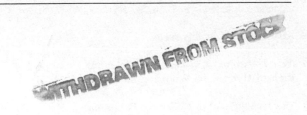

Warwick Studies in Industrial Relations
General Editors: G. S. Bain, R. Hyman and K. Sisson

Also available in this series

New Technology and Industrial Relations
Richard Hyman and Wolfgang Streeck (eds)

The Management of Collective Bargaining
Keith Sisson

Conflict at Work
P. K. Edwards

Managing the Factory
P. K. Edwards

Dismissed: A Study of Unfair Dismissal and the Industrial Tribunal System
Linda Dickens, Michael Jones, Brian Weekes and Moira Hart

Consent and Efficiency
Eric Batstone, Anthony Ferner and Michael Terry

Unions on the Board
Eric Batstone, Anthony Ferner and Michael Terry

The Changing Contours of British Industrial Relations
William Brown (ed.)

Profiles of Union Growth
George Sayers Bain and Robert Price

The Social Organization of Strikes
Eric Batstone, Ian Boraston and Stephen Frenkel

Shop Stewards in Action
Eric Batstone, Ian Boraston and Stephen Frenkel

Trade Unionism under Collective Bargaining
Hugh Armstrong Clegg

Shopfloor Politics and Job Controls

The Post-War Engineering Industry

Edited by
Michael Terry and P. K. Edwards

Basil Blackwell

First published 1988

Basil Blackwell Ltd
108 Cowley Road, Oxford, OX4 1JF, UK

Basil Blackwell Inc.
432 Park Avenue South, Suite 1503
New York, NY 10016, USA

British Library Cataloguing in Publication Data
Shopfloor Politics and Job Controls
  1. Great Britain. Industrial relations. Role
  of shop stewards
  I. Terry, Michael, *1948–* II. Edwards, P.K.
  (Paul K.), *1952–*
  331.87'33

  ISBN 0-631-15979-7

Library of Congress Cataloging in Publication Data
Shopfloor Politics and Job Controls

  Bibliography: p.
  Includes index.
  1. Shop stewards—Great Britain. 2. Industrial
relations—Great Britain. I. Terry, Michael, 1948–
II. Edwards, P.K. (Paul K.)
HD6490.S52678 1989 331.87'33 88-14658
ISBN 0-631-15979-7

Typeset in 10 on 11½ pt Times
by MHL Typesetting Ltd, Coventry
Printed and bound in Great Britain by Bookcraft Ltd, Bath, Avon

This book is dedicated to the memory of Eric Batstone

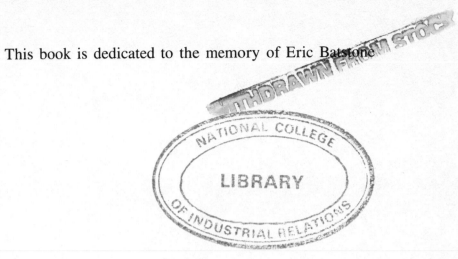

Contents

Contributors   ix
General Editors' Foreword   xi
Preface   xiii

1 **Introduction: Historical Analyses and Contemporary Issues**   1
   Michael Terry

2 **The Development of Shop Steward Organization: Coventry
   Precision Tools, 1945–1972**   24
   Michael Terry

3 **The Changing Face of Conflict: Shopfloor Organization at
   Longbridge, 1939–1980**   53
   Steve Jefferys

4 **Management Control and Labour Quiescence: Shopfloor
   Politics at Alfred Herbert's, 1945–1980**   84
   Ken Grainger

5 **Craft Unionism, Job Controls and Management Strategy:
   'Premier Metals', 1955–1980**   116
   Hugh Scullion and P. K. Edwards

6 **Job Controls and Shop Steward Leadership among
   Semiskilled Engineering Workers**   150
   Jacques Bélanger and Stephen Evans

7 **Wage Strategy, Redundancy and Shop Stewards in the Coventry Motor Industry** 185
John Salmon

8 **Conclusions: Another Way Forward?** 212
P. K. Edwards and Michael Terry

Bibliography 235
Index 242

Contributors

Jacques Bélanger, Associate Professor, Department of Industrial Relations, Laval University, Quebec.

P. K. Edwards, Principal Research Fellow, Industrial Relations Research Unit, University of Warwick.

Stephen Evans, Senior Research Fellow, Industrial Relations Research Unit, University of Warwick.

Ken Grainger, Doctoral Student, Department of Sociology, University of Warwick.

Steve Jefferys, Senior Lecturer, Department of Economics, Manchester Polytechnic.

John Salmon, Senior Lecturer, Department of Management, Manchester Polytechnic.

Hugh Scullion, Lecturer, Department of Industrial Management, University of Newcastle.

Michael Terry, Lecturer, School of Industrial and Business Studies, University of Warwick.

General Editors' Foreword

The University of Warwick is the major centre in the United Kingdom for the study of industrial relations, its first undergraduates being admitted in 1965. The teaching of industrial relations began a year later in the School of Industrial and Business Studies, and it now has one of the country's largest graduate programmes in the subject. Warwick became a national centre for research into industrial relations when the Economic and Social Research Council (then the Social Science Research Council) located its Industrial Relations Research Unit at the University. Subsequently, in 1984, the Unit was reconstituted as a Designated Research Centre attached to the School of Industrial and Business Studies. It continues to be known as the Industrial Relations Research Unit, however, and now embraces the research activities of all members of the School's industrial relations community.

The series of Warwick Studies in Industrial Relations was launched in 1972 by Hugh Clegg and George Bain as the main vehicle for the publication of the results of the Unit's projects, as well as the research carried out by staff teaching industrial relations in the University and the work of graduate students. The first six titles of the series were published by Heinemann Educational Books of London, and subsequent titles have been published by Basil Blackwell of Oxford.

This book marks a further stage in a long tradition of Unit work on shopfloor industrial relations. During the 1970s and early 1980s major factory-based studies of piecework bargaining, shop steward behaviour, and industrial conflict were conducted. These generally did not explore the historical roots of the practices that were investigated. A different strand of writing, focusing on the long-term development of labour relations and giving particular weight to managerial labour control policies, has emerged recently. A problem with this later work has been the concentration on the level of the industry or a few large firms, the broad sweep of the analysis tending to mask the detail of relations at the point of production. This book brings together the methodologies of the factory case study and historical analysis.

Five of the chapters are case studies of single factories, providing rich accounts of the development of shop steward organization and job controls and relating these to changes in competitive conditions and managerial behaviour. Each draws on detailed investigation of the plants concerned. Taken together, they give a unique picture of the growth of shopfloor industrial relations during the key period from 1945 to 1970, when the alleged problems of restrictive practices, unofficial strikes and militant shop stewards became a national issue. A sixth chapter focuses on a major issue of the time, redundancy, and compares managerial and union policies in the motor industry. The book's editors have written introductory notes to each chapter, in order to draw out its key features and its parallels with other chapters. Their substantial introductory and concluding essays set the case studies in context and analyse their implications for some major debates.

The book is thus much more than a collection of case studies. Its coherent analysis throws new light on such vexed questions as the origins and nature of shopfloor job controls, relations between shop stewards and union members, and the effect of workplace practices on productivity. The editors also argue in their concluding chapter that the pattern of shopfloor relations analysed in the book did not lead inevitably to low productivity and job loss. It contained within it an alternative in which craft traditions could have been developed instead of becoming the focus of confrontation between unions and managements. Hence, they conclude, the demise of manufacturing, and with it the weakening of steward organization, were neither inevitable nor as closely related as is sometimes alleged. This argument is as important in assessing the current state of British industrial relations as it is in the reconstruction of the past.

George Bain
Richard Hyman
Keith Sisson

Preface

This book draws together research material collected at different times for different purposes. It grew out of a recognition that there was a substantial amount of valuable material which was unlikely to be written up unless a vehicle was available. As work proceeded we became increasingly convinced that there were some important common themes tying together the various contributions, and feel that, despite its origins, the analysis offered by the book is a coherent one. We hope that in articulating such an analysis we have not done violence to the ideas of our contributors. We are very grateful to them for participating in the project, particularly since they all have many other demands on their time. As well as their intellectual interests they share close links with the University of Warwick. Steve Jefferys was a PhD student in the Industrial Relations Research Unit; Ken Grainger is completing a PhD in the Sociology Department; Hugh Scullion worked in the Unit for five years; Steve Evans is currently a Senior Research Fellow here; and Jacques Bélanger and John Salmon are former PhD students. The Unit established a reputation in the 1970s for detailed case studies of workplace industrial relations, and the present volume adds an historical dimension to this work.

A leading contributor to the Unit's work in the area was Eric Batstone, whose books (jointly authored with Ian Boraston and Stephen Frenkel) *Shop Stewards in Action* and *The Social Organization of Strikes* are widely acknowledged as path-breaking studies. Eric died suddenly in June 1987, so it is particularly fitting that we should dedicate this book to his memory. We are personally indebted to him for his example, advice and guidance over the years and, in the case of Michael Terry there was a period of close collaboration in a joint research project. The subject of shop stewards was one which Eric made his own, and anyone working in the area is indebted to him. Indeed the Unit as a whole owes a great deal to his commitment to scrupulous research.

Eric saw his work as contributing to the improvement of the lot of working-class people. We hope that, in a small way, this book can help in this by drawing attention to the dedication of those men and women who worked to build shop steward organizations in the 1950s, 1960s and 1970s. The task could be costly, as workers could lose earnings by taking up a steward's job and often ran the risk of managerial disfavour and even the sack. Much of the work, moreover, was not heroic but involved the difficult and barely appreciated job of pursuing grievances, attending meetings, and keeping an organization going. Our contributors acknowledge their individual debts to people who have helped with the research. We would like to add a wider note of appreciation to an often misunderstood group of people who made a remarkable contribution to the history of trade unionism in this country. We are also grateful to the editors of this series for their help and advice in bringing together this collection of essays.

Michael Terry
P.K. Edwards

1

Introduction: Historical Analyses and Contemporary Issues

Michael Terry

The subject matter of this book is shopfloor industrial relations in Midlands engineering factories in the period roughly between the end of the Second World War and the late 1970s. The significance of the subject, the dates and the industry selected will need little justification for most students of British industrial relations. In the late 1960s, Midlands engineering was seen by some as characterizing in extreme form developments in industrial relations typical of Britain as a whole. Thus, for example, the authors of the Donovan Report were accused by some of reducing the whole of British industrial relations experiences to those found in large engineering factories, many of which were to be found in the Midlands at that time (Turner, 1968: 351). Critics of the Report argued that the 'two systems' analysis presented by Donovan could only be found in such companies, if anywhere. Others, however, argued that the engineering 'model' constituted a particular form of union organization and industrial relations practice towards which other industries were likely to converge. In this way the 'Midlands engineering stereotype' became a dominant paradigm within industrial relations discourse towards the late 1960s.

But this preoccupation was not just coincidence. The Donovan Commission had been asked to investigate trade unions at a time of political and public concern over high levels of unofficial strikes, increasing wage drift, and increasingly poor economic performance in Britain's leading manufacturing industries. At that time, engineering was still paramount among them, and these alleged ills were seen as particularly prevalent in that industry, largely because of its particular industrial relations practices. The Donovan Commission undertook a great deal of research but, given constraints of time and resources, it could not undertake detailed historical study of the institutions it was trying to understand. Some commentators (e.g. Crossley, 1968) argued at the time that this was a major weakness in the Report. Twenty years after its publication this volume is filling that gap.

Earlier path-breaking work has been done in this area most notably by Tolliday (1985, 1986), whose work is cited frequently throughout this text. Our work builds on his, especially with regard to the Alfred Herbert company, which features in his work and in the present volume. Our studies provide both greater depth and breadth. The combination of access to copious management and union records, and interviewing, enables us to set out detailed and precise reconstructions of the development of plant-level industrial relations, and the range of companies extends outside the well-charted area of motor vehicles into a broader range of engineering (although all except one of our companies either made cars or supplied car components).

Our restricted choice of industry, region and time is deliberate, and not only in relation to the points made above. The restrictions provide a common core to the studies that enable some comparisons to be made and conclusions to be drawn. Thus, for example, the companies share certain characteristics of manual workforce composition, with skilled groups of workers performing broadly similar tasks in many cases. The industrial and regional concentration means that product and labour markets, important in understanding shopfloor developments, are not dissimilar between the companies covered. Finally, the trade unions involved in most cases are often the same, dominated by the Amalgamated Engineering Union (AEU) and the Transport and General Workers' Union (TGWU). The characteristic 'mix' of craft and general unions and their developing relationships provide a further common theme.

This volume brings together case studies by authors who share a common interest in the present subject. In several instances the chapters are based on material collected during the course of fieldwork research into contemporary issues and which did not fit easily into those accounts. (These chapters include those in which the company is identified pseudonymously, reflecting undertakings of confidentiality given at the time of the research.) The project grew out of a realization by the editors that a rich supply of unpublished material existed and that a book of this kind would provide an opportunity to publish detailed historical case studies for which no other obvious outlet existed. We have tried to ensure that all the chapters address certain common themes, such as the timing of the rise of shop steward organizations, their internal politics, and their dealings with management, but otherwise we have encouraged individual authors to concentrate on topics of special interest to them, or with particularly rich data. This has resulted in chapters which share common preoccupations while displaying differences in both the level and the focus of analysis.

The remainder of this chapter provides a detailed introduction to the development of interest in workplace industrial relations, and an overview of the preoccupations of writers during the period under review. In so doing it draws attention to the dominant themes in the book: the growth of shopfloor trade unionism and associated issues of trade union democracy, of the development of shopfloor bargaining, and of the relationships between shop steward activity, shopfloor bargaining and job control. There is no particular logic behind the ordering of the chapters, except that they move from a central preoccupation with the first topic — trade unionism — to concentration on the second — bargaining and job control.

A concluding chapter then tries to achieve two things. First it performs the conventional task of pulling together conclusions and inferences, and presenting, from a safe historical distance, an assessment of the strengths and weaknesses of both management and unions during the period. Second, and more controversially, the conclusion argues that there was an 'alternative strategy' for companies (and unions) faced with the emergent 'challenge from below' of the 1950s and 1960s, one that sought to build upon and develop the strengths of sectional, workplace-based controls, articulated through union organization rather than, as happened in most cases, either to resist or ignore these forces. We have attempted to do this for two reasons: first, to contribute an historical dimension to contemporary debates around employer and managerial strategies in a way we hope will be of interest to academics and practitioners alike. Second, we are concerned to argue the continuing relevance of detailed case study research, historical and contemporary, as a guide to good policy-making as well as to good academic practice. Relying on sloganizing, inadequately-researched accounts, and short-term journalistic and political preoccupation turned out in many cases to be a poor guide for prescription in the 1950s and 1960s. Now, as then, scholarly analysis might have provided a better source of information and ideas.

It is not part of the purpose of this book to argue that 'modern' shopfloor industrial relations somehow began in 1945, nor that they are confined to the engineering industry, still less to engineering in the West Midlands. We have no wish to intrude into debates as to whether the origins of the shop steward system and 'craft control' can be perceived in the medieval guilds. Not only are they beyond the scope of this book, but such an exercise would be redundant — and indeed impertinent — so soon after the magisterial overview of the broad historical sweep of industrial relations in this country produced by Alan Fox (Fox, 1985). It is, however, necessary for us to justify our choice of starting-point and of subject matter. In particular we are sensitive to the recent strictures voiced by Price who has argued that much industrial relations analysis of the period has lacked an historical perspective. In particular

the predominant emphasis is on the uniqueness of the post-Second World War developments ... the growth of informal bargaining tends to be treated as a distinctly new phenomenon responding to economic opportunities ... [similarly], the militancy of the late 1960s is ... seen as a response to ... sharpening inflationary pressures. ... The radicalism of that militancy — the way it demanded various forms of work control — is also seen solely within a limited time frame of the post-war era (Price, 1982: 181–2).

4

Price goes on to argue that, although there are novel features of the period,

> post-war industrial relations is composed of a distinct set of identifiable historical traditions whose significance transcends and informs the particular forces that conditioned and aroused its emergence in the 1960s.

While we would not wish to dissent from this general statement, we would argue that the novel features of the war and its aftermath are sufficiently marked to enable us to argue that it did represent a watershed in the development of shopfloor industrial relations. We would, for example, not dispute the persistence throughout the 1920s and 1930s of forms of shopfloor union organization, based around shop stewards, and a degree of autonomous worker job regulation, associated largely but not exclusively with the activities of 'craft' unions. But it does not follow that these structures somehow contained in embryo the developments of the wartime period and after. The existence of shop steward organization in engineering in the first 20 years of this century does not necessarily help us understand why similar structures should re-emerge 20 or more years later after a lengthy period of at best dormancy, at worst non-existence. Nor does the historical persistence of both craft and non-craft job controls in, for example, printing and the docks, automatically help us to frame an explanation of their emergence in post-war engineering. Recourse to broad accounts of working class traditions of opposition to the exercise of managerial authority provide us with one element of a starting point, but they are not sufficient to explain the rise and fall in patterns and structures of resistance, or their persistent non-appearance in certain industries such as footwear (Goodman *et al.*, 1977). Accounts of the social relations of production under capitalism that stress their antagonistic character may alert us to the fact of struggle in their working, but dynamic accounts of the development of the balance of class forces require more detailed attention to be paid to its changing manifestation and character rather than to its historical continuity.

With that as our starting-point the justification for our selection of material becomes clearer. The period following the Second World War (although admittedly with its historical roots in pre-war rearmament and the war itself) set the scene for an unparalleled development of shopfloor industrial relations in peacetime. Earlier manifestations of shopfloor union organization, again sometimes stimulated by war conditions as in the First World War, had shown themselves to be fragile in the face of peacetime fluctuations in demand and employer hostility. Outside a very few unions and companies, steward organization, if it existed at all, had been rendered largely impotent in engineering between the wars, and union membership itself often reduced to 'the maintenance of a habit' (Croucher, 1982: 24). Since then shop steward organization and shopfloor industrial relations have demonstrated a stability that persists to the present, despite some recent setbacks. It is a widely-shared view that the roots of this particular phase of industrial relations history may, especially in the engineering industry, largely be found in the events of the pre-war rearmament, the Second World War itself, and its aftermath. That these events in turn reflect the working-through of characteristics of work under capitalism that have a much longer pedigree is not disputed; all that is asserted here is that in themselves they are insufficient to explain the specific, and important, industrial relations developments of the period.

A Brief Background: Engineering and Industrial Relations

It is important to remember the extent to which large tracts of 'engineering' were relatively new industries in the 1930s, at least as large-scale employers. Armaments and shipbuilding aside, two major growth areas were motor vehicles and aircraft, both really only dating from the 1920s, with their thousands of attendant component suppliers. Their rapid growth and huge demands for labour sucked in workers from the depressed industrial areas into towns like Coventry, Oxford and Luton (e.g. Zeitlin, 1980: 125—8). Company structures were also changing through amalgamation and takeover, activities set in train especially during the 1930s but continuing well after the wartime period. Associated with these were shifts in managerial patterns and traditions as the original entrepreneurs came to be displaced by professional managers (see Hannah, 1983: 67—76; Croucher, 1982: 364). The rapid establishment of the so-called 'shadow factories' provided vast numbers of new engineering jobs, especially in Coventry, in a managerial environment often less hostile to trade unionism than the more established companies (see Jefferys, pp. 59—61 this volume).[1]

Into this situation of flux the exigencies of wartime production introduced two further factors of major importance. First was the direct impact of emergency wartime legislation. Order 1305 of July 1940 (Conditions of Employment and National Arbitration Order) provided for compulsory dispute arbitration and gave the government the power to require employers to observe 'recognised terms and conditions' within the district (Croucher, 1982: 88—9). Later, in March 1941, shop stewards received what Marsh (1963: 8) has described as virtual protection against dismissal under the Essential Work Order of 1941 which, although it strengthened employers' disciplinary powers, reduced their discretion to dismiss (Croucher, 1982: 116). Within that statutory context both government and employer priorities were for production above all else; cost, that vital peacetime criterion, mattered less.[2] And, second, although there has been much subsequent argument about the exact significance of the Joint Production Committees established during the war (approved by the Engineering Employers' Federation in March 1942), they provided a vehicle for steward attempts at involvement in managerial decisions; moreover, they provided a clear legitimation for steward activities in the eyes of (some) managers and, more importantly, of workers, both in trade unions and outside (Jones, 1986: 109—10; Croucher, 1982: 150—62). There is strong evidence that these factors contributed much to the growth of union membership, steward organization and plant-level collective bargaining of a kind during the Second World War, perhaps most notably in the aircraft factories, many of which had been established from scratch over only a very few years. That this process was patchy, incomplete and fragmented is equally clear, at least with hindsight.

Contemporary commentators noted the growth but, as we shall see below, attached interpretations to it rather different from those of more recent authors. More detailed evidence had to wait until the early 1960s, when Marsh (1963: 8) published figures showing that between 1947 and 1961 the number of AEU stewards had grown from 19,000 to 31,000 — on average one steward for every 37 members. By the same period the work of Marsh and that of Clegg and his colleagues was slowly beginning to build up a picture of shopfloor union activities (Clegg *et al.*, 1961: 154−61; Marsh, 1963; Marsh and Coker, 1963). A few years later a sudden flood of research, especially that connected with the work of the Donovan Commission, exposed the full extent of the steward-led processes of shopfloor collective bargaining (see especially McCarthy and Parker, 1968). In the shop steward pantheon, pride of place had to be given to the engineering industry, the subject of this volume.

Since then, a steady stream of research has extended our knowledge and understanding of the shop steward system. Surveys (e.g. Parker, 1974, 1975; Brown, 1981; Daniel and Millward, 1983; Millward and Stevens, 1986; Batstone, 1984) give us regular and precise information about the extent and influence of stewards across industries. Case studies, most especially those of Batstone and his colleagues and Brown (Batstone *et al.*, 1977; Brown, 1973) have given us a 'feel' for shopfloor industrial relations in engineering in the post-Donovan era. At the same time a number of historical studies began to widen our understanding of earlier development. But these studies have usually looked at patterns within an entire industry, usually the motor industry (e.g. Lewchuk, 1983; Tolliday, 1983; Zeitlin, 1980 and 1983; Lyddon, 1983). But few attempts have been made to go back to the level of the individual plant or company — arguably the most important level of analysis — to try to unravel the developments of the post-war period. Tolliday (1985) has made a start, and this volume is devoted to the same exercise, that of re-evaluating the historical case study material to enable us to understand better the factors at work in shaping worker organization and managerial actions in this important formative period. In so doing, however, we are concerned to move beyond accounts that frame their explanations in terms of broad factors such as the state of product markets or the weakness of managerial controls or, worse, that imply an historical 'convergence' towards an inevitable location of industrial relations decision-taking at plant level. Instead, we are looking to develop historical accounts of general aspects of trade union behaviour — problems of leadership, and control over work, for example — within a particular period of development. Thus we will attempt to produce historical accounts of the logic of management and union action and interaction within particular structural conditions, and show how these changed and developed.

Present Interests and Early Analyses

Modern ideas about the development of trade unions, the dynamics of collective bargaining, and the relationship between industrial relations and Britain's economic competitiveness frequently take as their starting-point, implicitly or explicitly, the changes in shopfloor industrial relations that occurred in the period between (roughly) the end of the Second World War and the late 1960s. Tolliday summarizes part of the story:

> trade union organisation established itself by the end of the Second World War, taking advantage of the tightening labour markets of the prewar rearmament boom and the favourable conditions of wartime production. In the postwar market ... firms found themselves facing a soft sellers' market ... and a tight labour supply at home. In order to achieve a continuous and expanding output, they conceded high wages and a considerable measure of job control to powerful shop steward organisations. By the time that international competition began to intensify in the mid 1950s, they had largely lost control of the shop floor and were unable to dislodge the deeply entrenched shop steward organisations that faced them (Tolliday, 1985: 108).

Other authors have added to this account, most notably those interested in union politics and government who have seen the development of shopfloor trade union organization as a response to the right-wing national union leaderships of the 1950s and early 1960s and, relatedly, as structures through which the Communist Party attempted to expand its industrial influence. Shopfloor trade union organization has loomed large in discussions of trade union democracy, and has been involved as the manifest refutation of Michels' 'Iron Law of Oligarchy' at least as applied to trade unions (Hyman, 1971: 32).

Detailed analyses of, among other things, inflation and economic decline, have been grounded in discussions of the importance of shopfloor industrial relations, especially in manufacturing industry. Debate has for decades been focused upon sectional wage bargaining, 'restrictive practices' and unofficial strikes. Several influential prescriptions for the improvement of economic performance, at factory, company, industry and national level, were based on (or at least contained strong elements of) proposals for the formalization of plant-level industrial relations: the introduction of proper procedures, recognition of stewards by managers and unions, and payment system reform (e.g. Commission on Industrial Relations, 1970; Parker *et al.*, 1971). At one time or another these reforms were seen as providing partial solutions to problems concerned with the maintenance of incomes policy, the removal of job controls with consequent improvements in business performance, the need for increased industrial democracy, and the enhancement of trade union democracy. They were in turn criticized by those who perceived these changes as being directed at the 'incorporation' of working-class leaders in order to restore managerial control over the intensity and organization of work. In short, shopfloor industrial relations has been one, and possibly the key element in the analyses of most important debates in industrial relations. Most of those analyses have, in turn, taken as their starting-point the view of the post-war developments summarized above.

This brings us to the central problem for such analysis and the primary purpose of this book: the period from the end of the Second World War until the late 1960s, allegedly among the most important in British industrial relations, has until recently been very little researched. Or, to be more precise, the early post-war studies note the existence of stewards and acknowledge their (minor) role in collective bargaining (e.g. Barou, 1947: 63—9; Roberts, 1956: 57—79), but the literature of the time barely hints at the fundamental changes in union organization and strength which, according to later accounts, were taking place during those years.

In some ways this lack of research interest is surprising, since it contrasts sharply with what was going on in the United States. In that country the 1950s and early 1960s produced important work in two related areas: research into collective worker behaviour, especially in the context of group restrictions on output and other working practices (the research of Gouldner, 1955 and Sayles, 1958 is relevant here); and industrial relations research into local union organization and 'fractional' bargaining (Chamberlain, 1948; Kuhn, 1961). With the exception of the pioneering work of Lupton and his colleagues at Manchester (1963), little or no work on output restriction was taking place in this country at the time, and none into shopfloor bargaining. One consequence was that views of British shop steward and worker activity were often inferred from American experience. Thus, for example, McCarthy, in his Donovan Research Paper on the role of shop stewards in Britain (McCarthy, 1966), uses the American work of Kuhn in talking about aspects of steward behaviour, and that of Slichter, Healy and Livernash (1960) in discussing output limitations and restrictions on working hours. Although there have been reams of paper devoted to analyses of British shopfloor bargaining activity and its implications for economic performance since the publication of the Donovan Report, the fact remains that our knowledge of the period 1945—68 remains slight. Prescriptions for change and their subsequent analyses are thus rooted in a series of assumptions about the nature of shopfloor industrial relations before the late 1960s rather than in empirically-grounded understanding.

This should not be taken, however, to imply that nothing was said about stewards and their activities for these 20 years — quite the contrary. But the preoccupations of many authors writing in that period, while anticipating some more recent themes, also reveal some major differences. Much of the literature of the period shares a common starting-point, namely that the war contributed much to the development of stewards and to their importance as local trade union officials. Several authors draw attention both to the formally-defined jobs of stewards as dues collectors and recruiters and to their informal role as providers of advice and representatives of members with local grievances (Barou, 1947: 63—5; England, 1950: 47—50; Roberts, 1956: 68—71), and there was a commonly-held view that their functions should be formalized and defined. Commentators drew attention to the inadequacy of provision for stewards in most union rule-books, and argued that this should be rectified (e.g. Collins, 1950: 118–19). Adherents of industrial unionism perceived the setting-up of Joint Shop Stewards' Committees in multi-union firms as an important means of achieving their eventual aim through the breaking down of inter-union rivalries (e.g. England, 1950: 32). But the key trade union issue discussed in the context of the shop steward debate was that of trade union democracy. Important though this topic undoubtedly was, and still remains, it is a very different preoccupation from those that have attracted comment since the late 1960s. And, although the 1960s witnessed the growth of concern at unofficial strikes and the part played in them by shop stewards (see, for example, TUC, 1960: 129–30), it was to be a few years before they were taken up in academic debate. More significantly, perhaps, economic factors such as wage drift and job controls, seem hardly to have affected pre-Donovan writers. The significance of this point is not so much the correctness or otherwise of analyses, but that the historical record suggests that there was little contemporary concern with the relationship between economic performance and shopfloor industrial relations. In the absence of such information and analysis, the absence of attention paid by unions, employers and government to what only subsequently became seen as an important issue is not surprising. The presence or absence of information is as much a part of the context of analysing behaviour as are product and labour markets.

Shop Stewards and Trade Union Democracy

To judge from the earlier accounts, the emergence of steward organizations during the war was, to start with, seen primarily as a strengthening of union democracy, with no real challenge to union constitutionality. Thus, for example, Collins writes (1950: 118):

> Fears that shop stewards . . . may cut across branch organisation . . . have usually proved ill-founded. On the contrary . . . the shop stewards may well enhance the trade union consciousness of members with resulting growth in attendance at meetings. Shop stewards are more likely to strengthen the branch machinery than to weaken it . . . for the workshop cannot, as things stand, replace the branch as the basis of union organisation.

But the outlines of the debate that was to fuel much later discussion were provided soon after by Flanders (1952: 57–8). Arguing the need for proper examination of the present state of workplace representation by the unions themselves, he commented that unions were reluctant to do this partly

> because the opinion still prevails that the strengthening of workshop organisation might undermine agreements arrived at nationally or on a regional basis or otherwise weaken the authority of the trade unions.

However, as he continues,

> The risks involved in the growth of any kind of 'factory patriotism' have
> to be weighed against the need for the unions to make their influence felt
> in the daily lives of the workers. Unofficial movements are usually a con-
> sequence of too great a gap between the top leadership and the active rank-
> and-file members.

Here we have an early statement of the potential tensions between two concep-
tions of union democracy that differs little from arguments three decades later.
Flanders, again anticipating many later debates, argues the need for increased
stewards' training, in order to ensure that stewards understand union policy, a
necessary precondition for acting in accord with it. Although Flanders com-
mended the steps being taken in this direction by the TGWU, the Ministry of
Labour, and the Workers' Educational Association, it may be a reasonable surmise that, then as now, education did little to resolve the problems. Certainly
the available evidence suggests that the 'gap' between national and rank-and-file
leaders grew rather than narrowed over the following years.

Early hints of possible conflicts between the two levels of union organization
were voiced by Roberts (1965: 460–4). While conceding the democratic potential of shop stewards, Roberts queried the validity of the more or less taken for
granted assumption that stewards will 'maintain close contact with their constituents, represent their views faithfully and report back conscientiously the policy
of the union' (Roberts, 1956: 460). He argued that stewards did not provide an
adequate link, and that they were subject to little membership control. To illustrate the ambiguity of the shop stewards' role, Roberts used the example of
the unofficial strike. While conceding that it demonstrated the healthy right of
members to refuse to accept without demur any situation pressed upon them, he
stated that 'the frequent exercise of this right is . . . a certain sign that the
machinery of union government and administration is not working effectively'.

There seems little doubt that it was the growing use of the unofficial strike
as a tactic that did more than anything else to foster the increasing polarization
within the union movement between these two 'competing' views of union
democracy, leading up to the major rows often associated with the TUC Conference of 1960, sometimes seen as marking the high point in the mutual disen-
chantment between national union leaders and shop stewards, and by that time
increasingly associated with alleged political divisions between left and right.
Thus in the wake of the 1959 Conservative election victory, according to
McCarthy (1962: 2), the 'left' attributed the defeat at least in part to 'TUC over-
caution, a failure to maintain contacts with the rank-and-file, and collaboration
with the employing class'; while the 'right' blamed much of the unpopularity of
the labour movement on 'the activities of "left-wing" bodies like the "communist controlled" National Council of Engineering Shop Stewards, which . . .
promotes unofficial strikes, undermines the elected leadership of the unions, and
fosters "chaos and disruption"'. The strengths (or weaknesses) of powerful
shop steward committees had been summarized earlier in the report of the

Cameron Inquiry at Ford as

> a private union within a union, enjoying immediate and continuous touch
> with the men in the shop, answerable to no supervisor and in no way offic-
> ially or constitutionally linked with the union hierarchy (cited in Beynon,
> 1973: 48).

The case for shop steward organizations was fiercely argued by, for example,
Jim Gardner, one-time General Secretary of the Amalgamated Union of Foundry workers. For him the attack on stewards mounted by both employers and
'right-wing' union officials indicated that they shared a common fear that
steward activities might disturb their cosy world. Once again the greater democracy of steward organizations was taken as their central claim to authority. For
shop stewards

> are the elected rank-and-file representatives . . . of the workers on the job.
> They are subject to recall and replacement if those who elect them are
> dissatisfied with their actions. . . . This is the source of their vitality, since
> where there is democracy there is strength; and no aspect of trade union
> organisation today is more democratic than the shop stewards and shop
> committees (Gardner, 1960: 32).

The case against was laid out in some detail by Wigham (1961: 90–101).
After conceding, briefly, that he was criticizing only a minority, he accused
stewards of flouting union rules and procedures, of manipulating members and
meetings, and of establishing their own small empires. It was left to McCarthy
to chart a middle route. Anticipating several of the proposals that were later to
be advanced by the Donovan Commission, he noted both the strengths and
weaknesses of steward organization, and advocated an increase in steward training in order to increase awareness of both procedural and union rules; the
development of local agreements with employers designed to 'legitimize the
steward's position in their particular factory'; and the increased use of
workplace branches to minimize problems of 'mismatch' between shop steward
and branch policies and institutions (McCarthy, 1962: 16–17).

In considering the attention paid to arguments about union democracy and the
role of the stewards and in understanding the powerful positions taken on this
issue, it is necessary to recall that one of the dominant concerns in the debate
in the 1950s and 1960s was the industrial role of the Communist Party (CP).
The fact that this issue has largely fallen from academic and public gaze should
not obscure its importance at that time.

Flanders, writing in 1952, launched a fierce attack on the role of CP members
in the British trade union movement, accusing them of (at least in the period
1947–52) 'magnifying industrial grievances in order to impede production by
stoppages of work' (Flanders, 1952: 146). However, he did not specifically
identify shop stewards with communist activities, concentrating instead on the
rule-changes of some unions, notably the TGWU in 1949, designed to exclude
party members from union office. Roberts, who did link CP influence to shop

steward activity, pointed out that 'consideration of the problems of local leadership . . . is made extremely difficult by the activities of the Communist Party'. He identified the strength of CP membership among engineering stewards in particular, but made the important point that the 'tendency among senior union leaders to treat all unofficial actions as merely the work of agitators' was wide of the mark, for it ignored 'the deeper causes of unofficial action, and . . . the weaknesses in union structures and governments' (Roberts, 1956: 462). Generally it appears to be the case that much of the discussion of the role of shop stewards from the early 1950s to the mid-1960s was shot through with claim and counter-claim for the role of the Communist Party. One consequence is that much of the analysis of union and steward behaviour is coloured by such debates.

Once again it is McCarthy's work that provides an early insight into a change of approach. He criticized such political debates as recipes for inaction, unlikely to contribute to the general health of the labour movement, and concentrated instead on proposals to reform the position of stewards in factories and in unions (McCarthy, 1962). Six years later the Royal Commission for which he was Research Director dismissed the 'agitator theory' of shop stewards. Stewards, according to Donovan, 'may be the mere mouthpieces of their work groups. But quite commonly they are supporters of order exercising a restraining influence on their members in conditions which promote disorder' (Donovan 1968: 29). On this analysis, the worst that stewards could be accused of was being excessively democratic, acting as workers' mouthpieces; at best they surrendered some of this and took initiatives to restrain membership action,[3] in either case a far cry from a view of stewards as fomentors of shopfloor discontent.

It may be argued that, in their keenness to sanitize the image of shop stewards (an objective for which there were strong political arguments), the Donovan Commissioners underplayed the importance of dedicated and motivated shop stewards in both building and sustaining shopfloor trade union organization. This is a theme dealt with in this collection, particularly in the contributions of Terry and Jefferys, the latter specifically touching on the role of CP members. But these chapters attempt to go further in that they use more recent approaches to the study of shopfloor trade union democracy — for example, discussions of the emergence of hierarchy and bureaucracy in shopfloor union organization — in an effort to cast light on an aspect of union organizational development whose contemporary analysis was to some extent vitiated by preoccupations with wider political factors.

Shop Stewards and Collective Bargaining

To modern audiences the relative neglect of the development of shopfloor bargaining in the two decades before the Donovan Report appears astonishing, especially in the light of that report's conclusion that workplace bargaining constituted nothing less than one of the two 'systems' of collective bargaining in this country; one indeed with more reality and relevance to the majority of unionists affected than the 'formal' system of national bargaining with which it was contrasted. This neglect also contrasts with the research attention being paid at that time to shopfloor bargaining — 'fractional bargaining' — in the United States. As noted above, early British theorizing (in the late 1960s) drew heavily on the American experience without, by and large, establishing the appropriateness of this experience for the UK.

The first edition of *The System of Industrial Relations In Great Britain*, published in 1954 (Flanders and Clegg, 1954) contains at most a few passing references to workplace bargaining. In tone it is very different from what appears to be one of the first books dealing with this subject published only one year later. It is perhaps no coincidence that this was written by a visitor from the United States. Fortunately for us, his book *Labor—Management Relations at the Plant Level Under Industry-Wide Bargaining* (Derber, 1955), dealt exclusively with the engineering industry in Birmingham. Derber looked at 10 plants and reached a number of useful conclusions. First, that they showed wide variation in both union membership and in management approaches to labour relations. Second, he concluded that, despite the importance of the national agreements in both substantive and procedural regulation, there was widespread shopfloor bargaining associated with issues of wage structure. These included such questions as the method of wage payment, setting the rate for the job (often in the face of tight labour markets for certain skills), the correction of inequities, and wage rate changes associated with changes in working methods or materials. He noted that the last of these was of particular importance given the speed of technological innovation at the time. Other issues that were the subject of local negotiation or consultation incuded redundancy, discipline and dismissal, recruitment and training, and health and safety, all issues untouched by the national agreements. Derber concluded that where unions were well organized, local collective bargaining was a vigorous process, with the 'bulk of stewards' activities . . . devoted to grievances involving new time studies and wage rates' (Derber, 1955: 102—3). On non-wage issues such as redundancy, promotion, and the introduction of new machinery, however, managements continued to exercise almost total control, although exceptionally their freedom of action in these areas could be curtailed through the resistance of strong shop steward organization (Derber, 1955: 100).

Three years later another American published a detailed study of shopfloor bargaining in another Midlands engineering factory, the Standard Motor Company in Coventry (Melman, 1958). Melman's famous account of the operation of the gang system, and the considerable influence on decision-making it afforded to workers through their stewards, does not need repeating here. It pointed to an extraordinarily sophisticated local institutional machinery for the formal joint regulation of a wide range of issues affecting not only wages and conditions but many aspects of the control and organization of production.

Of the two studies, it is without doubt the Melman work that has had the greater and longer-lasting influence. In Tolliday's view, at least, this has had unfortunate consequences for later students since it laid down the basis of the accepted view of post-war developments outlined at the start of this chapter, a view based on what is now seen as an untypical, possibly unique, example (Tolliday, 1985: 108). But the immediate impact of these two studies on industrial relations research and writing in this country appears to have been limited. It appears a reasonable surmise that the awakening of domestic interest in shopfloor bargaining in engineering owed rather more to the increase in strike activity. As Turner and his colleagues demonstrated for the motor industry, strike frequencies increased quite dramatically in the period 1958–64 (Turner *et al.*, 1967: 266). Several of the larger strikes had led to the setting-up of Courts of Inquiry, whose findings had provided startling evidence of the extent and nature of shopfloor union organization and bargaining.[4]

British academic interest in shopfloor bargaining can perhaps first be detected in the Clegg, Killick and Adams study of union officials (Clegg *et al.*, 1961: 154–61). But the major early studies were those of Marsh and his associates (Marsh, 1963; Marsh and Coker, 1963). Like the earlier American studies (but with little explicit reference to them) they concentrated on local-level collective bargaining within a context of national agreements. Their studies of shop stewards paid little or no attention to earlier preoccupations with union democracy and the role of political faction. Thus Marsh and Coker described the growth of 'domestic' bargaining in engineering, revolving around stewards, managers and supervisors, within national agreements that increasingly came to serve as a 'framework'. Evidence for domestic bargaining, informal and unwritten in nature, was found primarily in the phenomenon of 'wage drift' – the movement of the gap between rates (nationally negotiated) and earnings (affected by local bargaining). But it could also be seen in the growth of short unofficial strikes and in the development of personnel management. The increased significance of shop steward activity could also be perceived in changes in internal union organization as shop stewards came to supplant full-time officials in negotiations and other union functions.

Marsh also provided one of the earliest statements of an explanation for these developments that was shortly to become accepted as a basic orthodoxy. He argued that

> since the outbreak of the last war ... *general labour scarcity* has gradually extended to all workers the possibility of effective work group action which was formerly the privilege of a few. ... work group sanctions against management have gradually become effective, and 'management by consent' gradually necessary (Marsh, 1963: 18, emphasis in original).

This argument portrayed workers in general, and shop stewards in particular, as the prime movers for change. It was their demands and actions that were seen as having forced concessions in managerial practice. Unsurprisingly, perhaps, the role of management came to be seen as essentially reactive and opportunistic. Shopfloor bargaining was presented as a process that developed to fill the 'vacuum' created by inadequate local managerial control structures. However, it should also be recalled that the nature of the 'vacuum' was often held to be largely influenced, if not precisely determined, by the nature of the firm's product market and technology (e.g. Brown, 1973: 171). Action, whether taken by workers, stewards or managers, was relegated to an essentially secondary role at least in so far as it affected such diverse issues as the outcome of wage bargaining, the emergence of job controls, and the shape and cohesion of shop steward organization.

Nevertheless, the identification of weaknesses in managerial control structures led to a critical assessment of managerial competence in industrial relations matters. Managers, especially those at more senior levels in the company, were often held to be in ignorance of the 'realities' of shopfloor life, clinging to the increasingly untenable view that national bargaining continued to play a dominant part in the regulation of terms and conditions. This view was a central theme in the Donovan Report, which laid at management's feet the task of regaining the initiative in shopfloor bargaining. The 'managerial vacuum' analogy can be seen as persisting in some writings throughout the 1970s, and it evidently underlay many of the criticisms levelled by Michael Edwardes at his predecessors in British Leyland (Edwardes, 1983: 78 – 98).

The problem with this argument is that it is contradicted by much of the available evidence. The case study work of Derber and Melman showed clear managerial awareness of what was going on and the benefits conferred by local bargaining, especially in tight labour markets. The Melman analysis, in particular, showed management as an active agent in the process. A decade later the work of Turner and his colleagues showed that management in motor companies was clearly aware of the strengths and weaknesses of shopfloor bargaining and of their part in the process (Turner *et al.*, 1967: 214–16). Finally, the research undertaken for the Donovan Report showed a high proportion of management at works manager and personnel officer level to be satisfied with the present system. Indeed, 'three-quarters of managers thought that stewards were helping management . . . to solve its problems and run the plant more efficiently' (Government Social Survey, 1968: 96). An analysis of shopfloor collective bargaining based on ideas of managerial ignorance or inertia does not seem entirely to fit the facts.[5]

A more 'proactive' view of management in this process, as argued in the case of Standard Cars by Melman, found little favour elsewhere for many years. The idea that management in certain companies deliberately encouraged the development of shopfloor bargaining in order to facilitate its managerial priorities, although mentioned in passing by Turner and his colleagues, is a far more modern idea. For several years the favourite analogy for the growth of workplace bargaining was Topsy, who 'just growed' (Brown, 1973). As noted above, such analyses tended to depict the growth of shopfloor job control as an essentially passive process of worker controls filling a 'vacuum' left by the absence of managerial control, the vacuum in turn being largely specified by product markets and technology. It was not until the work of Friedman (Friedman, 1977) that the idea of a clear managerial dynamic was introduced. Friedman, in talking about the post-war car industry, argued that there were differences in managerial approaches between Coventry and the rest of the country:

Car firms which were not concentrated in Coventry reacted to the immediate post-war conditions of full employment and high demand by recognising the advantages of co-opting trade union leaders, primarily at the national level. Standard and other Coventry firms reacted by moving to Responsible Autonomy strategies which encouraged small groups of shopfloor workers to behave responsibly through loosening direct control. What they gained was flexibility within the workshop while introducing complex and continual changes due to automation (Friedman, 1977: 214).

It is not necessary to agree with the detailed arguments about Coventry and the importance attached to gang-working at Standard to appreciate the importance of trying to understand the post-war development of shopfloor bargaining within the context of wider managerial strategies. The recent work of Tolliday provides a helpful start in reworking historical material on several motor vehicle and other engineering companies (Tolliday, 1985, 1986). Several of the chapters in this book continue the development of this theme by going into greater specific detail in several companies, including some already covered by Tolliday.

There is much less variation in analyses of the role of management during the late 1960s and 1970s. For the purposes of this book it does not matter whether it was the publication of the Donovan Report and the establishment of government agencies such as the National Board for Prices and Incomes (NBPI) and the Commission on Industrial Relations (CIR) that contributed to the 'reform' of shopfloor industrial relations in the 1970s or whether these were changes already in train. The important point is the widely-held view that the late 1960s and first few years of the 1970s did indeed witness a transformation in the pattern of shopfloor industrial relations, with managements playing an important, though not unconstrained, part in this.

This 'formalization' of plant and company industrial relations concentrated heavily on procedural reform (Parker *et al.*, 1971) and, in some cases, on the associated reform of payment systems. Many authors have tried to analyse the reasons for these changes and their consequences. While there appears to be general agreement that, in purely procedural terms, the reforms achieved their objectives, this of itself tells us little, since they were purely a means to an end, the end being an improvement in substantive industrial relations. In particular the improvements sought were a reduction in unofficial strikes and 'inflationary wage drift' as managements regained control over 'decayed' payment systems. Finally, the reforms sought to improve labour productivity and economic performance generally, through the agreed removals of 'restrictive working practices'.

Attempts to evaluate the impact of the reforms in terms of these substantive indices have hitherto been at a pretty general level. Edwards (1983a: 213–14) has noted that there is little evidence of a reduction in unofficial strike levels that could be attributed directly to this reform. Indeed, both he and Hyman (1977: 183–4) argue that the very process of reform itself, by changing the *status quo*, actually precipitated an increase in such action. Batstone (1984: 128—45) has attempted to derive aggregate measures that look at both wage movements and labour productivity in this period. Despite some general problems with these measures, the broad conclusion that the procedural reforms had little, if any, impact on these gross economic indices appears inescapable.

The case studies presented in this volume permit, for the first time, a detailed plant-level evaluation of the impact of the processes of reform in the late 1960s and early 1970s. In particular they provide an opportunity to see them in an historical context of developing managerial and union strategies, often in response to dramatically changing economic fortunes. This in turn enables the authors to provide information on several key questions including, for example, the relationship between a reforming industrial relations strategy and wider priorities of production and maintaining profitability. For it was often argued during this period that reform of industrial relations provided a direct means of improving commercial performance; the pioneering 'productivity agreements' at the Fawley oil refinery (Flanders, 1964) were sometimes referred to as a paradigmatic example of their potential. The case studies presented here enable us to make a detailed examination of the relationships, and often the tensions, between the reform of industrial relations and the priorities of production. In particular, and in explicit contrast to some earlier analyses which postulated a relatively straightforward association between 'tight' product markets and 'tight' internal managerial controls, they illustrate the possibility of quite different industrial relations outcomes. As Bélanger and Evans show in the present volume, a market crisis may lead to a failure of managerial attempts to regain shopfloor control (see also Bélanger, 1987).

Shopfloor Bargaining and the Control of Work

Few topics can have aroused as much comment (and acrimony) as the issue of workers, unions, and job control. For some, 'restrictive practices', operated in industries such as engineering, by and through militant shopfloor union organization are one, possibly the largest, key to Britain's economic decline. To others they represent a proud tradition of worker resistance and hostility to the dominant priorities of capital, and show the way forward for an alternative economic structure rooted in workers' control of the means of production. For yet others, both on the left and on the monetarist right, they are simply an irrelevance, drawing attention away from more important structural accounts of the roots of economic decline.

In the aftermath of war, workers' and unions' actions were not generally perceived as damaging to productivity. Flanders who, as noted above, attacked the Communist Party for its alleged attempts to impede productivity in the years 1947—50, also commented favourably on the unions' non-insistence on their legal right to return to pre-war working practices that had been suspended by law since 1942 (Flanders, 1952: 128), although Collins (1950: 54—5) quotes an article in the AEU journal criticizing this position. (The wartime regulations had particularly affected the issues of dilution and skill demarcation.)

The publication in 1951 of *Productivity and Trade Unions* (Zweig, 1951), although it drew attention to the persistence of many forms of worker-imposed regulation at work, does not appear to have generated widespread comment. Nor, until the pioneering work of Lupton (1963) was there any real interest among British writers on industrial relations in the American 'human relations' literature of the period dealing with worker-imposed output restrictions and other aspects of group behaviour at work. But in 1961 two books, both written by journalists, dealt specifically with the topic of worker restrictive practices and the economic damage caused by their persistence. Both *The Stagnant Society* (Shanks, 1961) and *What's Wrong With The Unions?* (Wigham, 1961) had an impact, especially perhaps on the thinking of the Conservative Party. The impact on academic industrial relations and prescription was less direct, but two leading academic commentators turned their attention to this issue. Lupton (1963) followed in the footsteps of American academic interest in participant observer-based studies of group working and output, but the more influential was Flanders' study of the negotiated introduction of a productivity agreement at Fawley (Flanders, 1964). The latter was of particular importance because it sought to show not only the rational basis of most 'restrictive practices' but that they could be effectively removed, without opposition, through processes of open, detailed plant-level bargaining of a type to be advocated by the Donovan Commissioners a few years later. The investigation commissioned by Donovan into restrictive practices (Royal Commission, 1967) relied heavily on the research of Lupton and Flanders, and the prescriptions of the latter.

Since then the debate has rumbled on. For a brief period, job control and its pursuit by workers was celebrated as the means to heightened political consciousness (Mann, 1973: 21−2). Shopfloor bargaining over the regulation and cost of labour was also seen by some on the left as a major anti-capitalist force (Cliff and Barker, 1966; Glyn and Sutcliffe, 1972; Cliff, 1970). Successive government attempts to deal with the 'problem' of restrictive practices have tried persuasion linked to financial incentives, such as in incomes policy-linked productivity bargaining, and more recently have tried more direct methods of eliminating them in, for example, BL Cars (Edwardes, 1983), British Shipbuilding, and other parts of the publicly-owned engineering sector. It is still open to academic debate whether such attempts have been successful (see, for example, Willman and Winch, 1985; Batstone and Gourlay, 1986).

In recent years, attention has also shifted to wider debates about the relationship between shopfloor union power, as manifested particularly through restrictions on work and the introduction of new technology. Some (see Kilpatrick and Lawson, 1980) have used it to argue a general historical account of UK economic decline. Their analysis has been criticized as excessively one-sided by Hyman and Elger (1981) and, implicitly at least, dismissed as irrelevant by writers such as Williams *et al.* (1983) whose industry case studies attribute declining competitive performance almost exclusively to managerial failures. At the same time, a new school of theoretical and empirical interest has emerged in the wake of Braverman, preoccupied with the control of the labour process. This approach concentrates attention on individual and small group behaviour, and makes little or no effort to understand the role of trade unions (for partial exceptions see Rose and Jones, 1985; Wilkinson, 1983). From a different theoretical perspective, it returns to some of the traditions of the 'Human Relations' school.

The whole topic is beset not only with problems of partisanship, but also with those of definition. Recent analyses have, for example, introduced into the debate a concept rarely deployed in earlier discussions, namely the relationship between workers' regulation of job design and execution on the one hand, and the interests of employers and managers on the other. For many earlier writers, including several of those mentioned above, on both the left and right of the political spectrum, the mere existence of 'worker-based job controls' was taken to be synonymous with restrictions imposed by workers on management. More recently this has been questioned, in different ways, by the work of writers such as Burawoy (1979) and Hyman and Elger (1981), all of whom have suggested that at least some aspects of job control, at least in some specific periods, have not only not frustrated employer objectives, but may rather have *facilitated* the task of management. Indeed, Burawoy has gone even further and suggested that one element of managerial strategy is precisely to create scope for 'worker control', but to be exercised in a direction that facilitates efficient production. Friedman's concept of 'responsible autonomy', mentioned above, also stands in this recent tradition. Working within a more conventional 'industrial relations' framework, Armstrong and Goodman (Armstrong and Goodman, 1979) have argued that informal regulation of work, 'custom and practice', could be operated at least as much by managers, to enhance their discretion, as by workers, a point largely missing from earlier analyses of the phenomenon.

The crucial, but often ignored, issue of the relationship between shopfloor working practices, worker interests, and managerial strategies is one of the key topics confronted by several contributions to this volume, especially those of Bélanger and Evans, and Scullion and Edwards. These authors confront the general questions about the shopfloor politics of job control raised by Hyman and Elger (1981: 119), namely, 'within what material and ideological *limits* such controls are acceptable to capital; and in what way these limits alter over time'. The present contributions enable us, perhaps for the first time, to present detailed analyses of these issues by tracing in detail the emergence and development of shopfloor working practices over a long period, and within a managerial context that constantly redefined the significance of such practices.

A second, equally important, and largely ignored question with which this volume deals, is the *relationship* between the operation of shopfloor controls and the structure and behaviour of shopfloor trade unions. The question itself may occasion some surprise, since for many writers, especially those simultaneously either critical or supportive of job controls *and* shop steward organizations, the link between the two has frequently been taken as axiomatic. Nevertheless, closer examination of the material available reveals that the situation is by no means so straightforward. Early research hardly investigated the link, but Flanders' study of Fawley noted that most of the practices they were trying to remove were 'traditional practices' rather than 'union rules' (cited in Royal Commission, 1967: 51). Indeed it is noteworthy that the Donovan Report itself did not refer to the role of stewards in its discussion of such practices; this stands in sharp contrast to its treatment of wage bargaining. Lupton's studies made clear that several working practices operated independently of trade unions, even where the workforce was unionized, thus confirming the inference drawn from American studies of job controls in non-union plants, that specifically *union* organization of workers is not a necessary precondition for the creation and maintenance of job controls by workers. Nevertheless, it was the fervent hope of policymakers in the 1960s and 1970s that, even though shop stewards might not regulate these practices, they might be able to negotiate over them. Arguments that this might prove problematical precisely because of uncertainty over the 'ownership' of such rules (e.g. Terry, 1977) seem to have been confirmed by evidence that, even if the Donovan reforms have led to an increased formalization in dealings over pay, this was certainly not true over job control bargaining (Sisson and Brown, 1983: 149). There seems to be something peculiar about job control issues and their negotiation on the shopfloor. This again is one of the themes picked up by recent authors (e.g. Thompson and Bannon, 1985) and in contributions to this volume, where the highly problematic relationship between worker-based job controls and steward behaviour is fully explored. In particular, the problems for unions in building wider unity in the face of highly sectional working practices are discussed, as are the equally ticklish manoeuvres of seeking to maintain a good 'bargaining relationship' with management when union members are chipping away at the foundations of managerial prerogative through tactics seen by both managers and stewards as illegitimate.

Finally, several chapters contribute to current debates that examine both the particular nature of 'craft control' and its relationship to more general job controls. Many analyses have seen 'craft control' as operating in a manner rather different from other controls, depending upon possession by individual workers of particular and highly-developed skills. This has, it is alleged, put such workers into a strong position. Through their ability to control entry to the trade they have taken much discretion away from employers, who in turn become dependent upon craft workers' agreement to deploy their skills. Craft workers have little need to strike, since they are in a particular position of power with respect to their employer, a position quite different from that occupied by other workers. It has been argued that, in an attempt to achieve comparable power, semi- and unskilled workers have sought to deploy similar tactics and that some aspects of shopfloor controls can be explained by a theory of emulation. In this view, craft control has been particularly important, since it has been the 'model' to which non-craft workers have aspired. In that sense, therefore, job controls exercised by non-craft workers are nevertheless in the craft tradition, owing their lineage to their craft forebears. Engineering, as a traditionally craft-based industry, is an obvious area in which to test this hypothesis.

Analyses of this kind, alleging a direct process of 'transmission' or 'diffusion' of controls from craft to non-craft workers have been advanced particularly by Zeitlin (1980), and criticized in turn by Lyddon (1983) who accuses Zeitlin of having ignored significant differences between craft and non-craft control and of having relied too heavily on Melman's account of Standard. He seeks specifically to refute Zeitlin's hypothesis, arguing instead that, rather than reflecting attempts to emulate craft practice, emerging controls among semiskilled workers indicated that 'the attempts by workers to exert control over work is a structural feature of all capitalist societies, not the result of a prior tradition of craft control' (Lyddon, 1983: 137). Lyddon is thus stressing an account of the growth of job controls that derives from workers' common experiences of coercive social relations at the point of production. In his view, job controls have first and foremost a *workers'* logic rather than a *trade union* logic. The debate was rejoined by Zeitlin (1983) who conceded some of the points but insisted on the importance of prior cultural traditions and organizational practices in fashioning non-craft job controls. Again, both Bélanger and Evans, and Scullion and Edwards develop and expand these arguments, in opposition to Zeitlin, arguing that non-craft workers developed strategies and structures or organization and control independently of pre-existing craft forms.

Conclusion, and Plan of the Book

This chapter has done two things: first, it has drawn attention to the importance of the period under review, the views of shopfloor developments current at the time, and the gaps in the historical record; second, it has provided an overview of the importance of an understanding of historical developments to our present debate and preoccupations. What follows is intended to serve two broad purposes. By presenting a range of hitherto unpublished material, it seeks to plug a major gap in our historical understanding of twentieth-century British industrial relations. It focuses on shopfloor industrial relations in post-war engineering in the Midlands, certainly untypical in one sense of British industry, but prototypical as a 'model' of British industrial relations and, as we have seen above, highly influential in the development of both industrial relations theory and practice.

Second, the volume seeks to make specific contributions to a number of important theoretical debates, several of which have been outlined above. It should be stressed that each chapter was written as a free-standing essay reflecting the authors' data source and particular interest. It did not seem sensible to follow the usual practice of discussing in this introductory chapter the contribution made by each case study. This would be to imply a spurious unity of theme and method. The particular themes of each chapter, together with a brief discussion of the wider significance, will be found in its editorial introduction. What ties the contributions together is a concern to recover and analyse some key histor-

Michael Terry

ical developments. All but one, moreover, look closely at an individual workplace. The exception is Salmon's discussion of redundancy policy, which requires a comparative focus.

But what is the logic of this particular selection? What do the firms studied tell us about the issues discussed above, and how representative are they? The choice obviously reflects the availability of material, and the case studies are not meant to be comprehensive. But, as argued above, information is very scarce, so that any detailed studies must be valuable. The firms reflect, moreover, a range of situations. Longbridge is studied by Jefferys for its size and self-evident importance. Grainger examines Herbert's because the firm differed from the 'norm' of engineering. A study of why it was different can help to understand 'normality'. The pseudonymous plant studied by Bélanger and Evans can be taken to represent a fairly 'average' medium-sized engineering company. The firm in Terry's study occupied a specialized part of the market but was also affected by factors common to the industry. Scullion and Edwards' plant illustrates one extreme case of developed craft controls. By examining some neglected issues in all the car firms, Salmon is able to develop understanding of management—labour policy in them. In short, within the common environment of Midlands engineering, the firms considered display considerable variation: though not 'typical' they represent several important strands of development. The concluding chapter uses them, together with other material, to draw out the lessons that may be learned.

Notes

1. Under the 'shadow' scheme, 'specialist firms gave the benefit of their expertise to other engineering companies when ... expansion necessitated the building of new factories. The state bore the cost of building and equipping the new units, which were managed by private firms' (Croucher, 1982: 4).
2. The same emphasis on production appears to have been maintained for several years after the war, as the government struggled to deal with the financial crisis precipitated by the sudden American withdrawal of the lend—lease arrangements. The emphasis on production of consumer goods for export to generate income was backed by patriotic calls for production not dissimilar from those of wartime. In addition, several of the wartime legal controls were maintained during at least part of the Labour government of 1945—50.
3. The most thorough-going attack on the 'agitator theory' of strikes is in fact to be found in the work of Turner and his associates (Turner *et al.*, 1967: 287—92; Clack, 1967) who argue that it is simply inadequate to explain either strike patterns or the conduct of shopfloor industrial relations more generally. They are particularly dismissive of the role played by the Communist Party.
4. Turner and his colleagues make the important point that two of the Reports produced by these Inquiries — the Cameron and Jack Reports of 1957 and 1963 (both dealing with Ford) were 'taken as having a wide applicability to shop steward organization

in general' (Turner *et al.*, 1967: 215), despire the clear evidence of the special history and circumstances of that company.

5. For further arguments along these lines see Tolliday (1985). In passing it is worth noting that similar strictures could be made about the perceived importance of 'informality' in shopfloor collective bargaining. Calls for the 'formalization' of such bargaining were made in the face of a clearly-expressed management and union preference for the informal *status quo* without any clear statement of why, in the context of what was known about management and union contributions to shopfloor bargaining, such a change would produce any better 'results'.

2

The Development of Shop Steward Organization: Coventry Precision Tools, 1945–1972

Michael Terry

Editors' Foreword

Coventry Precision was a small, highly specialized engineering company that in the early 1950s became part of the Dowty Group. Terry uses data from the set of shop steward minute books to tackle the thesis of shop steward 'bureaucratization': the argument that sometime during the period 1945 to 1979 the nature of the relationship between stewards and their members changed from one of sectional activity co-ordinated by stewards on a basis of consent, towards a relationship of central control and direction, with stewards exerting an increase in internal discipline over sectional activity. Two factors are seen as central to this change; the increasing integration of stewards into official union structures, and the formalization of plant-level industrial relations by managers. Both are portrayed as external factors, introducing into steward organizations pressures to shift away from participative shopfloor behaviour.

   The data presented in the chapter show that, far from emerging gradually, the hallmarks of steward bureaucracy — formal procedures for election and accountability, centralization of authority — were present from the very early days of steward organization. While noting the contribution made by management and union officialdom, Terry argues that the main thrust to establish such structures came from the stewards themselves, with no obvious opposition from the membership. Contributory factors included the presence of only a small number of activists prepared to tolerate the earnings losses associated with union organization, the limited funds that members were prepared to donate to offset such losses, and the failure of early attempts by stewards to increase the base of membership participation. The argument levelled against crude versions of the bureaucratization hypothesis is that they concentrate excessively on external influences and fail to recognize that stewards' organizations are also the product of internal influence and decision-taking (see also Edwards and Heery, 1985). Centralization or decentralization of authority within shop stewards committees cannot be 'read off' from the actions of managers and union officials. This chapter may be contrasted with that of Bélanger and Evans, whose account makes it clear that stewards would have welcomed a degree of centralized authority — for good trade union reasons — had the workers in that factory been prepared to concede it.

In addition to this central preoccupation, the chapter provides information on other aspects of the Coventry Precision stewards' history. These include the building-up of the union membership and the establishment of 100 per cent organization, and the impact and importance of the rivalries between the AEU and the TGWU in the early 1950s. Both episodes left a deep mark on the steward organization. Terry also examines the influence of the payment system and of the policies of management on shopfloor politics. With the benefit of hindsight they can be seen as contributing to a tradition of formal relationships, both within the steward body and between managers and stewards, long before the days of the Donovan Report. The case study thus provides information on a company no less typical of Midlands engineering than large motor car factories, but much less thoroughly investigated.

The Bureaucratization Debate

The authoritative history of the union organization of engineering workers during the Second World War argued that 'the factory trade union organisation of the 1939—45 years was in many ways stronger than that of the 1970s. Although a lower proportion of the workforce in engineering was unionised at that time, communications between the shop stewards and their members were generally better' (Croucher, 1982: 377). It went on to suggest a number of general differences between the two periods that might account for this change. During the wartime period a recognizable shop stewards' *movement* was in existence, making use of large-circulation newspapers to involve the rank-and-file; there was a deep-rooted culture of workplace meetings drawing workers as well as stewards into activity; there was a constant need to defend the rights of factory representation; and shop stewards were able to assist members in a wide range of individual personal and domestic issues as well as industrial ones. By contrast, by the 1970s more sophisticated management strategies had started to open up gaps between stewards and members; there was a uniformly hostile press; and institutions such as the closed shop and checkoff of union subscriptions had reduced the routine contacts between stewards and members. In addition, the increasing use of written agreements had reduced the need for workers to exercise constant vigilance against managerial attempts to reclaim 'custom and practice' concessions.

In arguing this way, Croucher is elaborating a view widespread for many years among students of industrial relations (including the present author). In essence, the argument is that between, roughly, the end of the Second World War and the late 1970s, profound changes had taken place in shop steward organization and in the conduct and nature of shopfloor industrial relations. Hyman (1979: 57) points to 'the consolidation of hierarchy within shop steward organisation . . . a centralisation of control within stewards' organisations . . . [and] a significant degree of integration between steward hierarchies and official trade union structures'. Taking all these factors into account he argues that 'it is not fanciful to speak of the bureaucratisation of the rank-and-file'. While Hyman focuses attention on the decade since the publication of the Donovan Report in 1968, it has been suggested that the processes described had been in train well before that; that Donovan identified those processes rather than stimulating them (see, for example, Crossley, 1968; Turner, 1968). There are great problems of periodization here; most subscribers to the view would agree that stewards were not 'bureaucratized' in 1945 but were by 1979. The temptation to view the late 1960s and early 1970s as a watershed is strong for two reasons: first that the data, especially large-scale survey data, permit effective comparisons to be made over this period; second that this periodization neatly coincides the 'bureaucratization' process with the emergence of 'corporatist' developments at national level, thus allowing the finger of responsibility to be pointed at the 'reformist' Labour governments of 1964–70 and 1974–79 in particular.

But for many years the problem in all attempts at tracing historical developments before the mid-1960s has been an almost total absence of data covering the history of shopfloor trade union organization in the period between the end of the Second World War and the publication of the Donovan Report in 1968. Arguments about this period have therefore been necessarily speculative, but there has been a tendency to view much of the 1950s and 1960s as a 'golden age' of shop steward history, and this has sometimes influenced debate and analysis. Aware of the shortcomings of the data on the importance of this period of British labour history, scholars have recently been returning to this period in an attempt to fill the huge gap. When they do, as recent work by Tolliday demonstrates, long-cherished views — in this case that the period witnessed a general linear increase in the strength of shopfloor union organization in the motor car industry (Tolliday, 1985) — quickly have to be abandoned. But despite these recent important contributions, our knowledge of the development of shopfloor trade union organization remains partial. Tolliday's work confirms the need to reconstruct company histories in order to understand the emergence of particular patterns of shopfloor labour relations, but his work has only begun to touch on analyses of shopfloor trade union organization. In particular, his work does not deal with issues of authority and control *within* steward organizations, and *between* them and the wider union. It does not, therefore, help us a great deal towards an understanding of the emergence of 'bureaucratized' shopfloor stewards. We see shop stewards in 1945 who disappear into an historical void, only to appear twenty years later as the sophisticated and well-organized negotiators, especially in the motor vehicle industry (cf. Turner, Clack and Roberts, 1967), to whose activities a Royal Commission was shortly to devote a large part of its three-year deliberations.

Inevitably, perhaps, given the absence of data, the assumption was of a period of smooth and uniform development of shop steward organization, and this interpretation appeared to receive some support from such published research as did appear. The best of this (e.g. Marsh and Coker, 1963) seems to point to a steady growth in the number of shop stewards in engineering and a decline in membership constituency sizes, associated with other changes in shopfloor industrial relations.

On the face of it, there are no obvious reasons why the steward system developed and consolidated during the war should have continued unchecked into the years of peace. Although certain aspects of emergency wartime legislation which had been, among other things, helpful to shopfloor trade union organization, were retained by the Attlee Labour government, most was repealed in 1951. Economic conditions, while certainly more favourable to union growth than in the pre-war period, were by no means uniformly stable. Employers after the war were in many cases keen to reverse the shopfloor advances that had been achieved (Croucher, 1982: 386), and although their attempts to do so may have been less thorough-going than they might have been had the Conservatives won the 1945 General Election, there were significant attempts to weaken shopfloor trade union organization during much of this period (Frow and Frow, 1982: 314—61; Tolliday, 1985: 118—19; Beynon, 1973: 43—62). Finally, there was by no means general sympathy for shopfloor trade union organization within the national union leadership itself (Frow and Frow, 1982: 265—7; Tolliday, 1985: 133—5). It might appear that a hypothesis of uneven, partial, developments of shopfloor organization, stressing advances and setbacks, would be more plausible, and indeed the case study based work of Tolliday and of other contributors to this volume confirm the need to abandon straightforward assumptions about developments over this period.

Several of the contributions to this volume cast doubt on established assumptions by arguing that the movement of the 'frontier of control' was not the clear shift in favour of workers and unions conjured up by statements about 'custom and practice' encroachments into managerial prerogatives. This chapter will itself touch on these issues. But the central concern here is with another aspect of the conventional view of the changes in shopfloor industrial relations, namely the structure and activity of trade union organization itself. As implied by the quotation from Croucher at the start of the chapter, there is a widespread view that shop steward organization and plant-level industrial relations in the 1970s were in many ways significantly different from the 1940s and 1950s. This chapter will focus on one central characteristic of steward organizations that is often seen as typifying the periods 'before' and 'after' the process of 'bureaucratization'. It can be summed up by the argument that for much of the 1950s and 1960s shop stewards were 'genuine' workplace representatives, deeply enmeshed in the activities and preoccupations of those they represented. The relationship was seen as one of 'direct democracy' in which the stewards' policies emerged out of regular discussion and debate within the workgroup (for example, Kahn-Freund, 1979: 13—19). As part of this relationship the steward was seen as directly and constantly accountable to the membership and liable to summary removal from office in the event of inadequate performance. The notion of the steward as *primus inter pares* is characteristic of this view (e.g. Terry, 1983: 72). By contrast the modern steward is perceived as increasingly differentiated from the membership, trained and educated into the job, acting as a 'leader' rather than as a 'mouthpiece', whose relationship with the membership is based on the electoral 'representative democracy' of regular ballots. In particular the emergence of an elite cadre of full-time shop stewards and convenors has been perceived to be associated with an increasing hierarchy and centralization of authority within shop steward organizations. As Hyman has argued,

> In the past, joint shop stewards' committees have tended to fulfil the functions of co-ordination rather than control, to depend upon the voluntary agreement of various sections and their representatives rather than upon the exercise of sanctions. Today it is far more common for such committees to exercise a disciplinary role, forcing dissident sections of the membership into line, But at the same time, the small cadre of full-time ... stewards within a committee often possess the authority and the informational and organisational resources to ensure that their own recommendations will be accepted as policy by the stewards' body (Hyman, 1979: 57).

Two broad structural changes are held to have contributed to this change. The first is the changed relationship between shopfloor trade union organization and the external, 'official' union movement. The 1950s and early 1960s, in particular, are characterized as periods in which shop stewards' organizations — and hence many of their activities — were divorced from the official unions, who often strongly disapproved of their activities. Certainly there is no shortage of material to confirm the hostility that existed in some cases. Given the closeness of the relationship between workers and their stewards it appeared to many that stewards rather than official unions reflected more accurately the interests and aspirations of the rank-and-file membership, a point accepted by the 'pluralist' authors of the Donovan report as well as by Marxist and radical analysts. The period since then is seen by some as one of increasing 'incorporation' of the stewards into the official unions (Hyman, 1979: 57–8; Terry, 1983: 85–91; for a detailed critique see England, 1981 and Batstone, 1984: 83–120). The role of stewards has been recognized and codified in union rule-books, and union decision-taking structures up to national executive level have been increasingly opened up to lay representatives. The implication often drawn is that stewards and convenors affected by this process come under increasing pressure to reduce or modify their support for rank-and-file demands in order to accommodate national union policies. In that sense they are seen by some as being again less democratic and more manipulative of their members in the 1970s than they had been a decade or two earlier.

The second change often said to have contributed to the increased differentiation between stewards and members is the so-called 'formalization' of industrial relations; the replacement of unwritten understandings by formal, written agreements. Conventional wisdom stresses the informal nature of much of the bargaining and rule-making that took place between managers, especially foremen and supervisors, and stewards and members during this period. Regulation by custom and practice — unwritten, often uncodified agreement — is seen as almost a defining characteristic of piecework engineering factories in the 1950s and 1960s. As we have seen, this is allied with arguments about the structure of shopfloor union organization, for custom and practice (C&P) agreements were seen to be preserved as the property of the shopfloor, only defended by constant vigilance on the part of all workers against managerial attempts to regain lost ground. This too, therefore, was an important aspect of the 'direct democracy' of shopfloor union organization, as it required the constant and direct involvement of all workers in the defence of their gains.

It followed from this line of reasoning that attempts to 'formalize' plant-level industrial relations, as advocated by the Donovan Commission, could be seen as having the effect, intentionally or not, of reducing the democratic bases of relationships between members and stewards. The written agreements, signed by managers and stewards, that replaced C&P were the property of the stewards rather than the membership and hence reduced membership incentive to participate in their defence. Such agreements were seen as strengthening steward authority over members and reducing membership participation. In this way formalization may be seen to combine with the increased involvement of stewards in official union structures with the effect of differentiating stewards from their members and enhancing their central authority.

As noted above, the consequence of arguments of this kind has been to view the 1950s and 1960s as something of a 'golden age' of shopfloor trade union organization in which stewards reflected and articulated the interests of the members expressed through open democratic machinery, untrammelled by their involvement in the distorting 'bureaucracies' of national unions and formalized collective bargaining arrangements with management. Developments since 1968 or so are seen as contributing to a watering-down of this ideal, a weakening of the basic principles of democratic trade unionism.

An objection may be that the foregoing account is over-simple and fails to do justice to the sophistication of many accounts. But the purpose is not to be comprehensive, rather it is to make the general point that runs through much analysis, namely that shop stewards in the 1970s were less in touch with their members than in earlier decades; that one manifestation of this has been the emergence since the late 1960s of increasingly hierarchical, centralized shop steward organizations at plant level; and that major responsibility for this change must be laid at the doors of the official trade union movement and employers. This chapter will assess the validity of the periodization of events and the processes allegedly at work through a detailed examination of the history of one shop stewards' committee in a Coventry engineering factory between 1946 and 1972.

Coventry Precision: A Brief Introduction

The original company, the Coventry Repetition Company Limited, was set up in April 1937. The owner, Sir Harry Harley, already founder and owner of the well-established Coventry Gauge and Tool Company, was a flamboyant and well-known Coventry figure. The company produced highly specialized components, and from the start did much of its work for the Dowty company, which manufactured aircraft undercarriage legs and shock absorbers. The work done by Dowty increased greatly during the war, as did the amount of component subcontracting, especially in Coventry (Rolt, 1962: 40–5). The huge growth in aircraft business continued after the war, and Coventry Repetition grew. In early 1946 it changed its name to Coventry Precision Engineering and Repetition Company Limited, and in July 1951 was taken over by the Dowty Group, following the death of Harley early that year. As the range of components produced by the Dowty Group increased, most notably into the manufacture of hydraulic pit props, so too did the range of work undertaken in Coventry, although aircraft components for both civil and military customers remained the largest area of business.

In January 1966 it was merged with another Coventry firm acquired by the Dowty Group (Dex Machine Tools Ltd) and the new expanded company was moved from its original location on the Bedworth Road in Longford, Coventry, to a new custom-built site in Exhall, Coventry. The aviation subcontracting machining business (with which this chapter is concerned) was sold to Dunlop Ltd (Aviation Division) in September 1972 and this work was moved away from Exhall.

As a case study the company is interesting because it is quite different from the much larger companies – mostly in vehicle building – on which our present knowledge is based. It is often argued that, after the war, motor cars provided the ideal environment for shop steward development, with their combination of high product demand, tight labour markets, assembly-line technologies and, predominantly, piecework wage bargaining systems. This case study provides information on a company with fluctuating product demand and small-batch production methods and is thus a useful contrast to the motor car 'norm', now increasingly seen as untypical. It was, in addition, quite small. In contemporary accounts size is often seen as an important factor affecting shop steward organization; steward 'bureaucracy', crudely, is seen as more likely where there are large numbers of stewards — this itself is a 'bureaucratizing' factor. Finally, it is sometimes argued that the external union movement has had a greater interest in 'incorporating' the powerful shop steward leaders of large factories; the politically less significant leaders of smaller groups of members could be left alone. Thus this case study can be used to test an argument that a factory such as Coventry Precision might be less likely to have witnessed a process of steward bureaucratization than some others.

The data on which this chapter is based are the minutes of the factory Joint Shop Stewards Committee (JSSC), an almost complete run between December 1946 and May 1971. They provide a remarkably thorough account of steward organization and behaviour. In addition to providing detailed accounts of steward activities, the minutes regularly record the outcomes of steward elections, money granted to stewards in compensation for lost pay, and other data. This data core is supplemented by fragments of correspondence and other minor items, as well as by information gleaned from notes of interviews with the convenor and two senior managers when the company was the subject of a study by the National Board for Prices and Incomes in 1969. The account of the early history of the JSSC has been supplemented by information from two interviews undertaken by the author in 1977 with R. J. (Dick) Stynes, who joined the company in 1938, went on to become a TGWU shop steward in 1946 (having previously been an AEU member), and TGWU convenor in May 1948, a post he occupied until his resignation in July 1952. Since it is now 15 years since the factory closed, it has not been feasible to seek additional data from unions or management.

The factory was not large. The best estimate is that in the late 1940s and early 1950s the manual workforce numbered around 350, mostly direct male pieceworkers. Despite frequent revisions the payment system was time-based throughout rather than the more frequently found price-based system. Under such systems 'the worker is paid a basic time rate, a standard time is set for the job and a bonus is paid in relation to time saved in actual performance (or to extra output in the time allowed) ... a wage is negotiated in terms of units of time and the times allowed for different tasks are then fixed separately' (National Board for Price and Incomes, 1968: 4). The significance of this method for shop steward organization will be discussed later.

Much of the work was in small batches with long cycle and production times, which meant that there were frequent and lengthy interruptions for retooling and setting. Most of the work was highly skilled, although all the pieceworkers were officially classed as semiskilled. A more accurate count exists for May 1968 (after the merger with Dex and the move to the new site) when the company employed 350 direct workers (including 8 women) and 243 indirect workers (20 women). The toolroom and skilled machine tool fitters made up at least 25 per cent of the indirect workers, many being from the Dex machine tool workforce.

Building Up Union Membership

During the war union membership had hardly risen above its pre-war level of around 30 per cent. A majority of these, especially the toolroom workers, were in the AEU. This provides further confirmation for Tolliday's point (Tolliday, 1985: 108 and also contributions by Jefferys and Salmon to this volume) that the wartime period had by no means led to uniformly high union membership in engineering. There is evidence that in 1946 and 1947 the TGWU was making a recruitment drive in the company, spearheaded by Dick Stynes, with the assistance of Jack Jones, at that time a TGWU District Official and District Secretary of the Confederation of Shipbuilding and Engineering Unions (CSEU). In this the union was aided by the apparent lack of AEU interest in recruiting among the semiskilled workers and by the alleged inactivity and ineffectiveness of the AEU steward organization. The campaign of the TGWU was sufficiently successful to enable Stynes to apply for membership of the JSSC, having 'been elected by the TGWU members to the shop steward committee' (as minuted in the JSSC records on 23 January 1947). Stynes' testimony confirms the vital job done by Jack Jones in those early days. As Coventry District Organiser for the TGWU since 1939 he had, during and after the war, done much to boost shop steward organization in the city. His commitment to steward organization made him virtually unique as a full-time official in his union, and did little to endear him to the national leadership. It is clear that his vision of trade unionism contributed much to the development of steward organization in Coventry, both in the TGWU and in other trade unions. (For his own account of that period see Jones, 1986: 87−139.)

The AEU's apparent indifference to these developments changed as the TGWU stepped up its recruitment drive, and openly started to criticize the ineffectiveness of the JSSC, following the resignation of their one steward. The AEU response was rapidly to reverse their policy and to launch a recruitment drive of their own, although a proposal that they press for a closed shop was rejected, the committee not being 'unanimous in their support for 100 per cent TU'. Matters came to a head when the company declared two men redundant. The AEU-dominated committee was openly accused of failing properly to represent their interests, a view shared by some of the AEU stewards. The attitude of the majority may be seen in a minute that attempts to explain that one problem in representing the men arose in trying to understand whether he was 'a tool room man or merely a production turner' (4 March 1948). In May 1948, following an AGM to which all union members were invited, a new committee was elected, with TGWU stewards occupying the posts of convenor and committee secretary. Shortly after, following the intervention of the AEU District

Secretary, an AEU convenor was elected, although the TGWU continued to dominate the committee. From this point for two years the two unions co-operated and continued to recruit members.

In July 1950 the convenor announced that membership had risen to 85 per cent and that it was now time to press for a closed shop. This time the suggestion was approved unanimously. A printed slip was distributed to non-members informing them of this policy. By the end of August only 13 non-members were reported and in early September they were given a week's notice to join, with the threat of industrial action if they did not. The convenors met management to inform them of their policy and of the benefits they felt it would provide 'by having the help of the TU to cut out waste etc.' but to their regret management were not prepared to co-operate. A mass meeting attended by 217 members agreed overwhelmingly not to work with non-members unless they joined within 24 hours. All did, the last being the son of the managing director who was getting some experience on the shopfloor. Management appear at the last minute to have complained to the union full-time officials that the stewards were trying to impose a closed shop. The convenors in turn informed the officials 'that this was not so, but we had been trying to get a shop with 100 per cent TU membership'.

The crucial period as far as membership was concerned was therefore from 1948 to 1950. Important contributions to the success of the campaign were made by individual stewards, most notably from the TGWU, dissatisfied with the lack of effectiveness of the AEU committee. There is also evidence that the stewards were able to refer to campaigns for 100 per cent membership being waged in other Coventry factories. The apparent absence of managerial hostility to the recruitment campaign must also be recognized, however. The campaign took place at a time when there seems to have been no shortage of work and the stewards were able to obtain useful piecework concessions for their members.

Several points of particular interest emerge from this brief description. First, that whatever may have happened subsequently, relationships between stewards and the wider union, in particular district officials, were close and important. The union provided resources and advice. To that extent this shop steward organization was not independent of the wider union. Second, these early days already reveal the emergence of influential figures on the JSSC, especially the TGWU convenor and one of the three men who were AEU convenors during this period. These two factors continued to be important in the next formative phase of the steward committee. Finally, it is clear that the closed shop was fought for and won purely through worker and steward effort and organization (for evidence that this was typical of the period, see McCarthy, 1964: 119–22). The company's attitude was one of indifference, as far as can be ascertained. There is no suggestion of management involvement or connivance in the closed shop, and this clearly distinguishes this account from some more recent ones which have identified a clear managerial interest in 100 per cent union membership (see Dunn and Gennard, 1984: 78–9). The notion of a closed shop, partly enforced by management, as one element in a structured, bureaucratized, relationship between company and union, is inapplicable here. As Hart has noted, bosses 'came to love' the closed shop (Hart, 1979); they did not embrace it from the start, and although it is noted above that the Coventry Precision stewards attempted to enlist management support by pointing out the advantages they thought it would confer, it is hard to see this as in any way important to their successful campaign. The rivalry between the AEU and the TGWU has already been noted. The device deployed by the TGWU to obtain membership of the JSSC had been the rules of the CSEU (also known as the 'Confed'). The TGWU had decided that the committee were bound to act in accordance with Confederation Policy on Joint Shop Steward Comittees and hence would have to accept a properly-elected TGWU shop steward. Although the committee voted to ignore this request, most members were shortly to be voted out of office. As we shall see below, however, this was by no means the only time that formal procedural rules, especially those of the CSEU, were used in the battle that was to take place between the two unions.

The next clear sign of inter-union tension appeared early in 1951, and concerned an AEU member in arrears. His TGWU steward argued that he should be declared a non-member, as he was more than 13 weeks in arrears. The AEU objected, arguing that in their rules the period was 26 weeks, and even then a decision could only be taken by the District Committee.[1] The TGWU, with a majority on the JSSC, had their policy adopted by the JSSC, but even though the incident was patched up, it turned up again in October of the same year. Allegations of poaching followed, and in a heated exchange on 18 October the AEU convenor declared that 'the battle of AEU and TGWU was going on in every factory in Coventry but they were resolved not to do anything dishonourable'. According to the minutes he went on to state that 'The AEU is the largest and chief engineering union in the engineering industry. If a man is a skilled engineer the AEU is the only union for him to belong to'. Most TGWU stewards walked out, their convenor remaining only to state that in future the TGWU would operate on its own, representing only its own members. However, the clear impression is given that these were rather ritualistic moves, since even at this heated meeting the unions agreed to continue to liaise.

The rift was quickly healed at the AGM in November when the TGWU convenor read out the 1947 CSEU model constitution for JSSCs, saying that the TGWU were prepared to operate under it. It was overwhelmingly adopted. According to Stynes,

> Quoting the constitution was an attempt to bring the feeling into the membership that we should be united and that here was a procedural document which could bring us together again. It meant that there would be Confederation stewards on each section, elected by popular vote, with full powers to represent all the men on the section, whatever their union (interview notes).

The significance of this event goes beyond the mere settlement of inter-union differences. For the principle being accepted — that, for example, an AEU member could be represented by a TGWU steward — would have been rejected outright by skilled workers in many other factories at that time and since.[2]

The amicability of this settlement reflected a widespread desire for co-operation, a feeling within the factory that the two unions had worked well as a team and moreover that the unions were not strong enough to deal in-dependently with management. Furthermore the close personal and working relationships between Stynes for the TGWU and the long-standing AEU con-venor cannot be overlooked. According to Stynes' own account it had been the AEU man who had encouraged him into an interest in unionism, to the extent of pushing him 'into joining NCLC (National Council of Labour Colleges) classes, to get a couple of diplomas he thought would fit — he was a man who believed in this — me for the role of shop steward'.

The events described above demonstrate clearly the importance of the period from 1948 to 1952 in the creation of both a well-organized membership and a shop steward organization. The dates are of interest since the AEU and the TGWU both appear to have lost members in engineering and in the Midlands, at least in the first two years of this period (Tolliday, 1985: 122—3). But in Coventry at least, the scene had been set during the war by the organizing ac-tivities of stewards and Jack Jones, the TGWU and then CSEU District Secretary, noted for his rare commitment to the development of shopfloor organization. By this time most of the large Coventry engineering firms were effectively organized (Tolliday, 1985). At Coventry Precision, Jones's influence can again be seen in the efforts of the TGWU to recruit and organize and in this they, and later the AEU, were certainly aided by the presence of talented and committed individuals. Tolliday (1985: 112) notes the use of the tactic of slipp-ing activists into plants to organize membership. It is impossible from the minute books to discern the presence of such individuals, although twenty years later one long-serving steward stated in an interview that he had been 'sent in to organise the shop'. Whether or not this happened, there is evidence among the membership at large of a widespread predisposition to join a union. The speed with which 100 per cent union membership was eventually achieved, and the un-precedented size of the mass meeting that resolved not to work with the last re-maining non-members testify to this. The absence of any explicit managerial resistance is also noteworthy; although Sir Harry Harley had no reputation as a supporter of trade unions there were no signs of employer opposition (although later, after the 100 per cent unionism had been achieved, there were allegations of the victimization of one of the leading activists).

Nor is there any evidence of this changing as a result of the Dowty takeover. It would appear from the contacts later established with other Dowty Group stewards that much of the group had already been organized, but in any case the takeover was associated with no significant recorded changes in management personnel, and it was Dowty policy to give full autonomy to all companies in the group (Rolt, 1962). But it must be stressed that there is no evidence what-soever of any managerial *support* for the development of steward organization; the entire business of recruiting and of establishing the organization was undertaken through the activity of committed individuals, often putting in long voluntary hours and losing pay as a result. In that sense at least, the account differs from some more modern versions of recruitment that stress the supportive part that may be played by management both in recruitment and in the establishment of steward organization (see for example Terry, 1985; Willman, 1981).

These early days therefore saw a union organization created through its own efforts. Although management and others set the context within which this happened, it still seems reasonable to see this as a period of independent, internally-generated activity, in pursuit of the establishment of collective worker organization. Recent writing which stresses the role of management and ascribes less significance to the unions' own activities points to an historical difference or an indication that the present emphasis on the role of management in these matters has been overstated.

Three issues emerge from this period that will be taken up in later sections. The first concerns the relationship of the JSSC to the wider union. We have seen how in this period full-time union officials, the District Committees of the two unions, and the local Confederation of Shipbuilding and Engineering Unions all played an important role, as resources for the fledgling workplace organization, especially the TGWU, as sources of information, as courts of appeal and as resolvers of disputes. National union rivalries were played out on the local stage, and issues of union sovereignty − the JSSC versus the external union − were resolved. The second issue revolves around the means of that resolution, namely the adoption of the model constitution of the CSEU. This laid the foundation of the constitution of the stewards' body for the next two decades and marked the beginning of the great importance attached to constitutional propriety throughout the subsequent history. Methods of election of stewards, convenors and other officials, steward responsibilities, standing orders for meetings, and many more aspects of 'bureaucratic' procedure were all established in these early days. The constitution also pointed up and reinforced the third point to emerge, namely, the increasing influence of the convenor. The constitution conferred formal authority on the holder of the convenorship, thus confirming and extending the influence of this key individual within the JSSC.

Representation and Accountability

As noted above, there is a common view that early shop steward structures were more rooted in the membership through a process of 'direct democracy' than were later organizations and that, in turn, steward organizations tended to be subject to membership control and were prevented from making decisions and imposing them on the members. This section will examine these two aspects of local union organization, and will try to cast some light on whether or not any 'trend' to a more powerful and centralized steward body can be discerned.

One frequently used starting-point for looking at steward/member relationships is the system of steward elections. Central to the 'direct democracy' thesis is the view that stewards should act as advocates of policy worked out in collec-tive discussion; followers of the 'direct democracy' approach reject the sugges-tion that representatives, once elected, should have a degree of decision-taking autonomy. They therefore reject a 'parliamentary' model of regular election as the only basis for representation, preferring instead a model of 'constant accoun-tability'. It follows that such analysts place less stress on the technical pro-cedures of elections (although they are not discounted) than on a constant pro-cess of interaction between the collective and the representative. They tend therefore to stress membership meeting and debate, rather than formal elections, as the basis of shopfloor union democracy.

At Coventry Precision the earliest records of election procedures, early in 1947, reveal that the method did indeed seem to involve wide membership participation. The minutes show that the system adopted in the late 1940s was for each section to make nominations for shop stewards and to refer these for approval to a mass meeting of the membership, usually the Annual General Meeting. It would seem that the AGM had the technical power to reject a nominee put forward by a particular section, although there is no record of this authority being used. In between AGMs, sections could nominate stewards or, in the event of contested elections, hold a sectional ballot to put forward a name for eventual ratification. In April 1949 the convenor ruled that annual elections of this kind were 'unconstitutional' and that there was no ruling that a steward should resign at the end of one year or put forward for re-election. All that was required was an AGM to ratify new nominees. From the start, stewards' consti-tuencies were based on the work sections, with the exception of the TGWU members in the very early days (see above) and of the women operators who elected one steward to cover them all, a practice suggested in early editions of the AEU Shop Steward Manual.

This election practice was modified when the new constitution was adopted in late 1951. This required annual elections of a different sort. A nomination sheet was displayed on the union notice board and each section would put up the name of its nominees. In the event of a contest, there would be a ballot on the section, on a 'show of hands' basis. This system was abandoned in 1957, essentially because of the embarrassment caused by the public display of apathy shown by half-empty nomination sheets on the notice board. The response was to decentralize annual elections at AGM level to a show of hands at sectional level and there they remained. For as long as AGMs open to all the members were held, they retained the increasingly residual function of noting the nominees. But with the gradual demise of the AGM (see below) even this disap-peared and sectional elections, on an annual basis, became the norm.

However important election procedures may appear to be in the late 1980s, earlier authors tended to give them less emphasis and to stress other, less 'parliamentary' forms of relationship between steward and members, concen-trating on the members' ability to withdraw support from a steward, and on methods of report-back (accountability) to members. The only evidence we have on the former are data on steward turnover. The minutes mentioned the names of 182 stewards during the 25-year period. Comparing the lists of stewards recorded in the minute book each December/January we can show with some confidence that of these 71 (39 per cent) held office for a year or less, and a further 36 (20 per cent) only lasted between one and two years. Nowhere in the minutes is any reference made to the reasons for stewards (as opposed to convenors) quitting the job, but it may reasonably be inferred in the absence of other evidence that a proportion of these high turnover figures[3] reflected membership dissatisfaction. (Goodman and Whittingham, 1973: 117 suggest that lack of membership co-operation was by far the most common reason for steward resignation.) The turnover figures show no tendency to increase or decrease over the period studied.

Of equal importance to patterns of representation are arrangements for consulting members on a collective basis. The major set-piece forum for this, the Annual General Meeting, open to all members, was, as noted above, where steward nominations were ratified and the previous year's activities approved. Although important in the first few years, attendance was often low enough for the chairman to register disappointment (although attendances of 50 to 70 members of the workforce would not seem too bad by present standards, especially as meetings were held outside working hours). The general meeting was of great importance in convincing management of the seriousness of the 100 per cent membership campaign, and this was very well attended. But in 1950 the practice of holding an AGM open to all members seems to have stopped abruptly (or at least no further references to it appear in the minutes). The reasons were not given. It is important, however, not to overstate the democratic achievement of the mass meeting. The meetings were dominated by the policy proposals of the JSSC; contrary proposals from the shopfloor were rare and there is no record of any having succeeded. One clear example of the way these meetings could be utilized occurred in April 1959, when a special general meeting was called to enable the convenor to inform the membership of impending redundancies. Having advised them that the policy was that married women would be the first to go, the convenor referred to the extra strain he had been under during the previous few months, and suggested that perhaps 'a change would do him good. Now was the chance for workers to decide if they wished him to carry on . . .'. A vote of confidence was immediately proposed and carried unanimously.

Sectional meetings, by contrast, played an important part in the organization throughout. Not only did they become the basis of steward elections, but they were the main method of discovering members' opinions and of informing them of JSSC policy. Members' views were sounded out especially when the JSSC was contemplating industrial action and needed to know the extent of support. But more often the sectional meetings were used as 'top-down' channels of communication. Usually it was taken for granted that sectional stewards were doing this job in line with JSSC policy, although on one occasion the convenor rebuked the stewards for the fact that 'distorted versions' of JSSC discussions were circulating on the shopfloor. But this reporting back could be used deliberately to reinforce the JSSC's position, as for example in September 1958 when the convenor told the JSSC that 'it is the duty of all stewards to squash shopfloor rumours of acute work shortage', despite the fact that it is clear from the minutes that the rumours were justified. Information was also, on occasion, deliberately withheld, as when the convenor informed the JSSC that if the stewards received any information about changes on the shopfloor from 'efficiency experts' brought in by the company it should not be disclosed to the shopfloor.

On the basis of the evidence from the minutes, therefore, it would appear that, with the possible exception of the formative days of the union organization, the membership played only a limited direct role in the policy or decisions of the steward body. Attendance at meetings was also low and allegations of membership 'apathy', familiar to modern ears, date back to the early 1950s. Although some evidence suggests that there was a decline in the use of membership meetings as the constitutional and practical basis for steward decisions, this practice did not last long and was quickly replaced by an election procedure of sorts. Feedback to members was rarely discussed and it seems to have been partial and inadequate for much of the time. The convenor at least was concerned with the confidentiality of aspects of JSSC work. It is therefore difficult to sustain the argument that the period witnessed a gradual shift from 'popular' to 'representative' forms of democracy. The former hardly seem to have existed.

Steward Hierarchy and Convenor Dominance

As noted above, it is commonplace to view steward organizations of the 1940s, 1950s and early 1960s as less formal and hierarchical structures than those associated with post-Donovan developments. The emergence of bureaucratic structures is commonly associated with managerial moves to 'formalize' plant-level industrial relations. The 'golden age' of steward organization, by contrast, may be seen as a time when stewards operated on a basis of equality, with the convenor or steward acting as *primus inter pares*, exerting a benevolent influence of co-ordination based on consent and mutual support.

The pattern of organization at Coventry Precision does not conform to this model. As discussed below, both hierarchical steward structures and convenor dominance of steward affairs can be identified almost back to the starting-point of the organization. This section will analyse the history of these two aspects of steward politics in some detail.

Hierarchy
At the start it was the normal practice to hold meetings of all shop stewards on a weekly basis. Convenors and officers of the JSSC (chairman, secretary, treasurer, etc.) were elected by a full stewards' meeting held immediately after the steward elections. Convenors could, and frequently did, hold one or other of these offices. In late 1947 there were eight stewards, and that number had

increased to around 15 by the middle of 1950 when a shop stewards' committee of seven members was established, again elected annually by all the stewards, although several places were automatically allocated — to the convenors, JSSC chairman and secretary. From then on, for several years, the pattern of meetings alternated between 'committee' meetings of this smaller group and 'aggregate' meetings of all stewards. Although the pattern was irregular, the smaller group met more frequently than the aggregate meeting, although the agenda was the same. Frequent 'special aggregate meetings' were called during the first period of tension between the two unions.

In late 1951 the terminology changed slightly and the December aggregate meeting elected an executive committee with a chairman and vice-chairman (who also happened to be the two convenors), a secretary and a treasurer. The numbers were made up by three other stewards. The pattern settled into weekly executive and monthly aggregate meetings. Seven months later the stewards resolved to elect a negotiating committee of four (two convenors and two other EC officers). Within a month the management had agreed to recognize the 'authority of the negotiating committee as a body set up by and representative of the Shop Stewards' Committee'. Although the negotiating committee became a permanent fixture, the division between executive and aggregate meetings collapsed amid inter-union argument in 1952, to be replaced with a system of fortnightly aggregate meetings, because, in the view of one steward 'we were having too many meetings and getting on each others nerves and discussing trivial things'.

The authority of the negotiating committee was enhanced in late 1957 when the works manager agreed to monthly meetings. It is made clear in a later minute just how powerful this small body was by that stage. In May 1962 the committee was described as being 'vested with the authority of the JSSC to negotiate all issues to a final and binding agreement on conditions and wages affecting its members'. The membership of the committee became increasingly restricted to the office-holders. In 1961 the deputy convenor threatened resignation from his post because he felt that it should carry automatic membership of the committee, as it did for the convenor and the JSSC chairman. The JSSC agreed to this. In March 1970 the convenor argued that the JSSC Minute Secretary should also be an automatic member of the committee and this was also agreed although it meant removing one of the other stewards. By this time the committee effectively only consisted of officers elected by the steward body — convenors and deputies, chairmen and secretaries of the JSSC.

A degree of organizational hierarchy was therefore present virtually from the start, and it is difficult to account for this only in terms of the unwieldy size of the full JSSC. At its largest this never numbered more than 19, and was appreciably smaller than that for much of its early history, when the basic pattern was being fixed. Although there is some evidence that this structure became more rigid and ossified as time progressed, the committee structure emerged early and remained broadly unchanged.

Convenor Dominance

If the pattern of hierarchy appears at odds with some accounts of steward development, the emergence of the dominant convenor flatly contradicts them. Far from being *primus inter pares* the convenor of the Coventry Precision Company was, virtually from the start, the dominant shop steward. Between 1947 and 1952 five men held the position of convenor, four from the AEU and one from the TGWU. Of these, three who overlapped in office and came and went in the early days, were, from the minuted accounts, the dominant stewards on the committee. They were credited with initiating most of the policy debates that took place. Fragments of information testify to their abilities; most clearly the quality and literacy of the minutes they themselves took when acting as secretary. Dick Stynes, the TGWU convenor from 1948 until 1952, was four years later the Secretary of the Standard Shop Stewards Committee, Press Officer for the Coventry Trades Council and a member of the executive committee of the Coventry Labour Party (Melman, 1958: 245) — presumably therefore a highly able labour activist.

The inter-union battles of the early years, combined with the high financial costs of the convenorship, contributed to the high turnover. But even in this period the convenors had established their right to attend meetings of the District Confederation of Shipbuilding and Engineering Unions, as well as their own District Committees. In addition, they frequently chaired the JSSC meetings.

In 1952 a newcomer to the JSSC was elected AEU convenor. He was, according to one informant, a Communist Party member from London, and he remained convenor until 1960 when he was succeeded by his protégé, a man who had been a steward since 1950 and JSSC chairman since 1952. This latter man remained convenor until mid-1969. Between them these two appear effectively to have run the JSSC for seventeen years. The most impressive indication of their authority, but one difficult to use with precision, is the extent to which their activities, documented regularly under the agenda item 'convenor's report', come to dominate the minute books. But other, more formal, indices, confirm the impression. For example, it is recorded that, in addition to automatic membership of the committees referred to above, the convenor was made an automatic delegate to meetings of Dowty Group stewards ('combine' meetings) in 1953, and was elected 'press officer' in 1954. The convenor dominated the handling of individual grievances and other aspects of bargaining. In addition to handling matters referred to him through other stewards, he also had the responsibility of representing groups who could not find a steward themselves.

There were occasional signs of stewards attempting to curb this dominant role. In 1952 the JSSC agreed that the convenor should keep a record of all his activities, but there is no evidence that this happened. In 1960 a steward stated that the convenor was meeting management on his own too much, and thus leaving himself open to criticism (although he may have been referring to an isolated incident). In 1962 a motion of no confidence in the convenor was tabled by a steward but never debated. These minor and isolated events were the only references in twenty years that could indicate disaffection among the stewards.

Several factors contributing to this dominance can be identified. The first, as noted above, was the very high turnover rate among the stewards, which enhanced the convenor's pre-eminence as the most experienced steward present. Second, and of evident importance from the start, was the financial position of the convenor as opposed to other stewards. In the early days the shop steward funds were so sparse that in effect they could afford to compensate only one or two stewards (in practice the convenors) for loss of pay. Inevitably stewards passed grievances on rather than handle them themselves. Although stewards other than the convenor started to receive compensation in the early 1950s as the funds built up, the convenor always had the first and largest claim on the fund (for much of its lifetime it was called the 'convenor's fund'). While it is impossible to estimate the time spent on union activities by the convenor, it is apparent from the minutes that in 1948 he was guaranteed a minimum of four hours per week compensation from the fund, and that by 1960 he was spending 90 per cent of his time on union business. In that year the JSSC resolved to approach the company to ask that any steward elected convenor be put onto daywork at his section average, a device which effectively allowed the convenor to take time off without loss of pay. The company, which had earlier suggested making a donation to the fund, agreed readily. From then on the convenor's financial security was guaranteed.

Other management decisions also affected the convenor, such as, in 1952, conceding him the right to use company telephones, but the most important managerial influence on convenor dominance was the works and personnel manager's insistence, right from the start, that their dealings be with convenors rather than the other stewards. Stynes' own recollections confirm the impression gained from the minute books in this, and it may be that management's resistance to the sectional stewards was one reason for their high turnover. But the convenors themselves fostered this managerial approach, and this led directly to close links between the convenors and the man who became personnel manager in the early 1950s (he had earlier been the company secretary). These individual relationships were reinforced by the fact that this man remained personnel manager throughout the entire period, and he appears to have been given a relatively free hand in his dealings with the stewards.

Nowhere is the central role of the convenor more graphically illustrated than in the chaos in the shop steward committee following the resignation of the long-serving convenor in 1969. Problems in finding a steward prepared to take on the job led to a volunteer being found from the National Society of Metal Mechanics (NSMM) which had only three members in the plant. According to an (unsigned) document 'Chronicle of the 1970 Negotiations' he was immediately plunged into major wage restructuring negotiations with management and resigned a few weeks later 'after hearing of an alternative man being sought by some stewards to become convenor'. His successor succeeded in restoring stability and the 'Chronicle' referred to above spent considerable time emphasizing his part in the successful wage negotiations. But he too had to face a motion of no confidence within a year, following repeated complaints from the TGWU that they were not being properly represented.

This account provides ample evidence that shop steward hierarchy and, in particular, convenor dominance, are by no means innovations of the 1970s. At Coventry Precision they were present virtually from the effective start of steward organization in the early 1950s. The long-standing commitment to constitutional propriety reflected and reinforced this dominance, as shown, for example, by the role accorded to the convenor in successive versions of the JSSC constitution. But other forces underlay the convenor's position. We will examine three of them: the particular payment system in operation at the factory, the role of management, and the role of the 'outside union'.

The Roots of Convenor Dominance

Piecework Bargaining and Steward Structure
An account of relationships between stewards and members based on piecework bargaining draws attention to the bases of loyalties and antagonisms. At an individual level it is likely that, given the frequency of job timings and re-timings, a high proportion of pieceworkers would have made use of the services of a steward in negotiating a price. But while perhaps enhancing loyalty to an individual steward who 'did a good job' and encouraging the view that a representative structure is a necessary feature of factory life, it does not contribute to a perception of the union as a collectivity requiring mass participation for its effectiveness. To some extent that limitation may be transcended by sectional loyalties when sectional averages were being negotiated, as appears to have happened, for example, under the operation of the gang system at Standard Motors. But because at Coventry Precision the ability to improve sectional averages depended on continuous upward pressure on individual earnings, this process of piecework bargaining only occasionally engendered group activity. As for factory-wide loyalties, there were only rare moments when they were tested through wage bargaining. Even when this did happen, as with a claim in 1963 for 2d per hour for all pieceworkers, shopfloor views on industrial action to back the claim were elicited section by section with a 'lowest common denominator' outcome and a patchy response to a call for the minimum agreed action; a half-day strike one Friday afternoon.

The central political problem confronting the JSSC at Coventry Precision was in effect to develop a factory-wide policy in the face of continuing sectional and individual pressures. Two attempts were made by the stewards to negotiate a factory-wide revision of the piecework scheme, the first almost immediately in the wake of the successful push for 100 per cent membership when, it might reasonably be assumed, plant-wide solidarity was at a high point. A new scheme was introduced, approved by most of the pieceworkers, but heavily criticized by the dayworkers, especially the women. Constant pressure from the dayworkers led the JSSC to attempt a further reform in 1952, but this failed as a result of shopfloor indifference and management hostility. Managerial preference for maintaining the existing system and refusal to take seriously any further attempts at radical revision led to a decline in steward interest in this approach. They therefore were confronted with the need to balance sectional and individual interests. A requirement that all changes in piecework times be notified to the JSSC in late 1952 indicates an awareness of the need for regular information to monitor the situation.

The payment system was based on the negotiation, annually and/or at any other time that seemed appropriate, of section averages for groups of pieceworkers. Ratefixers timed each individual job and that time was then offered to individual workers who accepted it unless it was insufficiently generous to allow them to make at least the sectional average earnings. Rejection of 'tight' times was the main source of piecework grievance. Groups of dayworkers had their wages increased periodically in separate negotiations, but allegations that the stewards were paying insufficient attention to these groups, especially the toolroom, appeared periodically throughout the minutes, and were one reason for the occasional disaffection of the toolroom (and other groups) with the representation provided. The attention paid by the stewards to all aspects of piecework earnings was a clear indication of the importance attached to this aspect of their work.

It is clear from the early stages that in handling both individual and sectional claims the JSSC's approach was informed by political judgements of the appropriateness of particular claims and their potential 'knock-on effects', although the words 'differentials' and 'relativities' rarely occur. They were concerned to maintain roughly equal earnings in individual sections. Thus, for example, in March 1954, when a dayworker transferred to piecework was earning more than the rest of the section, the JSSC made it known that they would not oppose a re-time, leading to a cut in the man's pay. More generally, the minutes contain frequent references to situations where stewards were instructed to ensure members' acceptance of negotiated rates as fair. Sectional claims were dealt with on a similar basis. In April 1960 one section took industrial action, alleging it had done badly out of section average changes agreed by the JSSC. The senior TGWU steward threatened resignation should the agreement be jeopardized by their action. The JSSC agreed that they could not support such action and the section was informed of this by the convenor, at which they returned to normal working.

The maintenance of internal parities was just one part of the internal politics of piecework. The other side was shown partly by constant upward pressure on sectional averages through the negotiating machinery and also by defence by the JSSC not only of specific piecework grievances they considered justified, but of other aspects of working practices designed to help the workers' side in piecework bargaining. A constant stream of small matters relating to this started in 1947 with the JSSC backing workers' objections to the use of stopwatches for job timing and eventually agreeing with management that the watches should be face-down while timing jobs. In 1968 the JSSC supported the action of a worker who refused to sign a worksheet on which the ratefixer had applied times to separate motions, claiming that this was tantamount to time and motion study. Individual ratefixers were supported by the stewards in some cases, or complained about to senior management in others (according to a minute in September 1955 several ratefixers had been reprimanded as a result of such complaints). The factory-wide knowledge and appreciation of these actions by the stewards was one reason why the JSSC had a degree of support when it refused to support workers, for example in both 1957 and 1967 when workers were accused of causing excess scrap by increasing feeds and speeds to boost earnings. On such occasions, according to the convenor, 'it is not the duty of stewards to make excuses or defend men who have scrapped work. Their only duty is to see that the punishment is fair'.

Such an approach could lead to feelings among individuals or sections that they were not being properly represented, and this could come out as dissatisfaction with the section stewards, leading, on occasion, to their resignation. JSSC policy to try to maintain internal equity, although rooted in a desire for stability and fairness may, it appears, have had a destabilizing effect in some instances where individual and group interests were affected. It is worth recalling the quotation from Hyman cited above, in which the shop steward committee's function of co-ordination is *contrasted* with that of control, the former being seen as more typical of the early history of shop stewards. The evidence of Coventry Precision suggests that this may be a false dichotomy; co-ordination, over competing wage claims for example, appears to *necessitate* a degree of control, as indicated by JSSC incursions into sectional sovereignty. Without control, as suggested by Bélanger and Evans in this collection (see also Thompson and Bannon, 1985: 36–49), piecework bargaining becomes unco-ordinated and ultimately almost anarchic.

But this control was constrained by stewards' recognition of the pressure they were under from their members to maintain a degree of sectional independence. The ambivalence felt by the JSSC towards sectional action and autonomy was neatly illustrated by the 1967 pay negotiations in which each section was asked to respond, through its steward, to the JSSC proposals. At the same time it was agreed that no information on the progress of negotiations should be released to the shopfloor. A fortnight later the convenor claimed that stewards discussing and representing the views of their own sections in talks with management were 'undermining the effectiveness of the claim' and this led to a JSSC decision that in future only six stewards would meet management, a move that had the effect of reducing sectional contributions to the debate.

If the wage-bargaining system occasionally undermined the relationships between sectional stewards and their members, it acted to underpin the central position of the convenor. The *negative* reason for this was the fragmented nature of any opposition to the convenor; disaffected groups or stewards were often isolated. The *positive* reason was that the convenor handled all the tough individual and sectional wages issues; if he took it on there was a good chance of success. The wage payment system thus operated to enhance the standing of the convenor in the eyes of those on whose behalf he acted.

The Steward Organization and the 'Outside Union'

One aspect of the 'bureaucratization' argument, as noted above, was that steward systems, especially the leaders, had lost their early 'autonomy' from the official unions and had been increasingly integrated into official trade union machinery during the 1970s. The Coventry Precision minute books shows that the relationship between stewards and the wider union was more complex than this straightforward characterization allows. While the JSSC had virtually total sovereignty in deciding factory union policy, the wider union movement and its activities continually impinged upon steward behaviour, but often in such a way as to reinforce its own policies and priorities. There is very little evidence of tension between the two.

The role played by the full-time officials − of the TGWU in particular − in the recruitment and organization drive of the late 1940s and early 1950s has been noted. The close working relationships certainly persisted through the period of inter-union rivalry when the TGWU District Office, for example, helped to produce a Coventry Precision Stewards' Newsletter. Also noted were how differences in national union policy towards members in arrears became a basis for inter-union rivalry in Coventry Precision, and how a JSSC constitution drafted by the CSEU provided a basis for resolving it.

The branch and district levels of organization played their part in matters of internal union discipline, both against members in arrears and against occasionally troublesome shop stewards, as for example in late 1969 when a steward was threatened with being reported to the District Committee for refusing to attend JSSC meetings because he had 'no confidence in the shop stewards committee'. National union policies only rarely impinged on local activities, such as during token stoppages in support of national claims, most especially reductions in the basic working week.

But there was one issue of direct concern to the membership and the stewards that more than any other illustrated the relationship between stewards and the wider union − the working and allocation of overtime. From the start this was an area of potential friction between members and stewards and it was an issue over which the JSSC frequently used the branch and the district as a device for enforcing unpopular decisions on individuals or sections. In early 1951 the JSSC affirmed its continuing commitment to national policy on overtime − no worker could work more than 30 hours per month or 100 hours per year. In September 1955 two workers were reported to the branch for working excessive overtime despite warnings from the JSSC.

Well into the 1960s the JSSC was required to perform a balancing act between individual and group pressures for more overtime, and union policy recommendations from outside trying to restrict it. It is clear that the JSSC surrendered authority to the branch or the district committee to take disciplinary action against workers who had worked excess, but that they were happy when possible to take decisions that might be seen as popular with the shopfloor, such as in January 1965, when there was plenty of work coming in and the JSSC agreed to press management to meet this through overtime, rather than by taking on new labour. When overtime restrictions were adopted as JSSC policy rather than 'union policy' their weakness was shown when the JSSC refused to take any action against individuals who ignored it. This could lead to situations such as that which arose in March 1967 when the JSSC agreed that one section's refusal to lose overtime justified management's decision to declare redundancies — they had no alternative because of work shortages. In effect, therefore, the JSSC refused to take a consistent position on this issue, adopting an opportunistic stance throughout.

The JSSC's apparent unhappiness at dealing with overtime issues contrasts sharply with their confidence in piecework bargaining. The only explanation that seems sustainable is that the JSSC saw overtime as within the area of managerial prerogative, and hence not negotiable, at least not overtly. The same did not apply to piecework. One specific reference can be cited in support of this, namely in 1967 when the JSSC stated that 'it is not the place for a shop steward to organise or make out a rota for overtime working'; the implication being that it is management's task. More generally, it is quite clear that, as with redundancies, there were very few overt challenges to managerial prerogatives over questions of work organization, and this included not only managerial judgement over the need for overtime, but also the wide areas of flexibility and mobility of labour.[4] In this respect Coventry Precision stands in sharp contrast to Premier Metals and other factories described in this volume where stewards allocated overtime and, more generally, challenged managerial discretion over issues of job control. On the overtime question two possible answers can be suggested. The first is that because of the short-batch nature of much of the work, overtime tended to be needed in large amounts at short notice, causing problems for any JSSC interested in devising a fair and equitable distribution. Secondly, this highly formalized and constitutionally-minded JSSC had a long-standing policy of opposition to high levels of systematic overtime. Caught between that and pressure from members for overtime opportunities, it may have been more convenient for the JSSC to abstain from the issue, leaving it to managers and workers to handle between themselves.

From this brief summary of relationships between the stewards and the wider union movement we can draw a few general conclusions. First, that while the stewards enjoyed considerable independence, to describe them as autonomous does not apply to Coventry Precision. Relationships were formal, but generally cordial and supportive. Second, that there is no evidence of any change in the relationships over the years covered. Third, that the wider union was a convenient disciplinary resource for the JSSC throughout its history. Fourth, that being able to cite 'union policy' on issues such as overtime let the JSSC and in particular the convenor 'off the hook' in their dealings with management over areas that might have posed problems. It may be that this made the task of constructing close working relationships between the convenor and the management easier. It is to this that we now turn.

The Unions and Management: a History of Formality

The shop stewards' preference for formal procedures and constitutions has already been shown. The very existence of the minute books on which this account is based also suggests the long-standing preference for written records and codified behaviour. The same is true of the stewards' relationships with management.

In 1942 a formally constituted Joint Production, Consultative and Advisory Committee had been set up, along the lines agreed between the EEF, and the AEU, CSEU and the National Union of Foundry Workers. Although this structure staggered on after the war, putting in brief appearances in 1948, 1950 and 1952 it appears to have had no impact on steward behaviour. Given what we know, it is likely that the stewards were too occupied with the business of membership recruitment at this time. No further mention was made of the JPAC after 1952.

In May 1953 the first meeting of a new Negotiating Committee took place, and from then on the proceedings of this committee were regularly minuted. The composition of the committee is striking. It included the factory manager and the personnel manager, both of whom had already held their posts for several years and who were to remain in those jobs until the late 1960s. On the union side it included both of the long-serving convenors mentioned above (one in his capacity at the time of JSSC chairman). These two between them provided union continuity until 1969. The core composition of this committee, therefore, was stable for at least seventeen years.

The second point that emerges clearly is that the issues discussed at that first meeting included many which were to dominate union/management relationships and steward concerns for the next twenty years. The problems of short batch work, setting times, the timing of new jobs, and dayworkers' bonuses were all there and all ran like a thread through the subsequent history. Stability of membership and of issues discussed — many of the latter of considerable technical sophistication — provide the most fertile of environments for the development of what Batstone *et al*. (1977: 168−77) describe as 'strong bargaining relationships'.

However, although such 'strong bargaining relations' have frequently been seen as characteristic of informal systems of shopfloor industrial relations, at Coventry Precision they co-existed with a mutual commitment to formal agreements and, as we shall see below, the frequent use of formal grievance procedures. This factory, a 'classic' piecework Midlands engineering factory, seems to have been less characteristic of the 'informal regulation' described by Donovan than many others. The clearest evidence of this is the way the negotiating committee itself was used for handling individual and sectional piecework issues. In 1968 an NBPI researcher noted that 'requests for increases in piecework earnings are made ... through the Committee — and not squeezed out of the apparently vulnerable ratefixers'. One direct consequence was the development of detailed written agreements, covering subjects such as 'procedure agreed where a piecework price agreed on one shift is not agreed by the following shift' and 'definitions of what constitutes a short batch on different machines and consequent allowances'. Even more perishable items, such as agreement on the agreed rate to be paid on a machine that had developed technical faults, were written down and signed.

Although these are difficult to date with precision, the shop steward minutes provide information on when, in the view of the stewards at least, agreement had been reached on certain issues. Running from an agreement on ratefixers' use of stopwatches in 1947 through to an agreement on redundancy pay in 1971, the system generated a steady stream of agreements (a list of 27 identified areas is appended as appendix A). This steady output of formal agreements testifies to a consistent preference over the 25 years for written detailed agreements. The agreements reflect pressures of the time — so the 1958 redundancy agreement was reached during a period of heavy redundancies. But they do show an unvarying preference for recording and codifying agreements once reached, among both managers and stewards. Custom and practice (C&P), although referred to from time to time in the minutes, does not seem to have been the same dominant force here as in some factories during the same period.

The use of procedure provides some additional supporting evidence. Although records are scant, we know that in a four-year period up to mid-1968 the formal Engineering Procedure was used on 33 ocassions, resulting in 22 works conferences, 8 local conferences and 3 central conferences. Most of these were over simple wage increases for small groups (e.g. one central conference was needed to get management to raise a proposed increase for labourers from 2d to 3d an hour). This use of procedures suggests either a degree of managerial stubbornness or a desire on the part of management and unions to obtain an authoritative judgement on even relatively minor issues. It is well-established that use of procedure generally had increased during this period (see Hyman, 1972: 21) but a crude calculation based on Hyman's figures for those four years suggests that Coventry Precision, with a manual workforce of about 500 at that time (out of a Coventry engineering total of just over 100,000) (Thoms and Donnelly, 1986: 39) accounted for 2 or 3 per cent of all formal references to procedure, about four times what its workforce proportion might indicate.

Noted in the discussion on shop steward committee structures were the ways in which the establishment of a JSSC Negotiating Committee reinforced the authority of a small group, and the way in which the JSSC was on occasion prepared to turn down claims from individuals and groups. These aspects of steward politics were reinforced by the importance attached to formal bargaining. It is a truism that the use of formal procedures may act to reinforce shop steward heirarchy (e.g. Terry, 1983: 80) and their authority over sectional groups. At Coventry Precision this was clearly visible. Thus the (joint) negotiating committee minutes show the convenor saying of a demand for an increase by a machine section that the JSSC 'was not in agreement with this re-

quest, but obviously they must press it. They also deprecated the non-acceptance
of the agreement between management and the negotiating committee by the
operatives concerned'. Such remarks made to a joint committee can hardly have
improved the section's chances of success, and the failure of such a claim might
have strengthened the convenor's hand in dealing with the section in future. The
company's support for convenor discretion in such matters is neatly shown in
a letter from the Group General Manager to the convenor on his retirement, 'As
we are both well aware', he wrote 'the . . . procedure for avoiding disputes can
only work on a basis of mutual trust, and it has been a great help to me to know
that you have always tried to *apply your own standards to the many requests and
mandates you have been given by your members*' (emphasis added).

The company's preparedness to deal with stewards, and convenors in particular, from the start, has already been noted. We know from Rolt that the Dowty
Group gave considerable business autonomy to their subsidiaries (Rolt, 1962:
79) and a logical inference would be that this extended to industrial relations
matters.[5] Rolt also stresses the importance attached by the Group to personnel
issues generally (Rolt, 1962: 81—2) and we know that a pension scheme for
shopfloor staff dates from as early as 1957. The local management was never
hostile to 'personnel' matters, and it is perhaps no coincidence that the JSSC
itself devoted considerable effort to collections from the members on behalf of
various charities. The steward organization therefore developed in an environment that was broadly supportive. But the managerial environment equally
clearly encouraged the steward organization to grow in certain directions. As we
have noted above, they encouraged the development of 'responsible' convenors
from the start, and appear to have had clear views on what they were and were
not prepared to negotiate about. Both the procedural and substantive interests of
the JSSC can thus be seen to be in part an outcome of managerial preference
(although there is no evidence to support the view that this was a conscious
'strategy').

Conclusions

This case study has provided evidence that, at least in one Coventry engineering
factory, workplace industrial relations changed little in character between the
early 1950s and the early 1970s. The essential characteristics of shop steward
hierarchy, convenor dominance, formal and constitutional handling of both
JSSC affairs and stewards' dealings with management can all be detected from
the early days. There is little evidence to support a general view of increasing
'bureaucratization' during the period under discussion. All the essential
characteristics of a bureaucratic structure were present from the start.

Nor is there any evidence to suggest that these characteristics were the
outcome of any conscious intervention by either the outside union(s) or the
management, although we have shown ways in which the influence of both acted

to reinforce such tendencies. From the outset JSSC affairs were dominated by one or two individuals; the adoption of a constitutional form that reinforced this dominance was the outcome of *inter-union* problems, not managerial intervention. We have also argued the importance of the payment system and the particular politics of piecework bargaining in understanding the internal dynamics of the steward organization. That in turn reflected, among other things, the particular product market in which the company operated; the short-batch nature of much of the work. The product market was also an important influence on routine steward activity; piecework bargaining claims went up as product demand increased and order books were full. Finally, the high degree of skill involved in all the work, even that described as 'semiskilled' was also important. Thus all the factors typically claimed as important in understanding the dynamics of steward organization were at work.

But above all these we need to understand the part played by the stewards and workers themselves. This account confirms the need to pay greater attention than has recently been fashionable to the way in which the members themselves shape their own organization within the constraints undoubtedly set by the management, the technology and the labour and product markets. The chapter clearly shows how the development of the steward organization reflected a clear set of JSSC decisions intended to enhance, primarily, the effectiveness of the convenor in negotiating piecework wage issues.

Equally, however, it is important not to fall into the trap of equating such structures with 'undemocratic' behaviour. Insufficient data exist on membership views, and we have seen how participation by the rank-and-file, as conventionally measured, was never high. But we suggested that it was at least possible to infer a high degree of membership satisfaction with the success achieved by the JSSC in wage bargaining on their behalf. There is no evidence of a shift from control exercised by stewards on behalf of members to control exercised by stewards over members; both dimensions co-existed from the start. But the terminology itself is one which does not suit the steward/member relationship as indicated by the minute books. An analysis based on acceptance by the membership of the demands and priorities of the stewards would be more in keeping with the data. Formal indicators of democratic practice, whether of 'representative democracy' or of at least some versions of 'direct democracy' are incapable of estimating the stewards' claims to be representing the interests of most of their members most of the time. While they may be factors to be considered, their significance is shaped by the daily processes of shopfloor politics. In this case, for example, the nature of the work process, the payment system, and managerial behaviour towards the stewards were all contributing towards the shaping of membership and steward interests, and their bargaining priorities. Analyses of union democracy − at shopfloor level in particular − need to start from an appreciation of the political forces and constraints and only then begin to evaluate the importance of internal government procedures, both formal and informal.

Notes

The author is very grateful to Willy Brown for making available to him much of the archival material on which this chapter is based.

1. Archival evidence suggests that this issue of the length of acceptable arrears was a source of conflict in other Coventry factories.
2. The active role of the Confederation in Coventry under Jack Jones's secretaryship in this period was probably unique. In many places it was simply defunct (see Marsh, 1965: 30—3).
3. McCarthy and Parker (1968: 20) quote management estimates of shop steward turn-over between 13 and 17 per cent per annum on average.
4. The only clear exceptions to this appeared when managerial decisions challenged the white male exclusivity of the shopfloor. The JSSC resisted the recruitment of women, black workers and unskilled workers at various times.
5. The occasional references to Dowty Group Combine Committee dealings suggest considerable local IR differences.

Appendix A

Subjects and dates of agreements recorded in JSSC Minute Book:

1.	Ratefixing methods (stopwatch)	1947
2.	Canteen facilities	1951
3.	Facilities for convenor (telephone)	1952
4.	Time and motion study	1953
5.	Average rates for hospital visits	1954
6.	Apprentices' wages and conditions	1954
7.	Ratefixing methods (general)	1955
8.	Responsibility for scrapped work	1955
9.	Recruitment of new labour	1957
10.	Merit schemes	1957
11.	Consultation before overtime work	1957
12.	Retirement age	1958
13.	Redundancy	1958
14.	Job transfer/mobility	1958
15.	Pension scheme	1958
16.	Safety regulations	1959
17.	Discipline for lateness and absenteeism	1959
18.	Dayworkers' rates tied to Coventry toolroom average	1963
19.	Contracting of work outside factory	1965
20.	Authority of security personnel	1966
21.	Use of temporary labour	1968
22.	Foreman's authority in approving work	1968
23.	Interpretation of 'fatigue'	1968
24.	Length of tea break	1969
25.	Allowance for cleaning machines	1970
26.	Payment for salvage and rectification work	1970
27.	Redundancy pay	1971

3

The Changing Face of Conflict: Shopfloor Organization at Longbridge, 1939–1980

Steve Jefferys

Editors' Foreword

This chapter provides a broad overview of the history of shop steward organization at the Austin factory in Longbridge, Birmingham from the end of the war to the early 1980s. The central problem addressed by Jefferys is how a union organization as apparently powerful as the Longbridge Joint Shop Stewards Committee could be so rapidly and effectively swept aside in the period 1979–81. The answer, he argues, lies in understanding the essentially contingent nature of the power of the stewards. Thus, although shopfloor organization was able to grow, by fits and starts, through the 1960s and 1970s by exploiting market-based bargaining power and weaknesses in management's own structures, it was helpless in the face of the combination of rapidly declining business, anti-union management, and an increasingly hostile political environment.

The period under review cannot, Jefferys maintains, be understood except in the context of events that took place before and during the Second World War. The pre-war hostility towards unions shown by Austin himself and his senior managers led to the claim that Longbridge could not be organized, a claim soon refuted by wartime experience. During that period the critical events identified by Jefferys are the building of a nearby 'shadow' factory not affected by the Austin tradition, the impact of wartime legislation, the recruitment of large amounts of youthful, less deferential, labour, and the organizing role of the Communist Party. Towards the end of the war Dick Etheridge, the dominant character for the next three decades, was elected convenor.

After the war managerial attempts to turn back the clock were resisted by a union organization that had at least achieved viability, but the succeeding decades saw a period of entrenched shopfloor struggle as the company continued to resist recognition of shopfloor realities. Jefferys sees the continuation of an 'entrepreneurial tradition' in car manufacture and a failure to merge and amalgamate towards a modern car industry as evidence of the lack of strategic thinking within the enterprise. This found its reflection in multi-unionism, *ad hoc* shopfloor bargaining, and overt conflict never far below the surface. Jefferys contrasts this with the very different experience of the period in the United States and argues that the large differences in union organization between the two countries reflect differences in managerial strategy across a wide range of issues, including labour relations.

The 'blocking power' won by the unions — although never in a way that was able to inform a wider trade union strategy — created real problems for management and led the company to attempt a wide-ranging reform of collective bargaining in the 1970s. However, this too bore the hallmarks of haste, and the major consequence of the imposed structures was a weakening of links between the stewards, especially the convenor, and the membership, thus paving the way for the convenor's isolation and dismissal at the end of the decade.

The bulk of the chapter deals with the period 1945−72, and pays less attention to the period of reform and the dismissal of Etheridge's successor, Derek Robinson. This latter period is better-known and this account may be supplement by further material (Edwardes (1983); Willman and Winch (1985); Scarborough (1986)). Jefferys' chapter is broader in scope than most in this volume, and does not attempt the same detailed exercise. This enables it to touch on matters not dealt with in other contributions, including the formative role of the Communist Party (for a detailed description of the CP's analogous role in Coventry see Hinton, 1980). The author also draws attention to the importance of company structure, and the consequences of 'macro-level' decisions on such matters as merger, investment, and product range, although restrictions of space do not permit a full working-through of these processes.

Jefferys' analysis and conclusion are pessimistic in the sense that they clearly point to both the circumscribed and limited nature of shopfloor power, and to the extent of managerial influence on steward development. This helps us to understand the intractable problems stewards face when dealing with hostile managers in unfavourable economic and political conditions. The speed with which this powerful union structure was dismantled — Jefferys' starting pont — reinforces this analysis.

Introduction

The Austin Joint Shop Stewards' Committee, covering the giant Longbridge car manufacturing complex south of Birmingham, became known in the 1960s and 1970s as one of the most powerful of Britain's shop stewards' organizations. Yet in 1979 the committee's chief shop steward was dismissed more easily than was an earlier leading steward back in 1952. And by the summer of 1985 Austin Rover's director of employee relations argued that industrial conflict had effectively been eliminated from the plant.[1]

Recently much attention has focused on the significance and depth of the reorganization of industrial relations at the renamed Rover Group since 1979.[2] Short-term studies, however, tend to see change as a sequence of jerky movements, like a handcranked home movie. To get at the underlying historical dynamic, observation has to be speeded up and the perspective broadened. It has to range over factors such as managerial insecurities over the domestic and international markets, and workers' insecurities over employment, remuneration and work organization. And it has to stretch out to see the impact of the interaction of all these elements in a broader national political context. As this is done the image of a fixed frontier between two powers, management and workers, each exercising control over a distinct area of shopfloor practice, dissolves. In the place of clearly separated areas of 'worker control', 'management control' and 'joint control' and observation of their spatial competition over time, what appears is the continuous presence of opposed interests. This opposition is occasionally strident, highly visible and clearly articulated; more often it is confused, subdued and muted. Behind the appearance of worker restraints over managerial prerogatives or of unilateral managerial authority over its workforce is the complex history and active presence of articulate or inarticulate conflict.

In the USA, where the auto industry experienced rapid growth in the 1930s and 1940s, General Motors, Ford and Chrysler conceded 100 per cent unionization and gave manual workers seniority rights, high wages and pension schemes by the close of 1950. The effect of these reforms was to tie US car workers closely to their particular firm and plant. Formal collective bargaining procedures were introduced in the 1940s and 1950s which replaced much shopfloor bargaining and ultimately the shop stewards with legally binding plant- and company-wide negotiations. Conflict survived, but with a few notable exceptions, its articulation has generally been controlled within formal collective bargaining institutions (Jefferys, 1986: 32−3, 42).

Why has the expression of underlying conflicts of interest in the British car industry apparently been so different from the United States experience? At least three wider institutional factors played a part in delimiting the British experience of conflict: the British business tradition, the narrowness of British trade unions and the growth of the Welfare State. After the Second World War, British car output grew rapidly to 1950, from 1953 to 1955, from 1957 to 1960, and from 1962 to 1964. Yet the UK motor companies did not use these years of reconstruction and expansion to accommodate the unions and foster company loyalty. One reason for this was the presence immediately after the war of six UK volume producers competing for a much smaller domestic market than in the US. The four British-owned firms, Austin, Morris, Rootes and Standard, were particularly reluctant to raise labour costs and risk their short-term profits or the high levels of dividends they paid to their shareholders. Still run by the founding entrepreneurs or their chosen successors they were also particularly concerned to maintain their 'independence'. Thus a 1948 agreement on what the *Financial Times* called a 'complete technical merger' between Austin and Morris Motors collapsed in renewed acrimony between Leonard Lord and William Morris (Lord Nuffield) nine months later (see *Financial Times*, 7 October 1946; 13 July 1949). And when, eventually, a defensive merger between the two partners did stick in 1952, real rationalization of the product lines and plants was delayed another 10 to 15 years. The UK car industry from the 1940s to the 1960s provides a classic example of the impediments to the transition to modern corporate capitalism which Elbaum and Lazonick argue arise from the 'institutional legacy of atomistic economic organisation' (Elbaum and Lazonick, 1986: 15).

The post-war survival of the 'independent entrepreneur' tradition in British-owned car firms had significant industrial relations consequences. General management skills were largely absent from the self-made 'practical' men or members of a dominant family who made up the board, and the multidivisional management structures which were introduced in the United States at GM in the 1920s and Ford in the 1940s were absent from the British-owned car firms until the 1960s. The overlapping of day-to-day decision-making duties with overall executive responsibilities impeded the development of strategic thinking in all areas, and as long as industrial relations remained an adjunct of production rather than becoming a distinct area of management responsibility, any rational strategizing in this area was improbable.

A second structural factor tending to sustain high levels of open conflict in Britain was the nature and role of national union organization. Overall numbers of trade unionists grew rapidly in the 1940s, from 6 million in 1938 to nearly 8 million in 1945 and 9.5 million in 1951 (Bain and Price, 1983: 5). Yet despite this expansion, British *trade unions* remained weak as national organizations. This paradox was largely the result of two factors: in most sizeable workplaces this larger membership was divided between several overlapping unions with few full-time officials and little or no strategizing capacity. And secondly, employers who would negotiate with 'their own' unionized shopfloor workers continued to resist giving 'outside' officials a role, particularly as many of them appeared to be former militants or card-carrying Communists. The resulting organizational weakness meant the employers were not faced with a single authoritative union with which to negotiate, like the UAW in the United States. This, in turn, inhibited the formalization of British collective bargaining in the 1940s and 1950s. The UK car industry was only effectively 100 per cent unionized in the 1960s, between 10 and 20 years behind the US. When it happened multi-unionism continued to divide the skilled workers on traditional trade lines, although by the 1970s there were only two major unions still competing for semiskilled members. Before then national union leverage on British car firms remained highly localized, with little effective centralization.

Finally, the role of the national unions in post-war Britain in pressurizing managements to reform workers' conditions was weakened by the Welfare State. The fact that the government directly concerned itself with minimizing workers' insecurities over pensions, sickness benefits and unemployment pay, insecurities which in the US were largely accommodated within collective bargaining, had two important consequences. It narrowed the British workplace bargaining arena to the issue which highlighted conflicts of interest: unit labour costs. And it removed the wider bargaining issues to the arena of fierce party political conflict, where insecurities were dealt with by national political elections rather than by negotiation and accommodation. This politicization of welfare-related bargaining concerns, in the context of a Labour parliamentary majority until 1951 and powerful Labour oppositions thereafter, helped to sustain management's political anti-Labour stance at least until the 1960s when Labour took on (albeit temporarily) the appearance of the more progressive managerialist party.

Within this wider framework the focus here is on the origins, development and limitations of the powerful Longbridge shop stewards' organization over the forty years from the onset of the Second World War. This broad longitudinal sweep presents a view of a sharp class cleavage between management and workers which made cross-class bargaining institutions extremely fragile. In this context the frontier of shopfloor conflict moved easily and rapidly with market conditions and in response to workers' changing sense of what were legitimate means of expressing discontent and of securing effective remedies.

The Second World War was a watershed in the development of industrial relations at the Austin Motor Company's Longbridge plant and government intervention was crucial to this change. Before the war Herbert Austin had viewed union activity within his factory as unacceptable outside interference with managerial prerogatives. Yet the wartime Coalition Government's endorsement of collective bargaining forced the reluctant concession by Austin management of limited recognition to the factory's shop stewards. At the end of the war government policy reverted to its traditional largely passive role, and Austin top management's hostility to unionism survived intact until the early 1960s. But the shopfloor organization spawned in the war had grown too powerful in certain key areas of the plant to be destroyed in the boom years of the 1950s. It survived under conditions of pervasive managerial hostility into the 1960s and multiplied its shopfloor restraints upon managerial prerogatives. By the years of stagnation and decline in the 1970s these restraints were identified by management as a major factor in the company's crisis.

The grudging move away from the qualified managerial absolutism of the 1930s towards the acceptance of formal collective bargaining by management in the 1940s and 1950s had its corollary in the emergence of informal, shopfloor multi-union bargaining arrangements in the 1960s and 1970s. Later, the frontier of conflict moved dramatically in management's favour as economic conditions forced management to reorganize. After 1979 it reformed the payment system, cut manpower by more than half, and then removed most of the accumulated restraints on its prerogatives.

The 'power' of the Austin Joint Shop Stewards' Committee is, ultimately, found to rest less upon independent shopfloor activity *per se* − although without it managerial power would have remained largely unimpaired − than upon the 'spaces' conceded to workers' distinct shopfloor interests by a top management that alternated between antagonism and apparent disinterest. These spaces of omission and commission (Brown, 1973: 98−9) encouraged the organizational expression of workers' interests in opposition to management − as manifested in strikes, shop stewards, custom and practice etc. And the reasons for Austin management's propensity to fuel rather than defuse conflict are found in turn to have been formed in the interaction of management tradition, its policies, forms of organization and business strategy, and the wider economy and processes of political change.

From Early Days to 1945

Pre-War Anti-Unionism

Herbert Austin founded the Motor Company in 1905 and built a factory on a greenfield site at Longbridge in a semi-rural area to the south of Birmingham in 1910. By 1914 as many as three-quarters of Austin's 1500 engineering and 500 body workers were union members so the firm joined the Engineering Employers' Federation (EEF) to use its representatives to do any required face-to-face negotiating.[3] Austin did not intend to allow the unions to establish any kind of bargaining within the factory, but by the end of the First World War negotiations on piecework rates had begun and a Works Committee of shop stewards recognized. By 1921−2, when the company teetered on the brink of bankruptcy, the combination of job losses and the national lockout of the Amalgamated Engineering Union had indeed laid the Works Committee to rest. There would be no formal recognition of shop stewards in Austin's lifetime and, indeed, no recognition of a Works Committee representing the body of shop stewards at Longbridge until 1958.

Austin objected both politically and industrially to the labour movement and through C.R.F. Engelbach, works director from 1921 until 1938, and his successor, the former Morris Motors managing director, Leonard P. Lord, successfully impeded unionization of the Longbridge factory. The commonly reported view was that 'the Austin couldn't be organised'.[4]

Wartime Watershed

Rearmament and the Second World War changed Longbridge permanently, inserting government-inspired pluralism into a resisting unitary management structure and philosophy. In October 1936 the government decided to build a large 'shadow' factory to manufacture aircraft frames and engines on a site across the motor test track and flying ground area to the east of the main complex. Within a year the airframe section employed nearly 2000 workers while the aero engine section employed just under 750.[5] The appearance of labour shortages in the Birmingham area as the Aero's workforce rose to 6000 by mid-1938, together with the greater role played in aircraft production by skilled engineering and sheet metal workers payrolled by the government, soon led to the development of an effective union organization.

These consequences of Austin's management of an aircraft factory had an important knock-on effect at Longbridge. The successful unionization of the nearby Aero works and the growth of unions like the Amalgamated Engineering Union (AEU), which doubled its Birmingham membership between 1936 and 1939, greatly stimulated the small numbers of active unionists in the main Austin plant. In 1939, and without management permission, a group of about six shop stewards began to meet to discuss grievances and union recruitment. Wartime restructuring of the factory had major consequences for Longbridge's labour force, its traditional payment system, and the collective bargaining environment. Many of the factory's semi and unskilled male workers were conscripted. By 1942 new labour made up more than half the 16,800 manual workforce supplemented by approximately 5000 clerical workers and staff and including a significant proportion of women.[6] Gradually the new labour broke down the consensus of passive acceptance of managerial rights.

Wartime legislation (see the introduction) played its part in stimulating union growth, as did the formation of Joint Production Committees (JPCs). In June 1942, 50 workers' candidates contested the first election, and two weeks later the ten elected representatives held their first meeting with Leonard Lord and ten managers. Most of those elected were active trade unionists who had been given the backing of Shop Stewards Committee. The result was a boost to the prestige of union organization at Longbridge, although real doubts remained as to what the JPC meetings actually achieved as far as production was concerned.[7]

Despite these advances, at their wartime peak of strength trade unionists counted only a handful of departments as 100 per cent union, and throughout the factory as a whole they conceded there was still 'limited organization' — probably averaging around 50 per cent.[8] But by 1944 the cumulative effect of governmental backing for collective bargaining had led to over one hundred stewards being elected and organized into shop committees. Attendance at the stewards' regular Monday evening plant-wide meetings had also grown to between 20 and 30. Until 1943 when the AEU changed its rules to allow the recruitment of women, the policy of the stewards was to recruit the women workers into the TGWU, which then began to establish a significant membership in the factory. But the Austin Motor Company Shop Stewards' Committee was still dominated by the AEU.

One man in particular had come to the fore: Dick Etheridge. A semiskilled worker, he had a red AEU card, denoting his membership of the craft union's

TABLE 3.1
Wartime Influence of Birmingham CP

Communist Members of:	
National Union Executives	6
District Committees	20
Convenors of Shop Stewards	35
Shop Stewards and Branch Officials	200

Source: Birmingham District CP document, 1942, in
Etheridge Papers, Modern Records Centre.

new Section Five, formed in 1936. In most factories and for virtually the whole of the post-war period, a red card would automatically debar an AEU activist from being elected a shop stewards' convenor over skilled men. But Etheridge was not merely an extremely effective organizer, he was also a member of the Communist Party (CP). In June 1941 the Birmingham CP claimed the depth of representation in the trade union movement shown in table 3.1.

In 1944, when young men, particularly those who were good organizers, were in short supply on the Austin shopfloor, Etheridge's communism was widely viewed as a badge of honour, a sign of solidarity with the Soviet Red Army in its decisive battles against Hitler. The numbers of Communists in Longbridge were, as with national CP membership, at their high point, and the factory cell worked to ensure there was no skilled backlash against the CP candidate. In the winter of 1944, the stewards elected Etheridge as convenor.

In September 1944 the first factory-wide strike conducted by the shop stewards took place. The strike was not just about money, but about the more general fear that the Austin would revert generally to pre-war prices as soon as conditions permitted. With manual employment already 2000 below its 1942–3 peak, and workers anticipating considerable lay-offs in the last few months of the war, this was viewed by workers and stewards as an outcome to be resisted. A month later, the Austin Aero's 564 hourly-paid skilled workers struck for two weeks against a fall in their bonuses as the flow of new war work began to dry up. The AEU Birmingham District Secretary, A. Ager, pleaded with Austin management not to make 'concessions in industry at the point of a pistol' but instead to try and 'get a solution by negotiation'.[9]

The complex reconversion process of peacetime production involved the displacement of most of the plant's wartime women workers, the re-employment of ex-servicemen and the recreation of the pre-war structure of work organization. To smooth the process and ensure the support of the Ministry of Labour's National Service Officer, management conceded the 'fair' trade principle of 'first in, last out'. But the outcome was not a restoration of the pre-war labour force and pre-war labour relations. A solid basis of trade unionism had been established at Longbridge, and this proved sufficient to ensure the survival in key areas of the factory of the wartime organizational tradition of direct bargaining between the stewards and foremen and ratefixers over piecework prices and the 'fair' allocation of work to individual workers. Even the most hostile members of management could see there was little possibility of restoring intact its pre-war non-union strategy. So in 1945, under the interventionist eye of the National Service Officer, management negotiated the reconversion to peacetime production with the 'chief' steward, Etheridge. Austin management continued to refuse to call him 'convenor' since that might have wider organizational and bargaining implications, although they could no longer deny his and the other 100 to 150 stewards' existence.

Management had been forced to legitimate shopfloor unionism by the exigencies of war, and the election of a Labour Government in July 1945 gave this unionism additional justification. In September 1945 an historic meeting took place at Longbridge involving some 30 shop stewards, area superintendents and production managers. This agreed an overall 15 per cent increase in bonus payments to cover the transition from war-time to peace-time production. It was clear there would be no post-war return to the managerial absolutism of the 1920s and 1930s. Yet two months later Leonard Lord was elected chairman of the Austin Motor Company. And, like the late Herbert Austin at the end of the First World War, he had plans which did not include consultations with the unions and which specifically excluded the shop stewards led by Communists like Etheridge. Renewed conflict was on both management's and the shop stewards' post-war agenda.

Reconstruction and Readjustment, 1945–1951

The election in 1945 of a majority Labour government was not welcomed by Lord and the Austin Board. Leonard Lord's attitudes had been forged in staunchly anti-union Morris Motors, from where he had moved to Austin after a personal argument with William Morris in 1938. In November 1945 he decided not to take over the adjacent 'shadow' Aero factory because of continuing economic uncertainty, and at the first peace-time Annual General Meeting in March 1946 Lord bitterly attacked the war-time consensus on economic management. He argued that the war-time level of productivity would have to be improved: 'Can we accept the war effort of our factories as being good enough for the peace effort we must now undertake? He would be a bold man who would answer "Yes" without reservation'. And he challenged the direct controls maintained by the Attlee government:

Industry needs Freedom. Freedom from control and inexperienced academic planning, freedom from interference arising from departmental indecision or jealousy; freedom to apply the principles and experience of production on which the foundations of British trade and prosperity were built and on which it flourished (*Financial Times*, 27 March 1946).

This attack was followed nine months later by a public row between Lord and Emmanuel Shinwell, Minister of Fuel and Power, over Lord's informing the press of the likelihood of Austin shutting down in the fuel crisis before he informed the ministry.

Like Austin, Lord was ideologically opposed to government intervention, and particularly concerned that Labour might continue the wartime restrictions on dividend payments. But his fears were unfounded. While Austin's net profits in the four years from August 1941 to July 1945 averaged £342,000, they rose 360 per cent through the following six years of Labour government. Over the same period dividend payments rose from 16.25 per cent to 40 per cent of net profits a year.[10] The improvement in Austin's performance, particularly in 1950 and 1951, was largely due to the Labour government's directive to the car industry to sell 75 per cent of its output in the highly profitable export market. As early as 1946 Austin took over a large flight shed adjacent to the wartime flying ground for packing and despatching exports and in 1948 Austin moved into a third of the Aero area, which subsequently became known as the East Works. By 1950 Austin's manual labour force was some 42 per cent above the temporarily depressed 1945 level, as shown in table 3.2.

The growth of Austin's labour force between 1945 and 1950 in a period of Labour government reduced job insecurity and encouraged the renewal of the unionization process. In a few key areas of the factory, where the workers exerted considerable economic leverage over the whole production process, such as the West Works body shop, 100 per cent closed shops for particular unions were fought for and then tolerated by management. A strong union identity was particularly important for the two sheet metal workers' unions who used it to

TABLE 3.2
Longbridge Labour Force, 1942–1959

	Manual Workforce at Austin Longbridge, 1942–59		
Year	Manual Workers *(000s)*	Year	Manual Workers *(000s)*
1942	16.8	1951	16.9
1943	16.8	1952	17.2
1944	14.8	1953	17.1
1945	12.5	1954	18.3
1946	14.1	1955	19.9
1947	15.0	1956	14.7
1948	15.5	1957	16.7
1949	16.7	1958	16.6
1950	17.8	1959	17.1

Source: Etheridge Papers, MSS 202/3/4, Modern Records Centre.

set and maintain a ceiling on piecework earnings. In June 1946 the Birmingham and Midland Sheet Metal Workers (BMSMW) in the West Works struck to force an AEU member put on a job planishing a back seam with lead filling to join their union.[11] The sheet metal workers struck again on their own in October 1950 in protest against management laying off 150 line workers for two shifts, after previously redeploying workers when demand for the A70 car had fallen. They were using their closed shop in particular areas and occupations to impose restrictions upon management's unilateral prerogatives over hiring, firing and moving labour.

Other groups found the closed shop equally important in creating effective bargaining units capable of restraining a hostile management. The National Union of Vehicle Builders pursued a long and ultimately successful campaign in 1946 through the official procedures and on the shopfloor to secure an enhanced hourly rate for all its members 'the proper rate, however much the work may be split up by mass production methods'. In December 1948 the 40 AEU lorry body shop workers struck when one of their number decided to join the SMW.[12] Unlike the situation in the US, where the mid- and late 1940s saw auto companies conceding 100 per cent union shops in exchange for the national unions agreeing to discipline their members, at Austin the closed shop arose out of shopfloor workers taking sectional industrial action themselves.

Better financial returns and the withdrawal of the protective presence of Ministry of Labour and National Service officials after 1945, however, exerted countervailing pressure on Austin's top management to revert more closely to its pre-war industrial relations style. The result was that unionization developed in a context of daily conflict in which each new stage in the construction of a collective bargaining system was achieved in conditions of open conflict or covert suspicion. For example, when in May 1946 Lord announced 6 per cent across-the-board price increase on Austin cars, he publicly blamed the engineering unions for negotiating a national wage award which had raised the company's wage bill. He then refused to pay the national award in full for another six months until a National Arbitration Award was made against Austin.[13] Again, in January 1947, when the worst winter weather ever recorded settled on Britain, the company first responded with a good time-keeping bonus 'to maintain production'. And then in February when power cuts and supply problems made production virtually impossible, despite 70 per cent of the workforce having kept good time, Lord had no hesitation in issuing a week's notice terminating the contracts of all its 15,000 production workers to save the company from paying £37,400 a week in minimum wage guarantees.

Lord was as much an autocrat in the area of industrial relations as Herbert Austin, so although the presence of 170 shop stewards was acknowledged by the Personnel Department in 1946, top management rarely consulted them. In January 1948, for example, when management declared 600 Longbridge workers redundant, the stewards were angered by the absence of any forewarning or discussion. The stewards' convenor, Etheridge, repeated to the press the demand for effective collective bargaining arrangements:

We are not looking for trouble, but we are not afraid of it. We are extending the hand of friendship in the interests of production; but if the firm does not want it that way, they can have the other (*Financial Times*, 17 January 1948).

Top management maintained an ostrich-like posture after the war. It tried to ignore the increased legitimacy of the shop stewards through denying any status or role to their in-plant organization. In 1947 an agreement on a $42\frac{1}{2}$-hour working week, in keeping with Austin's pre-war policy of offering slightly better conditions than in the national agreement, was reached with Etheridge, but was then signed by management and the local Confederation of Shipbuilding and Engineering Unions' (CSEU) full-time officials.[14] The company acknowledged the existence of the 'chief' steward, Etheridge, but refused to recognize his deputies or the senior shop stewards of other unions with significant membership in the factory and it continued to use every opportunity, especially in periods of cyclical downturn, to undermine union organization.

Lord's anti-union philosophy could not consistently be sustained by front-line supervisors on the shopfloor. Under pressure from senior management to maximize production in the export drive, they increasingly found themselves obliged to make local deals with effective pockets of union organization. Within days of the January 1948 redundancies which provoked Etheridge to denounce top management's rejection of his 'hand of friendship', his offer was welcomed by his own supervision in the no. 2 machine shop. Four men, who had been fired for booking in more piecework items than they had actually turned out, were reinstated. This was on the basis of an agreement which ensured greater fairness all round. In future work would be shared out by the men so that no-one would feel obliged to make fraudulent work bookings because they were on a poorly-paying job or one which involved too much waiting time.[15]

Initially the foremen agreed to this self-regulation of job booking and work distribution because it ensured a better-running shop and higher production levels. But within this 'space' it did not take long for the practice to become fully legitimated in the eyes of the workforce, and hence a potential restraint upon management if it wished subsequently to change it. Shopfloor informal bargaining had begun as wartime *ad hoc* on-the-job encounters between a worker and steward on one side with a foreman and ratefixer on the other. But with the introduction of the post-war models in 1948 this basic bargaining level was supplemented by more formal meetings in the foreman's office. Frequently more than one foreman would be present, with ratefixers and sometimes the departmental manager as well. They might face several stewards belonging to different unions whose constituencies were also sometimes multi-union, and who were often in competition with each other for union members and influence. Imperceptibly, shopfloor bargaining developed from personal relationships into an institution with informal but clearly defined rules regulating the visibility of conflict.

A major challenge to this process of conflict regulation through shopfloor bargaining occurred in August 1948. Management used a demonstrator rather than a worker of average ability to fix a piecework rate on a new multi-spindle gear cutting machine. This breach of past practice was an attempt to establish new methods of piecework price fixing on the first post-war models. It aimed to overcome the problems Austin faced of either timing workers who were deliberately working more slowly to try and 'fix' a better rate, or of timing workers who had not had sufficient time on the new job to pick up speed along the learning curve. The result was a new rate which the stewards claimed would mean a loss of 25 or 30 shillings a week. The machine shop workers then staged a stay-in strike which spread rapidly into a three-day plant-wide stoppage.[16]

In 1948 while the Labour Government was desperate to maintain its export drive, the Cold War and anti-Communism were also becoming major factors in trade union and Labour politics. The TUC immediately denounced the loss of exports involved, complaining of 'the disloyalty and irresponsibility displayed by a minority of the workers who allow themselves to become involved in unofficial strikes'. The AEU Executive Council was equally blunt:

> Such unauthorised actions can only have the effect of undermining the authority of the Union. The EC desires to issue the strongest possible warning that calls for unofficial stoppages of work made by shop stewards or District Committees will not be tolerated.

These reactions from national union officials were, however, irrelevant. The threat to immediate production in a highly competitive market place was already too great and Austin rapidly retreated. The strikers resumed work when management agreed to drop the new practice of 'fixing prices by demonstrators' times'. Austin also restored the original piecework prices 'until negotiations are completed'. An important feature of the settlement was that it was put by the Joint Shop Stewards' Committee to a mass meeting of 10,000 strikers for their endorsement. Without considering the longer-term implications of its actions, management had provided the stewards with an issue on which they established the credibility of factory-wide industrial action with the whole workforce and, perhaps more crucially, with front-line supervisors. The result legitimated the existence of a major restraint upon management's ability to control unit labour costs.

This confirmation of post-war shopfloor bargaining between shop stewards, foremen and departmental managers was reinforced by another aspect of Austin's traditional anti-unionism. This was management's denial of exclusive bargaining rights to the two or three unions which theoretically could have represented most of its workers. Unless they worked in one of the few closed shops, foremen rarely intervened on the issue of which union new employees should join. If new workers were already members of affiliated unions they simply retained their existing membership, and if they were not, then they could join the union of whomever approached them first or appeared most effective in bargaining with the foreman. It was a very different approach to that of US auto industry management which, after it failed to defeat the unions between

1939 and 1942, deliberately supported industrial unionism (Jefferys, 1986: 24–6, 83–7). The result was that by 1950, when Longbridge had more than 20,000 employees, about 70 per cent of the 17,800 manual workers belonged to 13 different unions and elected around 220 shop stewards. Roughly 40 per cent of the plant's white-collar workers belonged to four staff unions with ten elected representatives to act for them.[17]

Austin management's refusal to funnel workers into one particular union effectively fostered the spread of multi-unionism among semiskilled workers within Longbridge. There is no evidence that this was an intentional policy aimed at keeping the unions weak. Management's attitude to its employees joining unions was generally just negative. It did not want the largest union, the AEU, to get too powerful,[18] nor did it wish the more militant National Union of Vehicle Builders to get a strong base within Longbridge, and if at all possible it wanted to reduce Communist influence within whatever unions it manifested itself.

Holding the Hard Line: The 1950s

Austin top management were disinclined to risk major disruption of production and losses of profit during periods of rapid expansion of sales by challenging shopfloor unionism and restraints on its rights. But it did act when sales slumped in 1951–2, following the onset of rearmament and a domestic squeeze, and again in the recession of 1956. Indeed the link between managerial economic insecurity, stimulated by falling sales or declining market share or both, and the reassertion of shopfloor management prerogatives was to be (and still remains) a constant feature of Longbridge's industrial relations.

In January 1951 Austin heralded the end of the post-war boom by dismissing 100 trim shop workers 'due to a model change and a new technique' (*Financial Times*, 20 January 1951). Throughout the year it continued to chip away at its Longbridge manual labour force to bring the total nearly 1000 below the 1950 level, while simultaneously attempting to introduce new working practices. In June 1951 management altered a job in the well-unionized no. 5 machine shop from a two-part component to a one-part component. All the surplus workers were redeployed except for seven AEU members who were given a week's notice. It was clearly not an accident that the seven included two well-known plant militants, one of whom, S. Pegg, was an AEU shop steward, the Secretary of the Longbridge Communist Party branch and a strong supporter of convenor Dick Etheridge.[19]

On 19 June 1951 Austin works manager Joe Edwards met Etheridge about the alleged victimization and rejected the Austin Shop Stewards Committee (ASSC) ultimatum that the dismissal notices be withdrawn. As a result the ASSC called on the workfore to down tools and stage a stay-in strike at 10 am the following day. This was the first strike formally called by the ASSC and marked a test of union strength which the stewards clearly lost. Austin's report to the

Birmingham Engineering Employers' Association shows that the strike grew in strength for the first three days:

Pegg and Bills Strikers, 1951[20]

Wednesday	20 June	6,881
Thursday	21 June	9,659
Friday	22 June	10,439
Saturday	23 June	10,456

But on Saturday the strike lost momentum and that evening a local newspaper launched an anti-Communist witch-hunt with a call for a return to work by a member of the strike committee, shop steward Charles Hewing. On Monday 25 June the stewards called a mass meeting in Cofton Hackett Park adjacent to the Austin works. This was attended by an estimated 10,000 strikers, many of whom cheered a return-to-work demonstration staged by the leading Boiler-makers' Union steward, Dick Nester. To many ordinary workers it appeared that the leading stewards were fighting for Pegg because he was a Communist. The fact that Nester was also chairman of the no. 5 machine shop stewards com-mittee gave additional credence to his assessment: 'For 18 months I have been watching Communism in this firm'. George Varnom, the strike committee chairman, eventually put the stewards' recommendation to remain on strike to the meeting and declared it carried. Roars of disapproval then forced him to order the physical separation of the workers for and against and the new count showed a three to two margin for a return to work.

In the lengthy unfolding of the York procedure agreement which followed, the case went to Works Conference in September, to Local Conference in October and finally to Central Conference in December. By then the sales recovery had allowed Austin to rehire 760 employees 'shaken out' earlier in the year, but of the seven dismissed in June, Pegg and Bills were the only workers never rehired. The strike was a clear defeat for the stewards and a reaffirmation by manage-ment of its rights to hire and fire. The only concession granted by Austin management was that in future it would notify CSEU officials in advance of any large-scale redundancies.

Etheridge remembered that defeat throughout his 24 remaining years as con-venor: 'After the Pegg and Bills strike I never called another mass meeting' he said in 1980.[21] It was such a crushing defeat of an unofficial strike that Ed-wards wrote to the Executive of the AEU in an attempt to get it to withdraw Etheridge's and Varnom's shop steward credentials. A telephone memo at the EEF records that the Birmingham Association 'was very glad about the outcome of this trouble which had been engendered by the Communist shop stewards and a Communist convenor'. Inside the plant the defeat bolstered a caucus of Catholic and anti-Communist right-wingers. W.J. Sullivan, a 50-year old North Works TGWU body mounter steward, tried to form a committee to organize a secret ballot on the question: 'Will you allow Communists or known followers to hold an Executive position, either in your shop or in the branch of your

Union?' When this failed he formed an anti-Communist group of stewards called the Trade Union Education Committee. Subsequently, he and another TGWU steward, W. Davies, who had spoken against the JSSC recommendation at the Cofton Hackett meeting were refused entry to the joint stewards' meeting. This led the TGWU to pull out of the JSSC until 1956 when Sullivan had left the union and Davies was no longer a steward, and a new full-time TGWU District Organizer, Les Kealey, was appointed for Birmingham. The shopfloor union tradition which had developed continuously at Longbridge since 1939 was thrown on the defensive by the Pegg and Bills strike. And the Conservative general election victory of October 1951 helped it to stay that way.

Another factor which impinged on industrial relations was the merger with Morris Motors. This was a defensive move, Lord told the trade unions, partly precipitated by the 1950−2 sales downturn:

> The company (BMC) is mainly a finance company. . . . It was felt, however, that there had to be some standardisation if the Austin and Morris Groups were to meet the competition (not just British companies but foreign and continental companies) and that this had been the main reason for setting up the BMC.[22]

The merger took place in 1952 and led to the formation of the British Motor Corporation (BMC), the fourth largest car company in the world after the US giants GM, Ford and Chrysler. The merger drew Austin's top management into a new industrial relations environment.[23] Morris Motors broadened its single-plant horizon with a multi-site dimension of considerably greater complexity, and the new BMC's 13 different engines and 23 different body styles also placed the rationalization of product and production facilities on the long-term agenda.

The same year Edwards, the work manager, approved a second assault on the stewards' organization.[24] On 13 August 1952 the company informed the CSEU's district officials that the following day some 700 manual workers and 100 staff employed on the A90 would be given notice of discharge to take effect in the next four weeks. Seven shop stewards were among those made redundant, including the leading shop steward of the National Union of Vehicle Builders, John McHugh, who had only been moved to the A90 line in June.

The NUVB's National Executive believed McHugh's transfer to a 'doomed' section was another clear case of victimization. McHugh, it felt, was targeted because he had earlier called the Chief Factory Inspector into Longbridge over its poor safety precautions and had successfully kept men on seat assembly work when the company wanted to use women. The NUVB had also negotiated a higher basic rate of 42 shillings a week for its semiskilled members than had other unions, whose members received between 36 and 38 shillings a week. McHugh was secretary of the ASSC, chairman of the newly formed Austin Morris stewards' Merger Committee and president of the Northfield NUVB branch, which as the central column of table 3.3 shows, had been growing rapidly since 1945.

The NUVB took McHugh's case through the official procedure to York,

TABLE 3.3
NUVB Union Membership, 1940–1960

| | *Northfield (Longbridge) NUVB Branch Membership 1940–60 (December figures)* | | | | |
Year	*Members*	*Year*	*Members*	*Year*	*Members*
1940	290	1947	1211	1954	1647
1941	402	1948	1486	1955	1904
1942	444	1949	1643	1956	1614
1943	403	1950	2027	1957	2526
1944	501	1951	2004	1958	2775
1945	550	1952	2122	1959	3131
1946	1188	1953	1408	1960	3687

Source: NUVB *Quarterly Journal,* 1940–60.

where Central Conference eventually recommended that McHugh be re-employed. When Edwards refused to do this, despite hiring more than 600 new starters, the NUVB called an official strike which started on 17 February 1953.

BMC publicly maintained that it treated McHugh no differently from other workers. At the Court of Inquiry towards the end of the eleven-week strike Edwards argued that the problem was created by the threats made to the company by the Communist NUVB Area Organizer, Evans:

> In the company's opinion, there was no justification for preferential treatment for a shop steward. That is a principle which we do not and never will accept ...

> If Mr McHugh had been left alone the same as the other people were left alone, including quite a few shop stewards of that particular Union and of other Unions, there is no doubt at all that Mr McHugh would today have been working in Longbridge. ... But while the Union was holding a pistol at the head of the company, we certainly did not entertain the possibility of re-employing Mr McHugh under these conditions.

Edwards' views were eventually adopted by the Court of Inquiry, but the reality was much closer to the NUVB's version of events. Behind the scenes John Barraclough, president of the Birmingham Engineering Employers Association, told a different story to the EEF. Explaining on 13 February 1953 why BMC had ignored the Central Conference recommendation that McHugh be re-employed, he wrote:

> If ... anyone is in doubt as to the right line to take in this matter, it is necessary only to consider the repercussions which would result if McHugh were re-engaged. McHugh is a Communist and a very troublesome one. He belongs to a Union which is Communist controlled

— a Union which habitually flounts National Agreements wherever it suits them to do so. . . . Any sign of weakness on the Employers' side would have disastrous results and could not fail to boost the prestige of this very undesirable Union.

And ten days later the Birmingham Association sent the EEF a private report from the Regional Director of the Economic League. It claimed:

The inside story of the Austin strike is that there is not the slightest doubt it is a cleverly-concealed Communist attempt to hold up production in this important plant.

John McHugh, the man whom this strike is about, is only a 'stooge'. . . . He is closely associated with Dick Etheridge, who is the Chief of Shop Stewards at the Austin Motor Company. He was the Communist candidate at Northfield in the 1950 General Election . . .

There is no evidence tht McHugh himself is a Communist though he has certainly played the Party game with great fidelity.

The evidence suggests the McHugh dismissal was a deliberate management attempt to weaken the NUVB, the Austin Shop Stewards Committee and the left-wing in the factory in the aftermath of the Pegg and Bill strike. In the process BMC also reasserted what Barraclough called 'The right of an employer to engage or discharge workpeople' without 'preferential treatment being accorded to Shop Stewards'.

The strike was defeated still more decisively than was the 1951 Pegg and Bills multi-union strike. The NUVB had kept the McHugh strike as an official single-union stoppage to avoid the risk of being outvoted by workers from other areas and other unions. But this tactic ensured that the 7000 workers laid off felt no involvement with the strike while the 2200 NUVB strikers felt they had been let down by the workers not laid off, half of whom crossed the picket lines. The NUVB strike leaflet carried a desperate message: '1939 — We fought Hitler. 1953 — We fight Lord'.

The inter-union bitterness that developed during the first month of the strike allowed management to take a further initiative when a mass meeting of NUVB members voted on 23 March to ask for a Court of Inquiry. Edwards then issued an ultimatum threatening to dismiss any workers who remained on strike as from 27 March, and on 30 March he recalled all the laid-off workers and attempted to resume full production. Nearly 600 NUVB members returned under this threat, but another 1500 held out for a further five weeks until the Court of Inquiry completed its findings. When they eventually reapplied for their jobs BMC used the opportunity to get rid of 34 of the original 50 NUVB stewards and 200 other workers. Neither McHugh nor any of the seven stewards who gave evidence to the Court of Inquiry were taken back. Etheridge, the only non-NUVB member allowed to attend strike committee meetings, was only recalled to the plant three weeks after the end of the strike on 5 May, and new restrictions were imposed on his movements. When he returned it was to a plant whose management had successfully dismissed about one in every six shop stewards, and in which non-unionism was thriving. Late in 1953 union density in the plant temporarily fell back to almost its post-war level of roughly 60 per cent, some 700 former members of the NUVB alone refusing to continue to pay dues.

Longbridge management's hard line on industrial relations in the early 1950s reflected in part the return to Conservative government and the encouragement this gave Lord and Edwards to recover the ground they felt had been lost to the unions under the Coalition and Labour Governments of the 1940s. Under the Conservatives direct controls on industry and over industrial relations gradually gave way to Lord's 'freedom from controls'. Above all, volume production for the home market was finally allowed to take precedence over exports. Between 1951 and 1955 domestic sales grew by 37 per cent a year (Dunnet, 1980: 61). Another factor encouraging belligerency in employers was the arrival of 'stop-go' economic management which accentuated the cyclical car sales pattern. This made long-term planning more difficult and it increased short-term job insecurity. In 1951, for example, average manual employment at the Austin fell 5 per cent below its 1950 average, while in 1956 it fell 26 per cent below its 1955 peak (see table 3.2 above). Besides imposing a penalty on the company of higher unit labour costs if labour was not shed rapidly, each 'stop' period offered, as we have already seen, opportunities for anti-union managements to roll back the shopfloor challenge to its prerogatives.

BMC's board of directors remained committed to putting shareholders' dividends before what were arguably the company's own long-term interests and those of its employees. In the aftermath of its 1951 and 1953 victories over shopfloor unionism, the company saw no reason to change its bellicose attitude to the national unions. This short-term perspective ensured that a formal, 'civilized relationship' with the anti-Communist national union leaderships of the AEU and TGWU was much more difficult to achieve than in the US. BMC failed to capitalize upon the weakness of shopfloor unionism by taking any initiative which would have enhanced the prestige and role of the major national unions.

As car sales improved between 1953 and 1955 BMC's aggressive approach to both national and shopfloor unionism effectively stimulated a revival of the tradition it had attempted in 1951 and 1953 to kill off. The revitalized shopfloor unionism at Longbridge was organized by and was dependent upon the network of elected sectional shop stewards. Following the debacle of inter-union strife which accompanied the McHugh strike, this network was also specifically legitimated by the CSEU. This occurred when in July 1953 the CSEU District Secretary formally summoned a meeting of an Austin Joint Shop Stewards Committee (AJSSC) to elect a CSEU Secretary and Chairman and a small executive committee. If this was an attempt to mobilize the right-wing against Etheridge and Varnom, it failed. They were duly elected Confed Secretary (convenor) and Chairman and carried on pretty much as before. Thereafter, one or more local

CSEU full-time officials attended every shop stewards' AGM to ensure propriety with the only substantive change being the later establishment of a seven-
strong multi-union works committee.

BMC senior management's covert anti-union stance was fairly consistent —
and successful — until the late 1950s. Yet departmental and line supervisors
found this policy full of contradictions and especially difficult to maintain in the
boom years. It was impossible to draw a rigid line between sorting out direct
production issues with the stewards, such as the number of men on a job and
the piecework rate, and the same bargaining process over indirect issues, such
as who worked overtime and what was 'fair' discipline. In Feburary 1954, for
example, supervisors put additional men on to the tracks to boost production.
But when this provoked a stoppage by workers who stood to lose a proportion
of their gang piecework bonus, the extra men were immediately withdrawn.
Despite the defeats of 1951 and 1953 verbal agreements on both direct and
indirect issues made between stewards and foremen increasingly appeared
legitimate to workers in the well-organized body and machine shops. And with
this recognition from line management in key areas of the Longbridge complex
so the influence of and support for shopfloor unionism grew in the plant as a
whole. Subsequently, when middle or senior management tried to renegotiate informal agreements or to withdraw custom and practice concessions, their actions
appeared illegitimate and a justification for sectional strike action by the workers
involved. Frequently even the foremen and departmental management were em-
barrassed by their superiors' breach of informal agreements. At times it seems
to them as if the top managers did not particularly care what happened on the
shop floor just so long as production kept going.

In the sales slump of 1956, BMC top management exposed the continuing
weakness of the unions by keeping its factories open during the first officially
called, multi-union company-wide strike. This was called to protest at BMC's
dismissal of some 15 per cent of the labour force, including 3000 Longbridge
workers, without concern for seniority or provision of severance payments
related to length of service. Most BMC workers ignored the picket lines, including virtually all Longbridge's NUVB members. Only a small minority of
Austin's workers stayed out the full week before pressure from the government
and the threat of blacking of its cars at the docks led BMC to agree to re-open
formal negotiations on the redundancy terms. When the minority returned to
work after the strike they knew they had lost the immediate battle. BMC did not
back down on reinstatements, and it only agreed to make token additional redundancy payments to a very small number of long-service employees. And to add
to the activists' discomfort, many skilled AEU non-strikers joined a breakaway
union, the National Association of Toolmakers (see chapter 7 in this volume for
a more thorough account of this dispute).

BMC's success in achieving such widespread dismissals at a very low cost and
in exposing the union's weakness was, however, short-lived. The returning
strikers soon found they had won the moral ground. BMC's actions appeared
unfair and illegitimate, even to many of those who had lacked the confidence

to join the strike. They felt that BMC had ignored what was becoming a common practice among other employers (most recently at the Standard Motor Company's Coventry plant) of making redundancy payments to dismissed workers. And the fact that even the Conservative government openly criticized the company's lack of thought for long-service employees also had an impact. Perhaps of still greater significance was the very rapid economic turnaround from slump to boom in the 12 months after the strike. This helped to undermine what was left of the credibility of management's hard line. By the winter of 1956/7 front-line supervisors in various areas of the plant were again making repeated concessions in the face of as many as two or three strikes a week, while by the summer of 1957 the breakaway toolroom union was 'almost extinct'.[25]

Extension and Consolidation of Bargaining, 1957–1968

In the ten years after the 1956 strike the Austin shop stewards' organization was given full recognition by management and reached the plateau of its influence over managerial shopfloor decision-making. The union revival at Longbridge of early 1957 was dramatically reinforced in the autumn by a national dispute between the CSEU and the EEF. This proved to be a major catalyst in the unionization process. In a dispute on wages the unions launched a series of regional strikes which for the first time demonstrated effective national union strength. At the factory level the simple direct national call for strike action to improve basic wage rates gave union activists a legitimate demand on which to unite workers who were otherwise divided by both skill and payment system. In the post-Suez balance of payments crisis, Prime Minister Harold Macmillan wished to prevent the dispute affecting the economy's leading export industry. So the government put pressure on the EEF to settle with the unions before the strength of Midlands regional support for the strike was tested. On the shopfloor the early settlement was viewed as proving trade unionism's vitality. The victory coincided with the return of job security generated by the sales boom of 1957 to 1960 when BMC's production of cars and commercial vehicles rose from 363,000 in 1956/7 to 669,000 in 1959/60, and then to 859,000 in 1963/4. At Longbridge, where BMC's best-selling Austin mini model was launched in 1959, the boom led to the rehiring of those workers dismissed in 1956. The EEF climb-down in 1957 helped legitimize union membership among those workers who still doubted its value or feared management hostility. Afterwards the fear of being victimized that had kept some from joining unions or from standing for shop steward virtually disappeared at Longbridge for some 20 years.

Workers' job insecurity diminished in a local context of considerable shopfloor bitterness with management over the 1956 redundancies and in a national context where the Conservative government was seeking to strengthen formal collective bargaining and tripartism in an attempt to grapple with the emergence of rising inflation from 1957. In 1958 Longbridge management finally conceded formal recognition to the Austin Joint Shop Stewards Committee and its Works Committee. This meant it would negotiate with other senior stewards besides the 'chief' steward Etheridge, and would also call members of the Works Committee in to meetings on issues which could not be resolved by the individual steward and foreman. By 1960 union membership among Longbridge's 16,000 manual workers had climbed to over 80 per cent. The advance to over 90 per cent came in the early 1960s when the factory's day workers finally took action to reduce the gap between their wages and those of the plant's 60 per cent of pieceworkers. In 1958 a fully skilled inspector received 20 per cent less than the minimum skilled toolroom worker on peicework, and 15 shillings (75p) less than the £15 weekly average earnings of AEU semiskilled peiceworkers. Lengthy negotiations to reduce the gap eventually led in 1961 to a strike for an improved bonus system by the hourly-paid dayworkers. This brought together those who had gained least in the spread of sectional piecework bargaining over the previous 15 years. Then in 1962 two one-day national official strikes were called in support of the CSEU's 1962 engineering industry claim. Both received nearly 100 per cent support from the whole Longbridge workfore, all of whom stood to gain improvements in holiday payments and overtime rates. Afterwards many of the remaining non-unionists at Longbridge finally joined a union. Full unionization (although not a 100 per cent closed shop) had taken nearly 20 years of conflict and was finally achieved, not as a concession by management, but through a combination of shopfloor and national union industrial action.

In the 1960s Austin management found itself faced with five tiers of bargaining, four inside the plant and one outside involving the EEF and externally-based union officials. At the top level were occasional references of disagreements to the monthly procedural meetings held at York between the national union officers and the national representatives of the EEF. Within the plant local EEF and Confed officials would also hold frequent procedural works and local conferences while outside the procedure senior factory managers held regular meetings with the works committee or its senior officers. From 1961 to 1965 the Longbridge convenor Etheridge reported to the monthly AJSSC meetings on an average of 35 factory items each month, most of which had probably involved at least two meetings with senior management. Beneath the plant-wide negotiating level, departmental managers bargained with the different shop committees covering all the major areas of the plant. Finally, foremen and superintendents also bargained with sectional stewards on an individual or group basis.

BMC's rising production (to 859,000 cars by 1963/4), the growing choice of car models demanded by a business policy premised upon maintaining a presence in every sector of the market from mini cars to luxury cars, and the increasing age of the machinery with which Longbridge workers had to work, all created a natural bargaining arena in which the more recently organized groups of semiskilled workers sought to emulate the informal agreements achieved elsewhere in the plant. Between 1962 and 1969 the introduction of national wage controls by successive governments tended to restrict national minimum wage rises while leaving a loophole for supplementary wage rises to be negotiated more or less informally at sectional level. This was not an insignificant loophole. At Longbridge half the workers earned locally-negotiated piecework bonuses which amounted to between 50 per cent and 70 per cent more than the nationally-negotiated minimum rates. After the 1961 strike the dayworkers received supplementary hourly payments which were also negotiated area by area within the plant. At the same time the introduction of new model lines, as well as the multiplication of consumer choice within existing model lines, created additional informal bargaining opportunities on the price of new work or new methods. Thus an unintended result of government wage restraint policy was to encourage Longbridge workers to rely still more upon their own shop stewards and the exercise of their right to strike to improve their wages, rather than on the national officials. Sectional strikes increased in number and became an increasing subject of concern for BMC management, the media, academics and the Labour governments of 1964–70.

Slowly, restraints on managerial authority were generalized section-by-section across the plant. Sometimes this was deliberately encouraged by a JSSC campaign, as with pressure in 1965 to secure the four-night week for all night-shift workers in the plant. At other times new restraints upon management were passed on as workers were moved from one area of the plant to another. At no time, however, did top BMC management make a detailed assessment of this development and try to construct a different form of industrial relations. By the time British Leyland was formed in 1968 manual union density at Longbridge was virtually 100 per cent and even among the 4000 white-collar workers in the complex it was over 75 per cent, and the number of informal agreements restraining management's freedom to implement changes in working practices ran into hundreds.

The spread of informal shopfloor union organization and the accumulation of restraints exercised over managerial prerogatives between the 1940s and the 1960s occurred in the context of chronic management failure. The 1952 merger between Austin and Morris had not eliminated long-standing rivalries and suspicion between senior managers and it failed to produce economies of scale or any really effective rationalization of car assembly or distribution. By 1968 the company produced seven entirely different model ranges with tens of variants of each model. Its best-selling model, the Mini, contained so many different components that for many years it failed to generate any profit at all. Senior management retained considerable contempt for university-trained recruits and BMC only began to recruit graduates in 1963. Perhaps most telling of all, BMC failed to invest at the rate of its major competitors: between 1954 and 1963 its net assets grew by 47.5 per cent compared to Ford UK's 73.6 per cent growth.

In the economic recession of 1966/7 when BMC vehicle production slipped back to below 700,000, the number of vehicles produced per employee was lower than at the time of merger in 1952 and BMC began to lose money. Its response was to replicate the employment insecurity and employee anger that occurred in 1956, through announcing 11,000 dismissals, of which 3754 were at Longbridge. Although covered by the Labour government's Redundancy

Payments Act of 1965, a measure directly prompted by the BMC sackings of 1956, the dismissals revived deep mistrust about management's loyalties to its workforce.

The consumer boom of the 1950s and 1960s brought to Longbridge workers rising living standards and improved working conditions, but it never removed their job and pay insecurity. Top management appeared to veer between aggressive anti-unionism and indifference to shopfloor issues. Both responses contrasted with government action in the 1940s and late 1950s, which specifically legitimated trade unionism. Instead of using the boom to create a sense of shopfloor job security and loyalty to the company, or of using it to formalize a close bargaining relationship with the national unions, top management at Longbridge allowed the material gains to be attributed to shopfloor unionism and in particular to the shop stewards' organization. This attribution of power and influence was to have far-reaching consequences in the years which followed the merger of Leyland and the BMC in 1968.

From Formal Bargaining to the Hard Line, 1969–1979

The takeovers and mergers in the car industry in the 1960s, which eventually led to the formation of the British Leyland Motor Corporation, were largely defensive. Like the original BMC merger it was primarily a marketing consolidation, intended to protect domestic sales from a rising proportion of imports, rather than to rationalize production or reorganize management. Under Lord Stokes the major weaknesses of the group were not tackled. BLMC's historically low level of capital investment and its sales strategy of maintaining a wide range of models which ensured low-volume production runs were left unchanged. What did change was that management increasingly blamed supply side factors and especially the blocking role of its unions for its problems. Virtually the only new policy top managers in the newly merged company could agree upon was that the shop stewards had become obstructions to effective management and that the piecework payment system they believed had spawned them should be removed. As if to mark its intention to give priority to industrial relations reform, BLMC appointed an industrial relations director to its main board. Management time and energy over the following six years was dominated by the removal of piecework and by the conflict and reorganization of work this entailed.

The introduction of detailed plant agreements under measured day work (MDW) was in line with the arguments of the Donovan Commission and, since the merger had been facilitated by a £25m government loan, it was good politics too. Ford UK's high profits made its hourly-payment and grading system appear a successful formula. At the same time the idea of moving from the continual bargaining which characterized piecework to annual formal bargaining sessions was highly attractive. A large number of executives were then recruited from Ford and added to the already large numbers of managers left over from the earlier mergers. But while BLMC had decided to implement a new payment system, it had not fully grasped that the achievement of MDW's potential was dependent upon the introduction of a totally new industrial relations environment, and in particular upon the reduction in scope for shopfloor bargaining.

At Longbridge the evident intention of management in 1972 to put the whole workforce on daywork was sufficient to persuade the senior stewards to adopt a negotiating response. Captializing on management's anxiety to introduce the new system with the minimum of disruption, the stewards agreed to the change and the establishment of just two pay bargaining units for the entire plant but in return secured the formalization of a whole range of consultative procedures. In place of the veto under pieceworking on new or different jobs which had not been properly priced or manned up, workers now claimed the right to refuse to carry out managerial instructions which had not been properly approved by the stewards in a clearly defined internal bargaining procedure. In tolerating this situation management unintentionally extended the range of issues on which shop stewards expected to be able to bargain. Plant-wide pay bargaining had been introduced but sectional bargaining over the pace and conditions of work had been formalized at the same time. Under these circumstances, the employment of additional numbers of supervisors to take over the disciplinary function previously provided by the pay packet failed to make any impression. Indeed, both car output per worker and quality plummeted as workers came to realise that they would get paid the same wage however hard they worked and for whatever quality of work. In 1975 a government study found that the assembly of the Mini at Longbridge took 2.3 times as many hours as it did at BL's Belgian subsidiary.

Acceptance of the introduction of MDW was achieved more easily at Longbridge than at several other BL plants. This was because its size and the multiplicity of tasks carried out there meant that half the workforce were already paid as dayworkers. In other factories, where car assembly pieceworkers made up the overwhelming majority, opposition was much more intense, even involving strike action, and the full transition to MDW was not completed until 1975. Another factor smoothing the transition to MDW was the improvement in status afforded the AJSSC after the election of new left-wing leaders to head Britain's two largest unions in 1967 and 1969. Both men, Hugh Scanlon of the engineers and Jack Jones of the transport workers, represented political and sectional forces in their respective unions which were strongly identified with the increasing authority of the shop stewards. Their encouragement of an enhanced role for shop stewards' committees dovetailed with management's interest in formalizing pay bargaining at the plant level.

By 1975 BLMC was effectively bankrupt and rather than allow it to collapse with total job losses (including those at its suppliers) estimated at over 750,000, the Labour government first commissioned a report into its viability by Lord Ryder, the chairman of the National Enterprise Board (NEB), and then agreed to purchase the company, which then became known simply as British Leyland (BL). Government policy was once more directly linked to developments in

Longbridge's industrial relations. The 1975 Ryder report was highly critical of BL's management organization and of its lack of investment and weak efforts at rationalization. The report also focused on its poor product range and on its bad labour relations record, but it concluded with an optimistic estimate of BL's sales potential. Ryder recommended that the government make some £2bn available to the company for a new model range and modernization of production facilities, and also that its collective bargaining and payment systems should be reformed again. The government funds, Ryder added, should be invested in tranches, conditional upon progress with these reforms and with major improvements in productivity.

The industrial relations objectives proposed by Lord Ryder were twofold. He argued that 58 manual employee bargaining units covering 34 plants were excessive and should be reduced and centralized with much greater synchronization of the separate renewal dates. And, in keeping with Labour government policy at the time, he suggested that productivity should be increased through an extension of industrial democracy. Workers' participation at British Leyland was not intended to diminish management's executive authority. As the document describing the 1976 agreement to a formal structure put it, the purpose was to 'increase the effectiveness of the operation of Leyland Cars to the mutual benefit of all its employees'. A four-tiered structure of joint management—union committees was established, covering the whole company, the volume car division, the Longbridge plant and the six Longbridge production units.

From the outset the experiment in industrial democracy reflected its origins in an imposed structure rather than as a direct political expression of workers' convictions that they could organize better than their management. The workers' side rapidly found there was little determination on management's side to make the system work and in any case the company's continuing crisis left the joint committees very little discretion. Within three years Ryder's main recommendations were effectively scrapped, and within five years BL had introduced company-wide pay bargaining supplemented by non-negotiable plant-wide productivity bonuses and had totally abandoned the rhetoric of workers' participation. Finally, in April 1980 management unilaterally and successfully tore up almost all the informal agreements restraining its shopfloor prerogatives and imposed new terms and conditions of employment on the entire workforce. At a stroke sectional bargaining was effectively eliminated, plant-wide bargaining was reduced to *post hoc* consultation and any remaining bargaining function occurred at company level. On the shopfloor the consequence was that collective industrial action in defence of shopfloor unionism's accumulated restraints over managerial rights became once again an illegitimate and risky response to arbitrary management action.

How was it that this transformation took place in such a short space of time? Several factors contributed to the change. The continuation of the company's economic crisis of 1974 illustrated by the collapse in BL's domestic market share from 31 per cent in 1975 to 15 per cent in late 1979 and early 1980, played a major role. This crisis worked in several ways. It legitimated management's statements about the risks to the company's survival if workers took strike action in defence of specific restraints. Equally it stiffened management's readiness to challenge and then ignore vetoes presented at what it saw as a superabundance of bargaining tables. The crisis heightened workers' job insecurities at a time when most national union leaders were unwilling to mobilize a political response that would embarrass the Labour government. In 1979 one of the major Conservative election slogans, 'Labour isn't working', capitalized precisely upon this sense of union failure.

The election of a Conservative government in May 1979 also played an important part in establishing what became known as 'the new realism' in industrial relations. Not only did the government repeal much of its predecessor's pro-union legislation but it enacted several measures designed to make effective industrial action more difficult to organize. The net result was the establishment of a political context in which collective bargaining and industrial democracy were identified as the problem rather than the solution to industrial relations conflict. More specifically, however, the election of a government with pronounced hostility towards the nationalized sector made both management and workforce more fearful that government financial support might suddenly be cut off.

Disunity among the unions was another factor in the very rapid transformation of the frontier of conflict at Longbridge. The divisions crossed in several different directions. They existed between unions representing craft and non-craft workers, between certain craft workers and production workers regardless of union affiliation, between different plants, and between the extensive layer of senior stewards who became more and more involved in negotiations in the 1960s and 1970s and the ordinary members. During the years of boom these divisions were largely obscured as both wages and plant and sectional bargaining autonomy steadily increased. But as management took steps to centralize wage bargaining, first with the introduction of hourly payment systems which allowed direct inter-plant and inter-grade comparisons to be made, and then with the commitment to pay parity in 1976, and as government pay restraint reduced differentials between high- and low-paid workers, long-standing tensions came to the fore.

In 1977 BL's toolroom workers struck unofficially in an attempt to secure separate bargaining rights. After the rest of the workshop crossed their picket lines the strike was defeated. But the strike had two important consequences: it forced management to adopt a policy for the rapid centralization of bargaining; and it led to the personal isolation in his work area of the Longbridge convenor, a toolroom worker and a Communist who had opposed the formation of a separate BL toolroom negotiating committee. Two-and-a-half years later, after Derek Robinson had been dismissed for continued opposition to the company's latest Recovery Plan, the lack of support from his fellow toolroom workers was an important factor in denying him the backing of plant-wide strike action. An equally important factor in Robinson's dismissal, itself symptomatic of the industrial relations transformation, was the public reluctance of his national union leaders to give him support. His union, the Amalgamated Union of Engineering

Workers (AUEW), had recently elected two right-wing officials to its top posts, and as in the period before Scanlon's term of office, they were much less supportive of shop steward autonomy generally.

In the period of the emergence of self-reliant shopfloor organization the opposition of the national union to strike action against victimization would not have made much difference. The year 1979, however, followed ten years of increasing reliance by shop stewards' committees on the national AUEW and TGWU leaders for support. Equally, the establishment of company-wide union— management committees on workers' participation (1976) and on collective bargaining reform (1977), and the close relationship maintained by the then leaders of the two major unions with the Labour government and its National Enterprise Board (NEB), had gradually brought the national officials to the centre of the BL bargaining process. In 1977, for example, Scanlon, president of the second largest union at BL, the AUEW, put his prestige behind the proposal to ballot the entire BL workforce on the company's proposals for centralized pay bargaining. This was the first of several such ballots which had as a more or less clearly articulated purpose the bypassing of the shop stewards and established bargaining processes. And later that same year the deputy-general secretary of the largest union at BL, the Transport and General Workers' Union, was a party to the NEB's decision to appoint Michael Edwardes as new chief executive with a brief to shake up BL's old management and implement a radical rationalization of the whole company.

The introduction of new top management in 1977 was a key factor in the transformation of BL's industrial relations. The historical overview presented above suggests that the 'strength' of the shop stewards' organization owed much to the 'space' left it by management. In the deepening crisis of the late 1970s, the new chief executive was able to use the narrowing of economic discretion to dismiss or force into early retirement large numbers of senior managers and appoint a layer of professional managers in their place. The reduction of available options also enabled Edwardes to advocate an unambiguous philosophy of managerial rights. Hard decisions would be taken and implemented. In 1978, for example, BL's most recently opened plant, the Speke no. 2 assembly plant in Liverpool, was closed in the face of union protest. And in January 1979 a promised parity payment was withheld from the entire BL workforce because management's productivity targets had not been reached. It was partly because Robinson led a one-week strike at Longbridge in protest at this decision that he was targeted for dismissal. But this calculated management decision, in November 1979, followed an 87 per cent vote by the workforce for an emergency Recovery Plan which involved cutting BL's manpower by 25,000 workers and major changes in work practices. This vote and the Robinson dismissal gave management at all levels a major boost in confidence.

In April 1980, after major lay-offs and the rejection at a mass meeting of the proposal to strike for Robinson's reinstatement, the company issued a unilateral ultimatum to its workforce. Employees were told that if they reported for work it would be assumed they had accepted an 84-page document spelling out new terms and conditions of employment. In this document management announced the end of all demarcation agreements, of any union restrictions upon the selection of workers for overtime or shift-working and of all agreements which restricted management's right to fill vacancies or move labour by suitability. If workers did not report for work it would be assumed they had voluntarily left the company and would not be eligible for any form of severance pay. At Longbridge the overwhelming majority of workers reported for work, but across the company as a whole some 12,000 workers struck for a few days against the ultimatum before the national union officials met the company and effectively called off the strike.

By the early 1980s a new Longbridge industrial relations system was in place. Unions remained recognized, but consultation only took place with their national officers. Informally, shopfloor workers had effectively lost all the leverage over the unilateral exercise of managerial authority they had built up during the previous forty years. Conflict had not been 'resolved'. It merely manifested itself in a new definition of workers' and managerial shopfloor 'rights'.

Conclusions

The ease with which the new industrial relations system emerged at Longbridge should not surprise us. Over the forty years of management—labour relations at Longbridge considered in this chapter the visibility of conflict reflects national and company-specific economic and political factors, interpreted via the organizational coherence of both management and workers. But these last factors were never equal in weight. Once market imperatives forced management to access its greater resources to secure the removal of shopfloor restraints there was little the shop stewards' organization independently could do to stop it.

Three other themes are worth returning to at the close of this brief historical sketch. One is that Austin management throughout has hardly held what could be dignified as a 'labour control strategy'. Very little evidence exists — even in the most recent period — of top managers calmly considering industrial relations as a long-term project over which they have to exercise a strategic choice. Rigid views on management rights and the need to police them by effective victimization of shopfloor opponents were held by Herbert Austin and most recently by Michael Edwardes. And in the intervening years top managers lurched from this hard line to toleration of a pluralistic set-up. But neither the hard line nor the periods of disinterest in and toleration of the shop stewards' activities were much more than predictable responses to market conditions and the business cycle in the context of changing national political considerations. Management decision-making appears, above all, as reactive rather than strategic.

A second point is that although this review of Longbridge industrial relations demonstrates the importance of market conditions in major turning points, the study also makes it clear that it is not possible simply to read off an outcome directly from the progress of car sales. Thus the boom of the 1920s and the recovery of the 1930s did not encourage the unionization of Longbridge, while the slump of 1956 did. The business cycle does not provide a sufficient explanation of industrial relations trends.

Finally the chapter suggests that the factors which historically have mediated the impact of the business cycle have been both organizational and political. At certain moments they ensured that workers would struggle for particular restraints over management, while at other times they did not. In explaining the dynamics of their interaction the emergence, rise and decline of the Communist Party in the plant clearly had a considerable influence. A core of perhaps 20 CP shop stewards from the 1940s to the 1960s raised expectations generally about what a shop stewards' organization should look like and stand for. As the national decline of the industrial base of the CP set in after 1956, the Longbridge CP failed to attract a younger generation of militants. Increasingly its strength was confined to the narrow base of the works committee, and its members lost their capacity to respond to and generate shopfloor struggle independently of the AJSSC. Other leftist groups who tried to fill the gap failed to do so. The result was that as originally successful, hard-fought restraints over management came to depend more and more upon management for their legitimacy and renewal, the steward organization slowly appeared to lose credibility. It was only under these conditions, in which in certain ways the steward organization atrophied from lack of struggle and mobilization, that the onset of the 1979 recession allowed it to be virtually cast aside. The experience at Longbridge suggests that the presence or absence of shopfloor restraints over arbitrary management is structured by the history of management but specifically created as the product of struggle.

Notes

This chapter is based upon research carried out by the author as a doctoral student in Warwick University's Industrial Relations department between 1980 and 1982. The author would like to acknowledge with thanks the helpful comments on an early draft made by Willy Brown and Dave Lyddon; the latter also generously provided the data on the Northfield branch NUVB membership from his own doctoral research. Thanks too to the Engineering Employers' Federation who generously allowed access to their archives, and to Richard Storey at the Warwick Modern Records Centre, which provided most of the historical documents used in the research.

1. Interview by author with Norman Haslam, Austin Rover Director of Employee Relations, Coventry 13 August 1985.
2. See Willman and Winch (1985); Marsden *et al.* (1985); Edwardes (1983); Williams *et al.* (1983); Tolliday and Zeitlin (1986) and Willman (1984).
3. Engineering Employers' Federation, Austin Motor Company Federation Document, 19 June 1914.

4. Dick Etheridge, 'Austin Joint Shop Stewards Report to Royal Commission on Trade Union and Employers' Organisations', July 1966.
5. Engineering Employers' Federation, Aircraft Shadow Factory, Membership File, Admission document, 1 January 1938.
6. Etheridge Papers, MSS 202/3/4/ Factory size.
7. Austin Shop Stewards' Committee, *The Report*, April 1944.
8. *Ibid.*
9. EEF Archives, Local Conference Report, 20 December 1944.
10. Austin Motor Company, annual accounts.
11. Etheridge, *op. cit.*, 12.
12. NUVB *Quarterly Journal*, June 1946. EEF Archives, Austin Local Conference, 31 January 1949.
13. List in Etheridge Collection, Modern Records Centre.
14. Etheridge, *op. cit.*, 12. An illustration of the complexity of the bargaining process is provided by the events which followed. When the national officers of the CSEU learned of the agreement they tried to get the local officers whose names were appended to it to force the stewards to accept the nationally agreed 44-hour week. The stewards refused and the local agreement survived.
15. AEU Shop Stewards Committee. Minutes, 16 February 1948.
16. The account of the 1948 strike which follows is based on these references: *Financial Times*, 21 August 1948, 24 August 1948, 25 August 1948; EEF Archives, Local Conference, 31 January 1949.
17. List of stewards, Etheridge Papers, MSS 202/3/4; estimate of union densities drawn from various interviews.
18. Thus the AEU District Secretary, S. C. Robinson, complained at a local conference in January 1949:

    At the back of some of the difficulties at the Austin Motor Company is the feeling that the company is developing an anti-AEU attitude, or preferential treatment for any Union but the AEU.

    EEF Archives, Local Conference, 31 January 1949.
19. AEU Shop Stewards Committee. Minutes, 23 March 1949.
20. The account of the 'Pegg and Bills' strike of 1951 which follows derives from five sources: EEF Archives, *Financial Times* and *Evening Despatch* reports, Etheridge interview and Etheridge, *op. cit.*, 13–14. The *Financial Times* puts the numbers of strikers much higher — at 80 per cent of 17,000 on day one and 90 per cent on day two when a first mass meeting backed the stoppage.
21. Etheridge interview.
22. Minutes of Conference between Austin Motor Company and Birmingham and Coventry CSEU officials, 1952. Etheridge Papers.
23. Part of the deal was that Lord Nuffield (William Morris) would retire soon as BMC chairman, which he did in December 1952 leaving his former rival Lord in charge; *Financial Times*, 18 December 1952.
24. The account of the 1953 McHugh strike which follows is based on EEF Archives; the Court of Inquiry report Cmd. 8839, contemporary *Financial Times* reports, Etheridge *op. cit.*, 15–16 and a brief synopsis in Turner *et al.*, 1967: 271–5.
25. *The Clarion*, January–February, May–June 1957.

Management Control and Labour Quiescence: Shopfloor Politics at Alfred Herbert's, 1945–1980

Ken Grainger

Editors' Foreword

The main feature of shopfloor industrial relations at Alfred Herbert's was in marked contrast to much of the Coventry engineering industry: piecework bargaining was very little developed and shop stewards had a very limited role in the production process. The firm plainly shows that shopfloor bargaining was not a natural product of the Coventry environment. A consideration of it can throw light not only on why it stood out but also on the conditions promoting bargaining elsewhere.

Two recent essays have discussed the firm. Davies (1986) analyses the early years of the twentieth century, characterizing Sir Alfred Herbert as a paternalist. Tolliday (1986) briefly considers post-war developments and the reasons for the contrast with other firms. He makes two main points. The limited development of bargaining was due to the firm's management style and its payment system. Managerial authority was vested in the person of Sir Alfred, and foremen continued to play an important role on the shopfloor. This reflected the nature of the payment system which was a form of group piecework in which prices were not negotiated but were settled between the chargehand and the ratefixer. Underlying this was a very slowly changing production technology which promoted stability. The second point is that the Herbert's pattern was not the tightly integrated system that it appeared. Had a more innovative production strategy been pursued or had stewards wrested the principle of mutuality from management during the Second World War, the paternalist tradition might well have collapsed.

In this chapter Ken Grainger provides the first detailed account of postwar industrial relations at Herbert's. He discusses several features which have remained hidden, notably the subordinate position of Asian and women workers. Apart from providing a richer description of the firm than has hitherto been available he offers several suggestions as to why the Herbert's system not only originated but also survived for so long. In addition to the factors identified by Tolliday, he draws attention to two specific features of the firm. The first was its production technology. Work processes were far less standardized than they were in the car firms with which Tolliday contrasts Herbert's, the result being that it was much harder for workers to identify common interests. Secondly, divisions by sex, race, and skill increased fragmentation.

Tying together the production technology, the payments system, and labour force segmentation was a distinctive style of workplace politics. Sex and race divisions, for example, are common enough but they had a particular salience here because they existed in a context in which those at the top of the hierarchy gained at the expense of the remainder. Similarly, the payment system continued to operate for so long because the skilled elite were able to wrest enough from it to satisfy themselves. The pattern of control was not just the product of factors imposed on the workforce. The leading shop stewards were active agents in creating and sustaining it. As Bélanger and Evans also argue in their chapter, traditions of factory politics develop logics of their own. Structural conditions create certain pressures but these have to be interpreted in practice. In the case of Herbert's a tradition developed in which stewards accepted much of the managerial control system and sought benefits for a small section of the workforce. This simultaneously reduced the likelihood that this section would want to disturb a cosy arrangement and made it difficult for other sections to mobilize to challenge it.

A reasonable inference is that the Herbert's system, although certainly not a tightly integrated package, was not a contingent and unstable arrangement which could fall apart at any time. The shopfloor organization was involved in creating and maintaining the system. As Grainger notes, several potential 'challenges from below', notably from Asian workers, came to nothing, and the style of shopfloor politics was still in evidence even after major efforts during the 1960s to reform the payments system and attempts during the 1970s to involve the firm in the Labour government's planning experiments. The bargaining relationship was a powerful cement holding together the disparate features of workplace relations.

Grainger calls Herbert's factory politics corporatist. This may be seen as controversial in view of the many meanings of the term corporatism. As he explains, however, he needed a label that encapsulated the character of factory politics. Some available terms have problems. To describe Herbert's simply as paternalist is to miss the fact that some bargaining did occur and to imply the presence of an unchanging moral order. The attempts at reform during the 1960s can hardly be seen as paternalist, and yet they clearly reflected earlier traditions of factory politics. These traditions were corporatist in that they involved the stewards' adoption of an ideology of shared interests with the employer. In his introductory remarks Grainger enlarges on how the term corporatism is to be understood. In the light of his definition, the term should not offer any difficulties.

Herbert's is perhaps best-known for its dramatic collapse during the 1970s. In order to provide a reasonably comprehensive picture of the firm Grainger describes these events, although without going into great detail. In the context of this book as a whole their significance is two-fold. First, and most obviously, the firm's difficulties cannot be attributed to 'excessive shopfloor power': severe problems of productivity need not stem from problems of shopfloor control. Second, the firm's efforts to rationalize its payments system had similarities with events in many other companies. Herbert's management, although 'in control' of the shopfloor in the sense that they were not dealing with powerful shop stewards, did not have a system of production management that was capable of surviving the hostile competitive environment of the 1970s. The firm shared with others problems of conservative designs and poor marketing, together with a dependence on a system of production organization that had outlived its usefulness. Its politics were distinctive, but it was not a different animal.

Introduction

This chapter analyses the evolution of industrial relations at Alfred Herbert's, the machine tool firm which had once dominated the industry but which collapsed in the 1970s. In 1983 the entire plant and equipment of the Edgwick site, the last vestige of the Herbert empire, went under the auctioneer's hammer. My research began as a study of the introduction of new technology but was diverted by the company's crisis. As I witnessed Herbert's approach to its second bankruptcy in five years, I was puzzled by the senior shop stewards' passivity. A 'sit-in' was eventually organized, but instead of broadening support for the action among local labour organizations the stewards asked the firm's customers to lobby the government on their behalf. This behaviour contradicted the convenor's left-wing political orientation. To understand it, I began to delve into the history of industrial relations at Edgwick.

A dinstinctive shopfloor politics had developed. In this chapter I concentrate on these politics, in particular the orientation of the stewards' committee, giving relatively little attention to effort bargaining. It should not be assumed that this bargaining was absent. Herbert's is often seen as a prime example of labour quiescence, with the inference that workers had no day-to-day effort controls. Workers in fact had many of the standard tricks for making their work easier. One example was the practice of skilled workers of keeping their own jigs and fixtures, which enabled them to do jobs more easily. It would be very surprising if skilled engineering workers in a large firm in Coventry did not develop such controls. But the key thing about them is that, unlike the controls which developed at Presswork for example (see the chapter by Bélanger and Evans), they were never aggressive: they remained private ways of affecting effort but they did not involve any organized trade union challenge to management logics. The key to this lies in the shopfloor politics of the firm.

These politics may be described as corporatist. I use this term not to characterize macro-political relations but to encapsulate certain features of factory politics. Shop stewards operated within managerial definitions. There was a belief in an identity of interest between managers and workers, and the stewards' ideology was a mixture of pragmatic accommodation with Herbert's system of labour control and an adoption of the values and attitudes of employers. There was an implicit acceptance of the unitary model of the enterprise. But managerial domination was not as total as some concepts, notably that of paternalism, can imply. Shopfloor relations reflected no simple quiescence. There was a process of negotiation and compromise between managers and the senior stewards. Corporatism is a convenient label to characterize this constrained negotiated order.

This chapter focuses on the years 1951–68, a period opened by senior management's moves to 'soften' its distinctive authoritarian style of employer paternalism and closed by more radical managerial reforms which were aimed at dragging Herbert's factory politics into the Donovan era of labour relations. This period provides a useful case study of a situation where transformations in the corporatist politics of a shop stewards' organization anticipated, instead of reacting to, changes in managerial policies on labour administration. More importantly, it shows that the weak shopfloor organization and 'somnolent' workforce at Herbert's were not simply the product of an authoritarian management; they also reflected the interests of sections at the top of the labour hierarchy in the plant.

The chapter has four main parts. The first sets the scene by pointing out the main features of Herbert's product market and management's response to it during the 1950s, and by giving a potted history of the workplace organization. The second discusses the shop stewards' response to management's cautious moves towards an accommodation with the workplace organization. The third part looks at the various sections within the workforce to explain its apparent 'somnolence' and its tenuous links with the shop stewards' committee. The fourth part examines the changes in shopfloor politics as the dominance of the toolmakers was finally broken. After these four sections, some concluding comments on the 1970s are made.

The analysis draws on a range of sources. Major documentary evidence comes from minutes of the shop stewards' committee and of meetings of the firm's board of directors. This has been supplemented with interviews with many of the leading figures in the plant. The minutes provide a particularly rich source of information and enable the chronology of developments to be established more accurately than is often the case in factory studies. Direct quotations given below are from minutes of meetings or interview notes; the context indicates which. I have also drawn on a study carried out for the Prices and Incomes Board in 1967 which provides valuable contemporary data, particularly on earnings (Williams, 1968).

The Firm and the Union

The Company
Sir Alfred Herbert exercised a dominating influence over the company. He and a partner bought an existing firm in 1888. Herbert soon assumed sole control. The firm grew rapidly: from 13 employees in 1887 to 500 in 1897 and 2600 by 1926. Herbert clung to power and continued to play a considerable role until his death in 1957. The centralization of control in the hands of one man created an idiosyncratic and increasingly outmoded organization. Later managers tried to rationalize and modernize, but in an increasingly competitive environment their efforts were of little avail. Redundancies began in earnest in the 1970s and continued unil the final collapse in 1983 (Davies, 1986: 103, 125–6; Tolliday, 1986: 224–5).

Davies (1986) has provided a detailed account of the company's labour relations during the first half of the twentieth century. This needs no repetition here, but the concept of paternalism which Davies places at the centre of his analysis needs some comment. For Davies, paternalism involves authoritarianism, discipline, and a hierarchy reflecting the mutual obligations of employers and employees. Herbert's is seen as a particularly well-developed paternalist organization based on an organic model of the firm. This plainly gave unions a limited role. There is much of value here, but it is also true that unions were not eliminated from the company and that a paternalist policy may be questioned from below. During the 1950s and 1960s an admittedly weak steward organization operated at Herbert's. As argued below, it represented the interests of one section of the workforce and was able to reach some compromise with the firm. Such facts fit uneasily into a strong model of paternalism, which can grant no role for sources of authority different from that of management. Herbert's in the post-war period was marked by a reworking of its labour relations, which took on a corporatist and not a paternalist character.

The Product Market
Unlike the motor firms which dominated employment in the local engineering industry, production in the machine tool factories was not subject to seasonal fluctuations in demand. Major shifts in demand were tied to the booms and slumps of national economies, movements measured over years, not months.

During the early 1950s, the company enjoyed a huge backlog of orders as a result of uniquely favourable circumstances: the revival of the defence industry; the dismembering of the German machine tool industry and the temporary elimination of other rivals in war-devastated Europe; and the fact that machine tool builders in both the USA and the USSR were oriented towards their own vast internal markets. Years later, a sales executive told Williams (1968: 29) 'semi-jocularly' that the company's attitude to its customers then was: 'We told them they could have a machine if they were prepared to wait a year for it and if they promised to look after it'.

It was a false complacency. By the middle of the decade, the revival of the European industry was well under way, a number of firms in the United States were establishing manufacturing subsidiaries in Britain as part of a drive to expand sales in Western Europe, and there was concern that the Soviet Union would inevitably switch some of its enormous productive capacity to export markets (Coventry Workshop/IWA, 1979). Herbert's products, increasingly uncompetitive both at home and abroad, were taking a declining share of those markets. The fact that it was still only a relative and not an absolute decline helped Sir Alfred Herbert to follow his own inclinations to resist pressure for change. Plans for the introduction of group technology were deferred indefinitely; there was minimal investment in new plant and machinery; and reports on the technical obsolescence of Herbert's designs were ignored. Sir Alfred's complacency during those years contrasts strongly with those celebratory accounts of his early years which describe his appetite for innovation, and his readiness to exploit new designs, new techniques and new commercial opportunities (Floud, 1976: 53; Aldcroft, 1966). The Chairman justified his conservatism by pointing to the backlog of orders and the continuing accumulation of profits.

Trade Unionism
The Edgwick site began life in the nineteenth century as a small foundry. In 1928, all production was transferred there from Herbert's old site at the Butts in the centre of Coventry. It remained the sole manufacturing plant until the war when 'shadow factories' were established at Exhall and Lutterworth. By the late 1960s, it was only one of eleven plants; but it was the largest and very much the centre of the Herbert 'empire'.

The fragile shop stewards' committee, which had emerged at the Butts during the First World War, did not survive the employers' offensive after the 1922 lock-out. By the early 1930s union organization had been restricted to the two craft enclaves: the toolroom and the patternshop. But Herbert's was among the first engineering firms to benefit from the rearmament boom. In 1932, it secured a major contract from the Soviet Union which reversed a pattern of short-time working into a routine of excessive overtime. Union organization was stimulated, but with the outbreak of war several leading activists quickly left to take advantage of the wages bonanza at local munitions and shadow factories. The new leadership was more accommodating to the limitations imposed by a 'grudging' management and possessed none of the radical hues of the pioneers.

Edgwick became and remained a stronghold for the right-wing AEU officials entrenched in the district's General Purposes Committee.

During the remainder of the war management made few concessions to the unions. The workplace organization was tolerated, but little more than that. The shop stewards had to wait until the national fuel crisis of 1947 before they were granted even the symbols of their authority on the shopfloor, such as a union notice board and the right to hold meetings on company premises. But this brief period of limited managerial support passed quickly, and the shop stewards' organization was plunged into despair once more as section stewards and members drifted away to seek better-paid jobs elsewhere.

Transformations of Corporatism at Herbert's

In the immediate post-war years, the shop stewards had to treat with a management which seemed determined to restore 'pre-war practices'. Towards the end of the 1940s, however, circumstances changed again when the government revived its defence programme, and the international product markets, briefly free of any serious competition from Herbert's major rivals abroad, expanded in response to the demands of Europe's post-war reconstruction. The new orders reversed Herbert's fortunes and, once again, the managers had to cope with a desperate shortage of labour, particularly skilled labour, at Edgwick.

At the beginning of 1950, management's initial response to the problem was to push for an increase in the night-shift; but this was quickly abandoned when the directors realised that it actually increased the exodus of skilled labour from the plant. Another tactic was to subcontract work but this, too, proved unsatisfactory. There were a number of technical difficulties and later complaints that the subcontractors' products were 'costing a great deal more than making them in our own works'. Eventually, and with obvious reluctance, the board reached the conclusion that it would have to offer higher pay to its employees.

The shop stewards' minutes show that these deliberations coincided with a gradual softening in management's stance towards the unions. In July 1950, the works director, Harrison, appeared at a meeting of the shop committee and spoke about the company's intention to implement a new bonus scheme which would significantly raise earnings. The available records suggest that this intervention was unprecedented. Harrison concluded his speech by expressing the hope that his visit would not be the last as 'he was prepared to meet the stewards at any of their monthly meetings and hoped by so doing to create that goodwill between management and men which was so necessary for the benefit of both'. For some reason, Harrison did not fulfil his promise; but the shop committee quietly waited for further news until October when the convenor warned that the 'men are getting impatient'. This appeared sufficient to prompt two directors and the 'industrial officer' to attend the next meeting and present the final arrangements for the pay offer — which the committee promptly accepted.

During the 1950s the senior managers attended only a few more committee meetings; but on each occasion they intervened on key issues. In August 1957 they attended one gathering to outline (and presumably justify) changes in the pay structure. Exactly a year later, they returned to explain why redundancies were necessary, and they came once again in February 1960 to present their plans for another major revision to the pay structure. There were other signs of the managers' 'softening' attitude towards the unions. In the early 1950s, the works convenor began to receive pay for time spent on union business. Shortly afterwards, the same concession was granted to the shop committee's secretary.

It is not difficult to imagine ways in which such a reconciliation could have proved very useful to the managers. Though Sir Alfred had reached his eighties by this time and visited Edgwick less and less frequently, he remained very much the firm's 'sole and governing director'. The other directors, all veteran Herbert employees, were careful to operate within the constraints set by his managerial philosophy. One of these constraints was Sir Alfred's determination to keep a tight control on piecework prices, even in the face of strong competition for labour. During the war, his managers had tried to resolve this contradiction by being 'liberal' on claims for non-productive work. Williams's research shows that the shop bonus, or 'Alfred Herbert Award' as it was called, was used to fulfil the same function in the 1960s. He found that increases in the shop bonus kept pay within 'striking distance' of the district average (Williams, 1968, especially graph 2). From the fragmentary data available in management and union records, it appears that this same device was used from 1950 onwards. (By 1960 the shop bonus made up 28 per cent of the standard hourly earnings of Herberts skilled employees.)

Of course, none of this explains why management 'awarded' those increases through negotiations with the unions. They could have raised the shop bonus without recourse to the shop stewards, but this would have been an unprofitable line to follow for three reasons. First, the increases were far too small to persuade workers that non-unionism 'paid'. Second, it suited management to maintain its 'hard gaffers' front — to keep tight control over job prices and a host of other labour issues — and that was more easily achieved if the pay increases were seen to be the product of tough bargaining with the unions. Third, the increases could be used to purchase an accommodation with the shop committee or, more precisely, with key members of it. In fact, the records indicate that senior managers fostered a special relationship with the AEU at the expense of the TGWU, and with a few shop stewards at the expense of others, in a way that must have been calculated to reinforce the sectional divisions between workers and to disable the shopfloor organization.

Shortages of skilled labour lay behind the limited accommodation with the stewards of skilled men, but management remained hostile to unionism among other workers throughout this period. For example, Phil Barnes, a middle-level manager, described the packers in a way in which sexist attitudes were tangled with ideas about hierarchies of skill: 'They were solely in TGWU, or something

— all the rest were in AEU, you see, skilled men, you see. . . . There were two distinct unions, you see. . . . None of the poles would meet. The women in the packing were just in TGWU — the scrubbers' union'. More tangible evidence of managerial opposition to the 'scrubbers' union' is provided by the firm's refusal to pay for any of the trade union activities of the deputy convenor — a position normally occupied by the senior TGWU steward — until some time in the 1960s despite the fact that the convenor and committee secretary, both members of the AEU, enjoyed this concession from the early 1950s.

In addition to opposition to the TGWU, managers also acted in ways that strengthened the position of the two senior AEU stewards, Feltham and Warr, within the shopfloor organization at the expense of the other shop stewards. The firm refused to compensate the section stewards for loss of earnings when they attended committee meetings. Shopfloor collections for charities — always an excellent excuse for stewards to get out and talk to their membership during company time — were banned. Even the more 'legitimate' forms of self-activity were discouraged; Vic Brown, a shop steward in the main fitting shop, recalled: 'they didn't like the blokes leaving the shopfloor, even the shop stewards to go up, you see. But [the convenor] was in the toolroom, and he could get up there'. But Vic did not question how this situation arose. The favoured status of the convenor seemed a matter of convenience. It appeared easier for management to treat with the convenor and the secretary — and pay them for loss of earnings while in negotiations — because both officers worked in the toolroom which had switched to a daywork system in 1950. Nonetheless, Vic felt frustrated by the limited scope to his work as a representative: 'You'd get nowhere. No matter what you took up, they took no notice of you; they would a convenor, but the shop steward didn't have a lot to say'.

If management's intention was to undermine the section stewards' self-confidence and make them dependent on the negotiating skills of the convenor, it appeared to work extremely well. On routine grievances, Warr was allowed to approach works management on his own. And even on major issues, such as the shop bonus, he was expected to fix some kind of deal. As Vic Brown put it, Warr was 'a cadger' who would 'give a bit to take a bit: He used to go up after something . . . and you didn't expect anything; but he'd come back with a little bit, enough to satisfy. And I think that he had a rapport with the management. They knew, you know. . . . They knew what the other was prepared to give and take, you know'.

From management's position, Herbert's corporatism was essentially a pragmatic response to the chronic shortage of skilled labour experienced by the company throughout the fifties. It involved a recognition of workplace organization at Edgwick; but it was a recognition that was very much on the company's terms. It suited the managers to encourage the 'sober trade unionists' (Lane, 1974) within that organization, those with a preference for conciliation rather than confrontation, those with an individualistic 'mister fix-it' approach to factory politics. From the little information provided by the minute books and the recollections of other workers, it appears that Freddy Warr, who resumed office as works convenor in 1950 and stayed there for the next 11 years, seemed to match management's needs more than adequately.

Warr had a knack of securing compromise deals that were sufficient to avoid a dispute. He was positively enthusiastic over the new corporatism, as the following incident suggests. In May 1959, Walter Shepherd resigned as Herbert's first Industrial Officer. At that time, the machine tool industry was in the depths of a trade recession and several hundred workers at Edgwick had already been dismissed (with plans for more to follow). But this did not discourage the committee from marking Shepherd's (voluntary) departure with the presentation of a stainless steel tray; nor did it mar the cordiality of the occasion. In his acceptance speech Shepherd said 'he was very pleased of this opportunity to thank them for the way they had conducted their business when he was on the Other Side of the Table'. Warr replied in kind with the comment that 'the firm was wrong in letting Mr Shepherd go as he believed that a useful job could have been done on both sides'. For much of his period of office, Warr dominated the shop committee. There were perhaps no more than three or four occasions when his leadership was openly challenged by other members of the shop committee.

During that period, the shopfloor organization demonstrated an extremely tenuous relationship with its membership which appeared to discourage it from organizing collective action. This is suggested by the rarity of debates about sectional issues. Instead the works convenor was usually left to resolve sectional grievances where possible or notify the district officials so that they could process the complaints through the formal disputes procedure.

It is not surprising that the shopfloor organization was reluctant to organize strike action. In the years up to 1961, there were a few 'demonstrations' over the shop bonus which usually took the form of walk-outs for works meetings or sit-down strikes. When the shop stewards did organize stoppages, they frequently encountered reluctance from sections of their membership. For example, in November 1953, a 'round robin' against one stoppage called by the CSEU was circulated. On another occasion, the committee decided to cancel a works meeting over the shop bonus because 'The stewards had not the confidence that the works were behind them, following the poor demonstration on Sat Jan 28th over the National Issue'.

The near absence of sectional stoppages cannot be explained so easily. In a plant where the piecework payment system was riddled with anomalies and wage rates were kept below the district average, a weak shopfloor organization might be expected to result in a noticeable level of sectional activity. But between 1945 and 1961 the minute books record only seven such protests, and the press reported one other; none lasted more than a few days. This suggests that the success of management's strategy towards the unions cannot offer a full explanation for this apparent somnolence. Similarly, the frailty of the shop stewards' organization and the character of its leadership — while consistent with management's objectives — cannot be attributed wholly to the managers' political skills. Instead, management's success was based largely on factors which inhibited the development of a collective consciousness within the workforce, and fractured it into hierarchies of gender, age, race and skill in which its elites were not inclined to support the politics of militant unionism.

Edgwick's Double-Sided Politics

It may help to think of Edgwick as two plants instead of one: a medium-sized foundry complex, and a large engineering factory.

The Foundry

The foundry complex employed a relatively small part of the workforce at Edgwick: 200 to 300 workers, or about 10 per cent of the total manual workforce on the site. In the 1950s, the patternshop was a small but significant enclave of craft labour. According to oral evidence, it employed nearly 40 patternmakers, 'a few real class cabinet-makers', and about seven craft apprentices. It seems to have been well organized from the beginning. Even during those years when the rest of the plant was a trade union desert, the United Patternmakers' Association (UPA) kept it a closed shop. There were regular elections for two 'committee men' plus a shop steward who, acting as a kind of senior steward, attended meetings of the Joint Shop Stewards' Committee and assumed responsibility for the first stage of negotiations with management over pay and individual grievances. The UPA exercised tight control over entry into the trade. Barry Doleman recalls that when he applied for an apprenticeship in the patternshop in 1950, he had to sit an entrance examination; some of the successful applicants were later 'weeded out' during their first months at Edgwick, and of those who completed the five years' training only one in three or four were offered a permanent job. Also in line with the classic model of craft regulation, management appeared to exercise very loose control over work itself, even with the apprentices. Unlike the experiences of engineering workers inside Herberts' toolroom, there is no evidence that management attempted to simplify the craft of the patternmakers, or impose a division of labour that enabled some tasks to be performed by semiskilled operatives.

Throughout the post-war period, the patternshop remained an area where skilled workers could take an intense pleasure in their work, which was associated with a strong sense of pride: 'I used to love to go to work in the mornings, and some nights I'd be loath to go home, really. And I wasn't the only one. There was a tremendous fellowship amongst the guys. A lot of respect for each other's skills'. The shop was 'a little protected world'. Yet, despite the high level of union organization in the shop the evidence suggests that the patternmakers earned significantly less than the other white workers in the foundries. Wage data for the 1950s are unavailable, but from Williams's figures, and Doleman's account of the struggle to restore differentials in 1964, it seems that only the Asians, confined to the grade of general workers, earned less than these craftsmen. An explanation for this paradox cannot be attempted until something is said about the other sections in the foundry complex.

In the 1950s there were just two foundries at Edgwick: no. 1, which produced relatively large castings such as headstocks and beds; and no. 2 which produced gears, spindles and some of the other, smaller components of machine tools. For both foundries, Herbert's probably employed between 60 and 70 skilled moulders and core-makers. Despite their 'skilled' status, they possessed few, if any, of the attributes of craftsmen. It is possible that most were members of the Amalgamated Union of Foundry Workers; but there is no evidence to suggest that by the 1950s they had organized a closed shop at Edgwick. The union exercised very little formal control over entry into these two trades. An apprenticeship system still operated for the moulders — the core-makers had trainees only — but this did not hinder management's recruitment of 'non-indentured' moulders. Their skills had become debased from the days when hand-moulding was a genuine craft. Now the difference between a good moulder and a bad one was, as Rimmer (1972: 34) notes, a few months' practice on the job. Core-making, if it had ever been a skilled occupation, had long since lost that status in other foundries in the Midlands. Instead, the job was probably given a 'skilled' status by management to justify the core-makers' high pay rates. In essence, both occupations were no more than repetitive, semiskilled work.

Not surprisingly, the oral accounts provide no evidence of a craft pride, and yet earnings were probably significantly higher than those of the patternmakers during the 1950s. Wage data for this period are unavailable, but if it is assumed that earnings were comparable to those in 1964 and 1967 — and there is some support for this assumption in the oral evidence — then it could be claimed that these two small sections of 'skilled' labour stood at the apex of Edgwick's pay pyramid. In 1967, for example, the core-makers' standard hourly earnings were 15/4d and the moulders' were 14/9d, compared to the 13/3d received by the patternmakers and 14/6d gained by the toolroom operatives who were the best-paid engineering workers on the site.

The high level of the moulders' and core-makers' earnings was management's response to the difficulties of labour recruitment. Work in the foundries was dirty, hazardous and subjected to great extremes of temperature. Better working conditions could be found easily elsewhere, and Herbert's was not the only firm where the managers felt compelled to offer higher earnings in order to recruit and retain semiskilled foundry workers (Rimmer, 1972: 10). This contrasted with the labour market for patternmakers where it seemed management enjoyed the benefit of strong competition for the few craft apprenticeships it offered and had no apparent difficulty in keeping the 'old gentlemen' who had gained their indentures at the firm. The second, major, reason for the moulders' and core-makers' relatively high pay is linked to the question of pay differentials.

The small group of semiskilled operatives who worked in the fettling shop, whose jobs entailed no more than sanding the burrs off castings, also earned significantly more than the toolroom workers. Probably numbering less than 20, the fettlers ranked amongst the best-paid pieceworkers at Edgwick. This must have disturbed both the moulders and core-makers who, if Rimmer's observations are applicable, would have been concerned to maintain some kind of pay differentials which reflected their 'skilled' status.

One should not place too much importance on the size of the differentials at any one time. As noted above, in 1957 the semiskilled fettlers were the best-paid pieceworkers in the foundries; but only three years earlier they had been ranked behind both the moulders and the core-makers. If data were available for 1970, they might show a return to the differentials recorded six years before. More importantly, these heavy fluctuations in earnings put a different perspective on the patternmakers' relatively low earnings. Their income may have been the lowest among the skilled foundry workers, yet they probably acquiesced in this situation not only because their work was infinitely more pleasant than the other forms of foundry work, but also because their earnings on a day-rate system were very stable. Pay was not dependent on fluctuations in the work load, shifts in 'informal understandings' about differentials, or the availability of excessive overtime.

Workplace Politics in the Engineering Shops
Two recent essays by Davies (1986) and Tolliday (1986) manage to discuss workplace politics at Edgwick without any reference to the foundry complex. This may be due to the foundries' double marginality, that is to say, they employed a relatively small number or workers and these had little influence on the politics of the rest of the site. Among Herbert's engineering workers, white women and Asian men were doubly marginal in almost the same way. They were proportionately few in number and apparently of little consequence to the trade union organization inside the engineering shops, so it is not surprising that both writers give similarly little attention to them. In Davies's essay, blacks are invisible and women are only mentioned in situations where, along with 'handymen and boys', they were seen as a threat to the skilled workers' fragile control over pay and conditions. Tolliday acknowledges that the subject of his study – the predominantly white, male skilled and semiskilled pieceworkers at four firms, including Herbert's – were 'at or near the top of the tree' among Coventry's engineering workers and that women and blacks were placed somewhere near the bottom (p. 208). However, he fails to follow up this observation with any discussion on how this labour hierarchy shaped workplace politics in his case studies. This is an unfortunate omission because the marginalization of women and blacks was very much part of the kind of politics that made the union organization at Edgwick so ineffectual.

Segregation. It is not known exactly when Herbert's began recruiting Asian workers. During the Second World War a few Indians worked in the main machine shop. However, it seems they were either technical apprentices or engineering students and their presence was a temporary one. By 1953, Asian immigrant workers were employed in sufficient numbers at Edgwick – both in the machine shop and the foundry complex — to cause unrest among the white employees and their shop stewards. All that can be said with any certainty is that when Williams visited the plant in 1967 clear lines of racial segregation had been established in both the engineering shops and the foundries. In the latter, Asian workers were confined to the unskilled and poorer-paid semiskilled occupations.

Williams's wage data give some indication of the strength of racism in the 'informal understandings shared by management and workers' on pay differentials in the foundries. For if the 'skilled' moulders and core-makers had difficulties in determining relativities with the semiskilled fettlers, they experienced no such problems with the general process workers. In both 1964 and 1967, Asian workers remained very firmly at the bottom of the pay hierarchy, though they did achieve a significant reduction in differentials in that period. For example, in 1964, their standard hourly earnings were equivalent to 52 per cent of the moulders' pay; three years later they had increased to 69 per cent. It is quite likely that this success is linked to the more turbulent shopfloor politics inside Herberts' engineering shops during the 1960s. Otherwise, the impression is that in the 1950s the Asian foundry workers did little to challenge these patterns of discrimination.

There are a number of possible reasons for this apparent quiescence. First, many were recent immigrants grateful for any employment they were offered. Besides, the availability of a phenomenal amount of overtime — double shifts and regular night work — offered some compensation for the poorer piece-rates they were given. Second, if they were recruited by a small number of English-speaking Asians who acted as 'go-betweens' — one form of labour recruitment at this time — this is likely to have had the initial effect of discouraging militancy by splitting people up into small ethnic groups each dependent on one or more 'go-betweens' who had a material interest in maintaining a passivity among their 'clients' (see Brooks and Singh, 1979). Third, until 1967 when 121 (56 per cent) of the 218 foundry workers were Asian, black workers probably constituted a minority of the labour force. The racist conduct of the other workers must have made them feel that they were very much an oppressed minority: there were the routine acts of harassment such as the display of racist graffiti, racist taunts, and the habitual use of clock numbers or racist tags such as 'Sooty' or 'Onion' as names for Asian workers; there were also, occasionally, acts of physical violence against black workers. In the absence of examples of protest elsewhere, it is hardly surprising that they chose to keep a low profile. Instead, they quietly joined the TGWU — rather than the AUFW which their white colleagues belonged to — and waited for better times.

The attitude of the shop stewards was also a factor. At a works conference in June 1953, Warr threatened strike action if any Asian workers were upgraded from labouring to semiskilled machinists' jobs, and in reply the managers gave an informal assurance to maintain the *status quo* (Works Conference Notes, cited by Tolliday, 1986: 207); but no part of these talks was even mentioned in the shop stewards' minutes. It was not until the Asian workers themselves challenged the colour bar that the whole matter came out into the open — and even then the works convenor tried to place a 'fig-leaf' over the committee's politics.

In the summer of 1961, a leading Asian steward, Rajmal Singh, clashed with the committee after he wrote to management to ask about 'the possible prospects for advancement of non-Europeans within the company'. The request may have been prompted by management's exceptional efforts at that time to recruit and train semiskilled labour and Rajmal probably wrote the letter as secretary of the local Indian Workers' Association, not as a TGWU steward; but the shop committee demanded a 'full and frank discussion'. At the following meeting the letter was duly censured. In October, the local paper carried the story of Rajmal's abortive appeals to both the Trades Council and the AEU District Committee to overturn the shop stewards' decision. The same article also carried Warr's denial that there was a 'colour bar' at Herbert's (*Coventry Evening Telegraph*, 20 and 21 October, 1961).

It is worth noting here that Rajmal did not attempt to organize any kind of industrial action to press his demand for racial equality. The Asian workers would have been reluctant to take industrial action because, like the women workers, they felt relatively powerless in the production process. Confined to jobs which serviced the direct workers and were commonly regarded as menial or, at best, peripheral, such feelings would have been understandable. However, events in the early 1960s were to demonstrate just how disruptive a strike by indirect workers could be.

A marginal sex. It is difficult to know how many women worked on the shopfloor at Edgwick during the 1950s. In February 1946, there were 738 women (17 per cent of the total workforce), but the stewards' minutes indicate that 199 women had left the plant in the previous twelve months and that the fall in numbers was continuing. With the revival of the defence industry in the late 1940s and the emergence of a chronic shortage of labour, women were recruited once more to take the places of absent men. Williams's study suggests that by 1964 women represented only 4 per cent of the manual workforce. While there is no doubt that this is a serious underestimate, it is obvious that during the 1950s the number of women who worked on the shopfloor at Edgwick continued to decline both absolutely and as a proportion of the labour force.

None of those women who were recruited and trained as semiskilled machinists to substitute for scarce (white) male labour — either during the war or in the early 1950s — ever gained skilled status; a similar group of men could not have been treated in this way without provoking serious unrest in the factory. It was a testament to the durability of sexism that this inequity was seen as unremarkable, a part of the 'natural order' of things in the engineering industry.

Similarly 'natural' was the practice of paying female machinists lower wage rates than males of comparable age and skilled status. Unfortunately, the only wage data available relate to the 1960s; but there is no reason to suspect that the situation was better during the previous decade. Williams claims that in 1964 the standard hourly earnings of women who worked as semiskilled machinists was equivalent to 71 per cent of that for male capstan operators and only 58 per cent of the pay of skilled turners. According to the shop stewards' minutes, matters had not improved by 1969 when the unions negotiated a scale of base rates for female semiskilled dayworkers which was significantly less than the rate for male labourers. Women's pay also remained abysmally low because they were less likely to participate in overtime.

Why was there no militant action by women in this period? There was either very little scope for militant unionism, as in the piecework gangs discussed below, or the work was regarded as peripheral to the production process. The women who drove the gantry cranes must have been among the few who were conscious of management's dependence on their 'goodwill and co-operation'. That is why, I suspect, they were the only ones who enjoyed equal pay with their male colleagues. The ambivalence of their male colleagues in the shop stewards's organization was undoubtedly another factor. In 1947, before the issue became tangled up with and then forgotten in national negotiations, the shop committee did press management for equal pay; and it is possible that this prompted the firm to make that unique concession to the crane drivers. But the traditional view of women as a subordinate part of the workforce to be displaced when men's employment was threatened remained strong. The minutes for 1961 record this expression of male privilege: 'Re crane drivers it was proposed we ask management to employ only male labour in future. This was carried.'

White, semiskilled workers: on the escalator. During the 1950s, the white men who worked as semiskilled operators on milling machines, drilling machines, grinding machines or lathes, were certainly not marginal to the production process. In 1967, Williams found that they constituted one of the largest sections of the workforce at that time. The figures he was given show that they outnumbered the fitters and amounted to two thirds of the operatives among the skilled, direct workers. The number of these workers at Edgwick, both absolutely and as a proportion of the total workforce, must have been even higher during the 1950s. Company records indicate that at the beginning of the decade semiskilled workers outnumbered their skilled colleagues by as much as 4:1. Yet, despite evidence of their numerical and technical importance, it appears that this group occupied a subordinate position in the firm's wages league.

In the 1960s Williams found that the structure of pay differentials broadly reflected the hierarchy of skills, that is to say, the toolroom workers enjoyed the highest wage rates, followed by the skilled machinists, the fitters, then the semiskilled machinists, and so on down to 'women's rates' among the unskilled dayworkers. In 1964, for example, Williams calculated that the standard hourly earnings of the semiskilled millers were equivalent to 83 per cent of those for their skilled counterparts, and 73 per cent of those in the toolroom. While comparable wages data for the 1950s are unavailable, there is strong indirect evidence to support the claim that the structure of pay differentials was broadly the same. First, there is Williams's observation that Edgwick's shopfloor was 'an ageing workforce' which had developed very strong norms on questions of pay, including differentials. Second, there is the testimony of the shop stewards' minutes which show that on each occasion during the 1950s when the shop committee initially campaigned for 'an all-round increase', they invariably settled on 'pro-rata' pay raises. Obviously, if all these calculations are correct, they raise some interesting questions. Why did the shop stewards and the semiskilled machinists allow toolmakers' representatives to retain the leadership of the shop committee throughout the 1950s when the interests of the former group were so poorly served? And why was there so little sectional activity among the semiskilled machinists in response to the shop committee's failings?

One factor which encouraged male machinists to identify with the skilled elites was the presence of opportunities for regrading. The vast majority of the machinists could, as at other engineering firms in Coventry, expect to gain skilled status in five years or less. The shop stewards' minutes record that ball-bearing drillers were 'the only grade of [male] direct machinists who [did] not automatically have the opportunity of progressing directly through the semiskilled grades to a skilled grade'. To a large extent, regrading depended on the attitude of the workers' immediate supervisors; but the union records provide testimony to the strength of the conviction among adult, male semiskilled machinists that they had a right to that chance. These high expectations were justified because Herbert's chronic shortage of skilled labour virtually guaranteed regrading for those prepared to stay with the firm. This is reflected in data which indicate that a major change in the ratio of semiskilled to skilled labour took place during this period: from 4:1 in 1952 to 0.6:1 in 1968. It would seem reasonable to suppose that this particular section of labour would have been less concerned about pay differentials based on skilled status than those kept off the skill escalator.

Skilled and Semiskilled Pieceworkers: Common Experiences

To explain how the common experiences of skilled and semiskilled engineering pieceworkers offered little succour to militant unionism, a useful starting point is Tolliday's (1986) article. Tolliday attributes the marginal position of the unions to a combination of factors: management's determination to run a 'classic anti-union paternalist shop'; the regularity of employment (which contrasted with the marked seasonal nature of work in the motor industry); and management's 'unadventurous approach to product innovation' which provided few opportunities for workers to raise earnings through piece-price bargaining. I would contest none of these points. But Tolliday does not consider the impact of technology on shopfloor politics — a curious omission since Herbert's was the only machine tool plant in his four case studies. His account of the firm's 'idiosyncratic payment system' also misses the mark in several important respects. Nor is there any comment on the fact that Herbert's toolroom operatives did not conform to the generalizations he makes about the toolmakers in Coventry's engineering industry. This section will explore these claims as a way of trying to explain the 'somnolent' character of the shopfloor organization.

Unlike the three motor firms in Tolliday's study, but in common with most machine tool factories at that time, the production process at Edgwick was highly fragmented. Thousands of different types of components were machined and assembled in small batches and, because of the layout of the plant and machinery, transported many miles back and forth across the shopfloor in the process. Machines were grouped together by type and not according to their function in the production process. By splitting the workforce into separate skill groups, the organization of work fostered divisions between workers. The material basis was there to encourage a sectional consciousness as opposed to a factory consciousness.

This form of organization also made it difficult (if not impossible) for any one section of the direct workers to effect an immediate disruption of production. This was demonstrated in 1968 when over 100 fitters went on strike for five weeks. This caused management to lay off no more than 150 operatives across the rest of the factory. The same point was even more relevant to the semiskilled pieceworkers in the machine shops. Unlike some of their skilled colleagues, they could not always rely on the labour market to keep their pay close to the district average; and unlike the track workers in the local motor firms they could not threaten powerful sanctions to press their sectional interests. They needed an alliance with the skilled workers. Indeed, one strategy that was open to them was to depend on the skilled elites, particularly the toolmakers, to secure pay rises which then became the subject of claims over differentials.

Tolliday's discussion of the firm's 'idiosyncratic payment system' contains three errors. First, it misconceives the politics of the gang system. Second, it misunderstands why this form of piecework resulted in low productivity in the post-war years. Third, there is no reference to Herbert's experiments with individual piecework between 1945 and 1960, though this system probably covered all the semiskilled, engineering pieceworkers during the 1950s.

Tolliday argues that, in contrast to the local motor firms, Herbert's management kept firm control of the shopfloor. This was not the case, at least not in the same way as firms such as Ford, where strenuous efforts were made to gain accurate measurements of, and secure detailed control over, the labour process. Despite some reforms at the end of the war, piecework prices at Herbert's remained, as one interviewee said, 'extremely phoney', and as late as 1967 Williams (1968: 16) found the rate-fixing department distinctly ill-equipped to remedy that situation: 'The personnel . . . are all from the shop floor. Not one has had any formal training in work study techniques. The stopwatch is very rarely used on the shop floor and prices are generally agreed by a straightforward bargain between the ratefixer and the chargehand'. Although management had a hard authoritarian style on questions of work discipline, the control of work itself was delegated, as far as possible, to the chargehands. This is an important distinction, particularly when, as in Tolliday's case, the analysis of factory politics at Herbert's hinges on an account of the firm's variant of the gang system.

Under this form of collective piecework, the chargehand was responsible for the allocation of work, supervision, and the negotiation of piecework prices. He also had a major influence on recruitment and dismissals within his gang, though he had no formal powers in this area. Furthermore, his financial responsibilities to the gang went much further than Tolliday's brief account implies. In addition to negotiating job prices with the ratefixer, he was expected to keep a record of work completed over a given period and ensure a stable and high level of bonus earnings from month to month. Often this involved the quasi-covert practice of keeping a kitty — getting the ratefixer to put aside some money when bonus payments were high to supplement poor earnings at other times — or, more rarely (partly because it was a dismissable offence), booking unfinished work.

Management gained several advantages from this form of piecework. First, it offered some of the benefits associated with internal subcontracting, namely delegation of control (*cf.* Littler, 1982 ch. 6) which generally reduced the costs of production control and labour administration, and provided a route for the upward mobility of key workers. Second, it had facilitated the exploitation of youth labour which had formed such a substantial section of the workforce before the war. Third, it was a system which encouraged every man to be a 'supervisor' to his colleagues (Schloss, 1892: 88) and, because the bonus was shared out unequally, with the actual supervisor receiving the largest portion, it gave that person a direct interest in increased production. Fourth, it was technically suited to specific elements of the labour process, such as fitting, where the calculation of individual piecework would have been 'special, elaborate and troublesome' (Schloss, 1892: 89). Lastly, the gang system aided management in keeping down labour costs without provoking serious oppositional activity among the pieceworkers. Workers were divided by the hierarchies within the gangs as well as between them. The tensions created by the low wage policy were frequently mediated through the chargehands and, by keeping together the formal and informal systems of job control, it limited 'the potential for the emergence of rival work-group leadership, such as ... shop stewards' (Littler, 1982: 92–4).

Tolliday's failure to grasp the distinctive politics of this form of collective piecework leads him into errors about its effect on productivity. He argues that the gang system 'had little to do with incentives' because the pieceworkers were excluded from the pay bargaining process and, through a complex grading system which individualized earnings, 'the main beneficiaries seem to have been the chargehands and the skilled workers'.

These are plausible arguments; but they are not supported by the evidence. First, during the 1950s none of the skilled workers could possibly have benefited from the gang system at the expense of the semiskilled. Second, instead of developing a deep resentment at their exclusion from piece-price pay bargaining, there is considerable evidence to suggest that many pieceworkers did not want to get involved in its mysteries. They were content to let their chargehands assume this responsibility so long as the bonus payments remained stable and at a level they regarded as fair. This would explain why, when given the chance through an agreement reached in 1966, workers in only 14 out of 78 gangs exercised their right to have a gang member present during pay bargaining between the chargehand and ratefixer (Williams, 1968: 1).

The conditions which made Herbert's variant of the gang system viable as a form of labour management in the past had considerably weakened by the 1950s. Firstly, the opportunities for employment elsewhere in Coventry made skilled pieceworkers less tolerant of any bullying tactics. Secondly, the opportunities for the super-exploitation of youth labour were increasingly limited after the war: Herbert's no longer attracted young workers in the numbers experienced before 1939; there were new government controls on vocational training; and the company needed to ensure that enough apprentices gained sufficient training to replenish its skilled workforce. Thirdly, and perhaps most importantly, the collective piecework system was supposed to be a form of payment-by-results. To operate effectively, the chargehands had to show that increased effort resulted in bigger bonuses, yet, since senior management appeared more concerned about keeping control over labour costs than encouraging increased production, there was little scope for this form of incentive. To retain their skilled employees in a tightening labour market, the managers discovered they were compelled to keep piecework earnings close to the district average, but, because of Sir Alfred's fierce opposition to higher job-prices, this had to be achieved, principally, through increases in the shop bonus — the Alfred Herbert Award — and systematic overtime. As the former caused piecework earnings to become a diminishing proportion of workers' pay and the latter practice encouraged workers to pace themselves, it seemed inevitable that these 'solutions' would transform the gang system into a weakened form of piecework which resulted in relatively low productivity.

Effort in many of the skilled jobs was extremely difficult to measure. Williams relied on subjective impressions — he thought the work pace 'looked' slower than at the other machine tool firm, Wickman's — and such indirect evidence as the fact that scrap and rectification costs varied between 1.6 per cent and 2 per cent of total direct wages compared to 8–10 per cent at Wickman's. Other evidence of this unhurried approach to work is suggested by Vic Brown: 'You had to keep at it . . . but you didn't have to rush to sacrifice a job, you know. It had to be done dead right . . . nothing bodged up or anything. It had to be done dead right'. The available evidence indicates that senior management recognized this problem at a very early stage. Some attempt was made to introduce individual piecework in 1942; but it collapsed quickly for reasons that are not entirely clear and it was not until 1945 that a more determined approach was adopted. By the 1950s, it is probable that an individual piecework system covered all the pieceworkers in the two machine shops; and so it remained until 1960 when the gang system was suddenly restored across the plant.

Despite the apparent scale of these changes, Tolliday's silence on the individual piecework interlude is understandable. There is only passing reference to it in Williams's study, and even the primary documentary sources say remarkably little on the subject. However, it is an unfortunate omission, as the story provides further evidence that the gang payment system was not the crucial feature of factory politics at Herbert's.

There is no evidence that this outcome of the pay reforms disturbed senior management. During the 1950s, particularly in the first half of that decade, management's tolerance of their employees' unhurried approach to work was understandable. If the work rate was low, it only meant that the customers had to wait a little longer for a Herbert machine; and if they grew tired of waiting, it hardly mattered as there were many more prepared to join the queue. This mood of complacency provided the dynamic for the relationship between managers and engineering pieceworkers at Edgwick. A former manager expressed it this way: 'If you can make a thing and sell it at a reasonable price and a reasonable profit, and the people who are making it are used to making it, and it doesn't require much effort on their part — they can rap them out quite nicely, they've got everything weighed up with regard to piecework prices and that — it's a hell of a job to change it, you know'.

A third flaw in Tolliday's argument is the failure to observe that the toolmakers at Herbert's did not conform to his general statement that 'in many firms the organization of toolmakers became weak and quietistic' (p. 234). He attributed this to the Coventry Toolroom Agreement (CTA) introduced in 1941. This linked toolmakers' pay to the average of all skilled workers in firms belonging to the Coventry and District Engineering Employers' Association and enabled toolmakers to rely on automatic increases.

Herbert's toolmakers did not conform to Tolliday's generalization for two main reasons. First, their recent history had not encouraged them to be 'quietistic'. Herbert's tradition of anti-unionism meant that they could never take it for granted that their position would be respected. During the war, for example, there had been prolonged conflict over the employment of female dilutees. Second, Herbert's toolroom was much larger than average, while the craft ethos was stronger than it was in other Coventry factories. The toolmakers were an elite within a craft elite that was relatively large. They thus continued to play a central role in shopfloor politics. Rather than quietly following, and through the CTA enjoying the fruits of, pay bargaining conducted by other groups, Herbert's toolmakers were pressed to the forefront. The CTA made them wage leaders and in the context of Herbert's factory politics the logical strategy of other groups was to seek increases based on the CTA.

In the mid-1950s, the hegemony of the toolmakers must have seemed a permanent fixture of factory politics at Edgwick. But this rested on an alliance that was not as enduring as it looked. Though few figures are available, it seems that the toolroom continued to dwindle in size during the 1950s; management was about to terminate the individual piecework experiment and restore the gang system across the two machine shops. Probably more importantly, a trade recession towards the end of the decade made it apparent that the interests of the skilled pieceworkers and dayworkers were being protected at the expense of the semi and unskilled employees, and that the representatives of the skilled workers were unwilling or unable to protect the interests of the semiskilled.

A severe redundancy in 1958–9 illustrated this. The stewards' committee defended the position of skilled workers. This shook the dominant assumption in factory politics at Herbert's — that the interests of the toolmakers (and other fragments of the skilled elite) broadly coincided with those of the majority of the membership. That assumption received a further blow in 1960 when the senior stewards agreed to the restoration of the gang piecework system in the machine shops. The deal created a new supplementary bonus, called the Special Alfred Herbert Award; but this was only intended to guarantee the earnings of those who had been high-fliers under individual piecework, principally the chargehands and a few skilled machinists. Remarkably, the semiskilled gained nothing from this agreement to compensate for the loss of their right directly to negotiate job-prices.

The redundancy crisis also signalled the end of Herbert's style of management. The long boom was over and the employees were reminded that the myth of 'jobs-for-life' had always been contingent on economic circumstances. Only months later, the managers dismantled another feature of Herbert's tradition: the non-contributory pension scheme for the shopfloor. Since, it has been claimed, this decision effectively wiped out all the contributions for employees under 37 years of age, its political impact across all sections of the shopfloor is not hard to imagine.

The toolmakers' dominance of the shop committee did not survive these events for long. At the end of the decade, the firm began re-employing large numbers of those dismissed a year before or even later. Ron Doughty was among those called back. He returned, probably like many semiskilled machinists, with a smouldering resentment of his treatment by management and some suspicions about the role of the senior stewards. As a veteran opponent of Warr's corporatist approach to factory politics, Ron had strong personal reasons for espousing a conspiracy theory to explain his dismissal in 1959. On his return in May 1960, he immediately resumed that oppositional role in the shop committee; but this time he could no longer be marginalized as an occasional nuisance and embarrassment. He quickly found allies on the shop committee in his challenge to the leadership. In February 1961, he replaced Feltham as committee secretary. Then in November he was elected works convenor and thus ended Warr's eleven-year-long period of office.

Conflicts and Reform in the 1960s: A New Regime?

Heightened Conflict
Shortly after the election, a series of strikes by clerical workers disrupted production in some of the local engineering factories. Herbert's management must have expected some kind of industrial action from those same sections within Edgwick's workforce, but it is doubtful whether anyone anticipated the size of the strike wave that rolled through the plant.

At first, the strikes were very limited affairs, both in terms of the numbers of participants and their duration. On several occasions in April 1962, the pinkers and sprayers struck for more pay — though only for a few days each time and never long enough to cause any lay-offs. In May, 23 storekeepers went on strike for two days to press their pay claim. Then, in September that year,

140 shop clerks — progress chasers, stock control clerks and storekeepers — walked out demanding an end to the merit award system and an increase that would reduce the widening differentials with the production workers. They did not return 'for meaningful talks' until 39 days later, by which time about half of the shopfloor was laid off. A year later, 39 shop clerks in the despatch department stopped work over the demand for a closed shop. This strike lasted 70 days. During that time, it was reported, a third of the hourly-rated workforce — principally the semi and unskilled day workers — had either joined the strike or been suspended for taking sympathetic action (*Coventry Evening Telegraph*, 29 September, 24 November, 1962; 3 October, 6 December, 1963).

On a few occasions, this new mood touched even the skilled workers, though the effect was hardly dramatic. For example, in April 1962, the test bay workers rejected a review of merit payments as a response to their wage demands. Just over a year later, anger in a fitters' gang over piece-prices encouraged the section stewards to raise the demand for a veto over piecework prices and during the shop clerks' strike in October that same year, the repair fitters narrowly voted against strike action over their pay claim. But the strike had disturbed the 'somnolent' character of factory politics at Edgwick only temporarily. Over the next four years only one sectional action — by foundry workers — was recorded in the minutes; none was recorded in the local press. Ironically, after 1966, its new politics may have even contributed to this apparent inertia when a Labour government imposed a wage freeze. The convenor used all his persuasive skills to pledge his committee's loyalty to this measure. It was also clear that the strikes did not cause a shift in the locus of power, or influence, within the shop committee from the skilled to the semi and unskilled workers.

The upsurge in industrial action was not a 'revolt' of all the semiskilled workers. The records suggest that, apart from the pinkers and sprayers, the semiskilled pieceworkers 'slept' through it all. Perhaps this was because of the 'escalator effect' of custom and practice which, in Herbert's circumstances, virtually guaranteed their rise to skilled status. Whatever the reason, there is no doubt that the massive disruptions to both production and distribution at the plant were caused not by white, male semiskilled machinists, but by non-manual employees and, among the manual workers, by white women workers and Asian day labourers.

Before the strikes, these last two groups had occupied the lowest levels of the labour hierarchy and were, politically, the most peripheral elements of the labour force. As they were isolated from the other semiskilled workers during the strikes, it is not surprising that, afterwards, their situation should remain unchanged. In the case of the Asian workers, it seemed that the politics of their oppression remained as powerful as ever. For example, in November 1965, when it seemed probable that more black workers would be recruited to deal with the firm's desperate shortage of labour, racism resurfaced in the union records. They read, somewhat cryptically, 'Imigrent labour — request gone to Coy'. Two months later that request was plainly (mis)spelt out at an Annual General Meeting: 'Re couler imigrent's Coy would not accept our points no more wag'.

When the strikes came, Doughty was probably unable and unwilling to emulate Warr's tactics. As a semiskilled grinder and a new boy at Herbert's — he started work there in 1950 — Doughty lacked the authority ascribed to men such as Warr, who was both a long-service toolmaker and an experienced Labour councillor. Also, unlike his predecessor, Doughty was not a 'cadger'. He was not prepared to try to fix some kind of quick compromise deal. He held a principled approach to factory politics. Furthermore, he endorsed the strikers' objectives: he was concerned about the low pay suffered by the shop clerks, women workers and manual dayworkers; and he saw closed shop agreements as a vital objective in trying to build an effective workplace organization.

The discontent felt by some of the skilled workers, as they went through the unprecedented experience of being laid-off through strikes — and, furthermore, strikes organized by people who occupied the lowest levels of the labour hierarchy — can be imagined. While it lasted, this mood must have sustained the tremendous pressure Doughty experienced in those first years of office. But by 1964, after the 'revolt' of the dayworkers had passed, Doughty quickly regained sufficient allies among the AEU stewards to disrupt Warr's attempt at a comeback. In January that year, the former convenor stood for the post of committee chairman. Eventually, he secured the post; yet only through the intervention of a district union official and after this 'victory' he never won another election. Later, Warr retired from union politics when he took a foreman's job.

The managers' reaction to the new leadership, and the strikes that quickly followed, was also predictable. Their tentative efforts to work with the stewards were swiftly ended. In May 1962, immediately following the pinkers' strikes, the shop committee was informed that the notice boards were not to be used for 'Union Propagander'. In September, restrictions were imposed on the movement of the TGWU senior steward and in 1963 the managers decided to 'tighten up custom and practice' on the movement of all the senior stewards. For their part, the shop stewards decided to stop the practice of making presentations to retiring managers.

In addition to becoming more restrictive on 'custom and practice', it seems that the managers also tightened up on pay. When he compared the average income of skilled workers at Herbert's with the district rate, Williams observed that 'a negligible differential in earnings in December 1960' had 'widened to 1/3d per hour in April 1965' and that at 'the present time [October 1967] this gap is 1/7d per hour' (Williams, 1968: 31). For the latter years, the Labour government's pay laws provided a ready-made excuse for the widening gap: the managers had only to conform to regulations when the wage freeze was imposed in 1966. But there is no such excuse for the earlier period. It is evident that in response to Doughty's 'straight' leadership and the surge of strike activity, managers became more reluctant to concede increases on both piecework prices and the shop bonus. Piecework earnings declined as a proportion of the skilled workers' total income: from 45 per cent in 1960, they slipped to 40 per cent in 1965 and 37 per cent at the end of 1966. This was matched by a corresponding rise in the proportion of earnings accounted for by the Alfred Herbert Award: from 28 per cent in 1960 to 35 per cent six years later.

In response to this situation, there is no doubt that a large number of skilled workers quit Herbert's and sought better pay elsewhere. According to Williams's figures, between 1964 and 1967 there was a net loss of 176 (15 per cent) skilled, direct production workers. Among the skilled pieceworkers who chose to remain at Herbert's, many were probably the 'satisficers' Williams described in his study: men who valued job security, a regular income and a relatively low level of mental and manual effort more than they valued the possibility of being among the top earners in the district.

From about 1966 anger grew among the 'satisficers' as the plant managers destabilized the effort bargain by introducing, in quick succession, a new range of radically different machine designs. That destabilization was achieved in two ways. First, the rush of new jobs exposed the technical inadequacies of the ratefixing department and the apparently arbitrary structure of piece-prices that had flourished under the gang system. Second, as Williams put it, the pieceworkers were 'faced by the mental stimulus of new work, new methods and new approaches'. In January 1967, Williams forecast that, in consequence, 'the predictability of the environment will decline and with it perhaps the somnificient (sic) atmosphere' (Williams, 1968: 24).

Crisis and Reform

At the end of 1967, preliminary steps were taken to devise a productivity scheme; but short-time working held up this work until May 1968. When the talks were resumed, managers seemed in no haste to conclude a deal. Then, in July, the crisis finally broke. Exasperated by management's delays, some 200 production fitters in the main shop struck work to press their demand for a daywork system and a pay increase that would raise their earnings to the district average. They stayed out for five weeks, sustained to some degree by a 'fighting fund' hastily organized by the shop committee.

When they struck, the fitters demonstrated one of the paradoxes of skilled labour in the engineering shops at Edgwick, namely that despite their position in the labour hierarchy and the fact that shopfloor politics mirrored their interests, most skilled engineering workers were very poorly placed to press their demands through industrial action. The fitters' strike lasted five weeks; but it seemed to have little effect on production. During the dispute only 150 workers were laid off, and another 30 were suspended for taking sympathetic action. The fitters returned to work on management's terms.

This paradox was central to the character of factory politics at Edgwick. Warr's 'cadgerism' was probably based on a pragmatic acceptance of that paradox: a recognition of the fact that, for the sections he represented, a strong workplace-based organization was a doubtful prize to wrest from a management fiercely opposed to shopfloor bargaining when those same sections were so poorly placed, strategically, in the labour process. Relying on the workings of the labour market and the interventions of the union's district organization secured a level of pay and conditions which kept his constituents reasonably happy: it was safer and more economical of effort. Furthermore, the absence

of a strong and assertive workplace organization could benefit the skilled sections at the expense of the others. The practical demonstration of this point came
during the trade recession in the late 1950s. A powerful factory-wide organization, committed to the CSEU's policy on redundancies, could have dissuaded
management from revoking the agreement on short-time working. Instead, the
shop committee did nothing to stop management from sacking hundreds of
workers so that some skilled men could continue to boost their pay with overtime
earnings.

The defeat of 'cadgerism', symbolized in Doughty's election in 1961, did not
radically change shopfloor politics at Edgwick. Doughty's repudiation of Warr's
cosy, quasi-secretive style as a negotiator brought an end to Herbert's variant
of corporatism; but much else remained the same. The foundry complex remained locked into its own politics. In the engineering shops the realization that those
who were kept at the bottom of the hierarchy before Doughty's election – the
women workers and the Asian dayworkers – were still there even after the
strikes in 1962 and 1963 had astonished observers, and probably themselves too,
with their ability to create havoc on the shopfloor. That power could radically
have reshaped politics at the plant. If those strikers had not been isolated by the
traditional practices and ideologies of their oppression, the outcomes could have
been very different. The struggle could have forged a powerful shopfloor
organization which the managers could not continue to marginalize. The strikers
remained isolated in their confrontation with managers who, being long-service
Herbert employees themselves, resorted to the 'hard gaffers' approach to labour
relations in their moment of crisis. Consequently, once the strikers' anger was
spent, Edgwick's 'somnificient atmosphere' was quickly restored and the shop
committee was forced to labour on in a political environment that had become
reminiscent of the late 1930s.

The company's new chairman continued to be concerned, however, about the
relatively low productivity at the Group's largest plant; but the issue assumed
greater importance when, from 1967 onwards, growing financial difficulties
forced him to look for economies. In October, the senior stewards were
presented with the 'road maps' for the Productivity Payment Scheme (PSS).
They were told that it would create earnings close to the district average in less
than nine months, possibly even more pay within 15 months, and that the
plethora of differentials would be removed in two years. That same month all
the shop stewards were taken to a week-long course at the EETPU's college at
Esher 'to understand and believe the tremendous proposals the co. have committed themselves to'. However, the hype did not impress those who had not
secured the fitters' award. Almost immediately after the section stewards' return
from Esher, another series of strikes took place.

Management's proposals were not all hype. PPS was a radical project. Directly modelled on the much-publicized, state-sponsored scheme tested at the Fairfields shipyards during 1966–7 (Alexander and Jenkins, 1970; Paulden and
Hawkins, 1969) PPS represented a comprehensive programme of reform. Corporate management said that within 14 months it would: create a wages structure

for the entire plant; eliminate gang piecework which, with its 'six broad systems and 143 variations', the 'men distrusted' and 'involved too many calculations for management'; establish the ground rules for negotiating job-times (all 200,000 of them); seek ways of increasing productivity through the reorganization of work; and measure enough jobs to be able to start a measured daywork system. But this was only the half of it. The senior managers had another, hidden agenda: to introduce a computerized shop loading and scheduling system (CLASS) which would enable them to take direct control of production and end the delegation of authority to the chargehands. In essence, management set itself the twin objectives of bureaucratizing the chargehands and incorporating the shop stewards' organization into a highly centralized and formalized collective bargaining procedure, thus transforming Herbert's from a relic of Edwardian employer paternalism into a corporation that embodied the very latest in managerial theory and technique, an enterprise 'remodelled for the seventies'. It was an ambitious reform programme. But, over the next two years, these plans were slowly unravelled by the effects of Herbert's wider corporate crisis.

Intimations of this outcome appeared very quickly. In June 1969, just six months after the final version of the PPS deal was signed, the production fitters struck to press for implementation of that first agreement made in August 1968 which, among other things, had promised the district average by the following April. The strike lasted ten days. Management quickly acknowledged the legitimacy of the fitters' claim, but only conceded another interim award because, according to the stewards' minutes, a 'grim two weeks of profitability' had placed Edgwick 'on the brink of closure'. This news confirmed the signs of crisis that had been evident on the shopfloor: the disruption of production caused by frequent design modifications to many of the new products; problems with component suppliers who 'seemed indifferent to orders placed by us'; and acute shortages of labour in some sections. It was apparent that the scheme would never raise productivity through the incentive of higher earnings.

The strike also provided senior managers with a sharp reminder that, unlike their counterparts at Fairfields, they were dealing with skilled workers who were becoming increasingly wage militant. This did not bode well for management's other project, namely the attempt to develop a measured daywork system. Though they must have been conscious of the near certainty that their actions would provoke hostility to the new job-times, divisional managers and the consultants involved in implementing the scheme were obliged – again because of the wider corporate crisis – to produce a much cheaper and quicker version of the measures adopted at Fairfields.

Probably the most damaging revision of the Fairfield 'experiment' was the decision to produce, as 'estimated times' for the second, transitional phase of the scheme, synthetics built from the old job-times developed by the now much-discredited ratefixers. A newly appointed divisional manager acknowledged that this technique was bound to 'cause disharmony between men and management'. When productivity bonuses fell, partly as a result of this device, managers had to guarantee bonus earnings for that phase of the scheme. Attempts to measure job-times for the third and final phase of the scheme were similarly affected by these revisions to the plan. By December 1970, a full year after the date when measured daywork was originally planned to come into operation, only 5000 out of 200,000 job-times had been measured.

The failure to develop accurate job-times inevitably undermined senior management's plans to use the computer as a means of reaching down and taking direct control of work. Without a reliable database, the computer could not provide an effective aid to shop scheduling. The entire project was, in any event, technically misconceived because of the state of the art in computers at that time. The computer could process information only in batch mode. This was entirely unsuited to the complexities of machine tool production. However, the computerization of the shop scheduling system added another dimension to the crisis at Edgwick. CLASS enabled senior management to readjust build programmes in response to changes in the market. Unfortunately, this facility was abused, particularly between 1972–4, when frequent and major changes were made to the schedules. In the ensuing chaos, the proportion of capital that was tied up as work in progress climbed to record levels.

By June 1969, the senior stewards must have realised that PPS was unlikely to fulfil, at least for the forseeable future, the promise of higher pay through increased productivity. Yet they continued negotiations on PPS for two more years to achieve two objectives: to ensure that the gang system with all the trappings of employer paternalism that went with it, such as the merit system, was completely dismantled; and to try to replace it with a measured daywork system in which section stewards would play a key role in ensuring that the new times were acceptable to their members. The first objective was achieved relatively quickly, since it coincided with senior management's own agenda; but when it became clear that the new corporatism did not embrace a strong sectional organization and that the managers were content to use 'estimated times' for the duration of this particular market crisis, the senior stewards finally yielded to pressure from their membership and began negotiations for an alternative payment system.

In the course of three years' negotiations over PPS, the shop stewards gained considerably from senior management's new corporatist policies. Since September 1968, they enjoyed exclusive use of an office with an external telephone line. Between that date and April 1969, the number of shop stewards rose from 40 to 65. Also in April, in talks on the disputes procedure, it was settled that the chargehands would be excluded from negotiations over job-times. In June, managers gave a 'gentlemen's agreement' on the unions' right to establish post-entry closed shops at Edgwick; objectives that trade unionists at Herbert's had dreamed of since the early war years were suddenly granted by management *fiat*. It is not surprising that the union records, through their exceptionally detailed accounts of union meetings and the PPS talks, display a new mood of confidence, even elation, as managers methodically dismantled a control system that had until then effectively marginalized the unions. But despite all these gains and the flurry of sectional strikes that had taken place at the beginning of the PPS talks, the shop stewards' organization remained generally weak at sectional level.

The interests of the skilled engineering pieceworkers seemed to have been, as ever, the senior stewards' dominant concern. Though the pay structure had been 'rationalized' in terms of the number of differentials, there is no evidence that efforts were made to tackle the complex hierarchies of skill, age, gender and race that lay behind that structure.

The resilience of traditional attitudes towards women and black workers has to be central to any account of the weakness of the shopfloor organization at Edgwick. They legitimated both the marginalization of those workers who had the most to gain from a strong workplace-based organization, and the hegemony of those who were accustomed to using the labour market and their district organization to defend their interests. All this may explain why, despite all the early warning signs — including the rumours of redundancies following the appointment of 'butcher' Raine as Chief Executive — the senior stewards were unable to organize effective resistance when the firm's corporate crisis finally broke in February 1971 with the announcement of over 800 redundancies across the Group, more than half of which were to take place at Edgwick.

Initially, things seemed to go well. Staff and shopfloor unions came together and organized a strike before management could issue redundancy notices to individual workers, thus avoiding one divisive tactic the company could have employed. But, at the end of the week, a works meeting had to be convened as a result of the sudden collapse of the staff's unions' opposition and the ambivalent stance of the AEU officials. By a majority vote, the membership decided to return to work. It should be noted, however, that Edgwick was the only plant where management encountered any resistance to the rationalization programme. Though it must have been little consolation at the time, the strike persuaded the managers to give only that plant extra time to find volunteers for redundancy.

In that first redundancy programme, the shop stewards experienced difficulties in finding volunteers. Given the news of redundancies at other local engineering factories and the very small *ex-gratia* payments Herbert's was prepared to offer, it is not surprising that management had to order some 200 compulsory redundancies. The psychological impact of these job cuts cannot be overstated. Though 'jobs-for-life' was a myth for semi and unskilled workers, for many of the older skilled workers it had been real enough. For them the cuts meant the end of a very powerful paternalist tradition which had given them a sense of their own worth and dignity.

When, in March 1971, a further 79 redundancies were announced at Edgwick to be followed by a brief period of short-time working, there was no resistance. The minutes only recorded the JSSC's decision not to convene a works meeting on the issue. In September, management offered a £1 increase on the base rate and the offer of talks on the possibility of scrapping the productivity scheme in March 1972. With that news, PPS was effectively dead, and with it management's promise of raising pay to the district average. In the post-Fairfield, post-Donovan era, the shop stewards were asked to accommodate themselves to a new economic reality: 'any extra on the wages bill could bring about further redundancies', they were told. Eventually, a settlement was reached on a £2 increase on the base rates of skilled pieceworkers, with *pro-rata* increases for the others. The minutes suggest that the managers wasted no time in demonstrating the equation between pay and jobs: the same works meeting that accepted the deal was also asked to support the shop stewards' demand for more time and higher *ex-gratia* payments to deal with the imminent closure of two large engineering shops in the plant.

It is not difficult to imagine the negative impact of these events on the workplace organization. The minutes record the outward signs of this pattern: the declining attendance at JSSC meetings; the EC's recorded 'disappointment and dissatisfaction' with sections that ignored the overtime ban; the rush of managerial initiatives that, initially at least, encountered little resistance on the shopfloor despite the absence of any prior consultation with the shop stewards. However, there is also evidence of the revival of a minimal level of resistance. On the shopfloor, the senior stewards were able to impose an overtime ban which, if not observed by all sections, did inconvenience management; and the threat of 'non co-operation' frequently persuaded the managers to reconsider their tactics over such matters as the transfer of potentially redundant staff and changes in work practices. This opposition provided the base for Doughty's efforts to politicize the issue of redundancies by appealing for some form of state intervention. However, the minutes indicate that, at this extra-factory level, political opposition was not based on what the DATA representative called 'that concept of class solidarity'. On the contrary, it had much closer associations with notions of employer paternalism in which industry is portrayed as a classless, corporate enterprise. Thus, when the JSSC decided to participate in the TUC's National Lobby on Unemployment in November 1971, senior managers were not only asked to fund a shopfloor delegation but they were also invited to participate.

In addition to conveying a corporatist message, Doughty's attempts to politicize the 'machine tool situation' was also a desperate plea for help. Implicitly, it was a statement of his organization's impotence, its inability to sustain from its own resources a level of resistance that would probably compel a positive response from others.

At the beginning of the PPS talks, when it seemed that Edgwick's politics were being turned inside out, the minutes conveyed the new mood among the stewards simply through the unusually rich details of the records. Now that the situation was changed once more, the minutes slid back to the terse, cryptic style of the 1950s. The secretary's very last entry for 1971 was, uncharacteristically, written in pencil and decorated with doodles. The next year, Jim Rollaston, a shop steward from the fitting shop, refused to stand for re-election as the JSSC's secretary.

Concluding Remarks: The False Dawn of a State Rescue

Particularly during 1974, the stewards regained their confidence as the company's demise seemed more certain. The answer to this riddle is that in the months leading up to Herbert's bankruptcy, the senior stewards had established contact with Anthony Wedgwood Benn, then Secretary of State for Trade and Industry, who responded to their appeal by asking them how they would spend additional state aid to restore the company. Benn also made it clear that if or when the managers approached him for assistance, he would insist that the shop stewards were involved in devising Herbert's survival.

In the event, the managers did approach the minister for more funds and, as he promised, Benn responded by offering aid on the condition that the company opened its books and involved its workforce in the formulation of 'a new corporate plan' (*The Observer*, 3 November 1974). True to their word, the managers talked candidly about the policies and practices that had contributed to Herbert's difficulties. During the next six months, they provided more than enough evidence to confirm the shop stewards' long-standing belief that the crisis was due primarily to managerial incompetence. But the process of 'worker participation' was given much less substance. Though each site had a joint committee of managers and workers' representatives (shop stewards and staff reps) which reported to a 'group committee' (that included a senior official from the DTI), 'worker participation' was severely limited in two ways. First, all but one representative agreed to restrict the flow of information from the committees to the membership because of the alleged commercial sensitivity of much of the data. Second, workers in only one union, TASS, tried to formulate their own plans for Herbert's survival (and even that was little more than a reformulation of the senior engineers' proposals); the others were content to limit their 'participation' in the planning process to criticizing the plans devised by others, the managers and accountants appointed by the DTI.

These were critical weaknesses in the participation process. Since the 'corporate plan' which finally emerged had been devised over the heads of the workers, they were unlikely to make great sacrifices to defend the 'plan', if, or when, it was threatened by other forces. On the contrary, their very passivity in that process, their continued dependence on others outside the plant to come up with a 'rescue package' during those months, almost guaranteed that they would react to any such threats with a hopeless fatalism. Those threats materialized very quickly.

In August 1975 Benn was transferred to the Department of Energy. His successor, Eric Varley, acted quickly. Raine made a 'surprise resignation' on 8 August and Walter Lees was appointed the following day. When, in October, Lees began to implement his plans by announcing 550 compulsory redundancies at Edgwick (and the imminence of 700 more cuts at the Red Lane plant), the shop stewards approached Varley for help (*Coventry Evening Telegraph*, 10 and 24 October, 1975). He made it clear that he had no intention of 'interfering' with the management of the company even though it was on the brink of becoming the state-owned National Enterprise Board's first subsidiary.

This cycle of events was repeated in 1976, 1977 and 1978. Each time, management presented the redundancies as part of a desperate remedy. Each time, the senior stewards protested against the cuts and sought the intervention of MPs, government officials and the NEB chairman. Each time, they were rebuffed with the argument that management must be allowed to manage, and each time a crisis was averted by the discovery of a sufficient number of volunteers.

In June 1980 Edgwick was put up for sale. For more than a month, the senior stewards simply waited for a buyer. There was only token resistance when the foundries experienced the first batch of compulsory redundancies. The convenor put his energy into staging a demonstration in London. The symbolism of that demonstration probably said more than he intended. The 'coffin' of Alfred Herbert Ltd was carried through the streets of Whitehall, followed by 100 workers. They maintained their bearing as 'mourners'; but their placards protested at the imminent closure, at the way 'loyal', veteran employees were being cast onto the scrap heap. The banner that dominated the procession bore the image of a huge, grinning yellow face looking over a gate. The legend read: 'KEEP HIM OUT; KEEP HERBERT IN'.

Eventually, a buyer was found — a small business called Tooling Investments — but it had plans to employ only 500 workers at the plant it had acquired at Red Lane. A few section stewards retained their jobs after Tooling Investments had closed down Red Lane and moved into Edgwick. However, they soon had the feeling of 'living on borrowed time' as they witnessed the rapid transformation of Herbert's new managers from self-appointed 'saviours' to asset-strippers. It took just three years for TI to bring Edgwick to its third, and ultimate collapse and leave Coventry's labour movement with more doubtful legends.

5

Craft Unionism, Job Controls and Management Strategy: 'Premier Metals', 1955–1980

Hugh Scullion and P.K. Edwards

Editors' Foreword

As noted in chapter 1, job controls in the post-war period have important continuities with previous controls, and a powerful force in this link has been widely seen as the craft tradition. In this chapter, Scullion and Edwards address several questions which arise: how have craft controls operated in practice; how far have these been unchanging traditions and how far have they been developed and amended; what has been their relationship with the activities of non-craft workers; why did management accept them and what benefits did it gain; and what have been their implications for productivity? The plant which they study is particularly useful for examining these questions since it was dominated by a union with a strong craft tradition. The factory is certainly very untypical of Midlands engineering, but precisely because of this it provides a case which is ideal for examining the nature and impact of craft controls.

The authors' material on the period up to the mid-1950s is limited, and they are able to do no more than sketch in the origins of craft controls. But their rich and varied sources for the period since then permit a detailed analysis of bargaining relationships together with some important insights into managerial thinking. Craft controls are seen, not as monolithic and unchanging 'restrictive practices', but as resources which were drawn on to meet new circumstances. In some aspects they were strengthened but in others they were operated flexibly in response to the economic circumstances facing the firm. Although the stewards could impose powerful sanctions on management, they often chose not to do so, and the discipline and workmanship that were core elements of the craft tradition contributed to productivity.

In addition to these central concerns, the chapter contains information relevant to other contributions. Wage data are analysed, and conclusions that support Salmon's argument, that extensive job controls are not necessarily associated with high levels of earnings, are drawn. Most importantly, aspects of union organization are considered. By the 1950s the 'Craft Union' had a clear steward hierarchy and an influential leadership. These were the products of its own efforts and not managerial sponsorship. These points echo Terry's argument in chapter 2 that hierarchy is not necessarily an invention of the 1970s and that early forms of it do not fit the model of managerial sponsorship. Scullion and Edwards also discuss relations between stewards and members. Stewards were authoritative figures who at the same time depended on shopfloor support and who were in close contact with their members. This picture may be compared with that given by Bélanger and Evans, in whose plant these relationships were less clearly defined and where the authority of the stewards was precarious. It may be that the less confused position at Premier reflected the long-established role of the Craft Union in the work process, for this enabled expectations about authority and the appropriate roles of stewards and work groups to develop.

The factory studied by Scullion and Edwards has now closed. However, the analysis of how craft controls operated is of continuing importance not only in reassessing the past but also in consideraing the future. The craft tradition had a strong productivist ethos, and notions of discipline generated order on the shopfloor. As suggested in our concluding chapter, these features of the British tradition should not be neglected.

Introduction

The Nature of a Craft
The craft traditions of British trade unions have long been seen as important factors shaping the character of the union movement as a whole. Fox (1985: 64) identifies the origins of what he calls the craft heritage in eighteenth-century combinations. The basis of unions in craft traditions was common to European labour movements, but

> what marked the British scene was an emphasis on restrictive and demarcative regulation which was later to be widely emulated where possible by occupational groups with no background of craft tradition and apprenticeship.

Zeitlin (1980: 120) concurs, seeing the peculiarity of Britain as lying not in the 'prevalence of shop steward organization, job control, and restrictive practices', for these things exist in other countries, but in 'their diffusion throughout the industrial structure' as compared to their limitation elsewhere to skilled workers. The restrictive practices associated with craft unions have also been widely seen as responsible for Britain's poor productivity record (Kilpatrick and Lawson, 1980). Although this view is highly controversial (*cf.* Hyman and Elger, 1981: Williams *et al.*, 1983), it raises questions about the actual operation of craft unions that warrant investigation.

Other chapters in this volume explore the job controls (or the lack of them) associated with non-craft workers. In this chapter, we look at craft control itself. A major question concerns the nature and dynamics of this control. Both Fox and Zeitlin equate it with job control and restrictive practices. One problem is that such things are difficult to define, for what, to management, looks like restriction may be seen by workers as a reasonable defence of their interests. It is, moreover, a commonplace of industrial sociology that many groups that no-one would classify as craftsmen can practise such forms of 'job control' as output ceilings and collective effort standards (Roy, 1952; Lupton, 1963); union membership is not an essential ingredient for such practices (Mathewson, 1969).[1] There is also a danger of circularity: craft unions are identified with restrictive practices, while these things are also used as evidence for the existence of craft unions.

Difficulties with the use of the term 'craft' have led some writers to abandon it. Thus Turner (1962) has argued that the category is not a useful basis for classifying unions and that the degree to which a union recruits openly, or alternatively restricts membership to particular trades, is a better criterion. But even he gives 'craft' some meaning: 'the classic craft union is distinguished by the apprenticeship system, the restricted entry of boys solely as learners into an occupation to which the union confines itself' (p. 233). And to say that it is difficult to classify unions according to the degree to which they have craft traits is not to deny that the claim to craft status has been an important characteristic of some occupational groups. The craft ethos remains a crucial part of their self-identity.

Cockburn (1983: 113) has analysed one key element of this ethos in her study of a group of workers for whom craft is a very powerful notion, namely printers. This element is skill, which for Cockburn has three aspects: the skills that reside in the worker, the skills needed to do a particular job, and the political dimension of defending successfully a group's claims as against employers and other groups of workers. She argues that technical change has eroded the first two aspects so that the third is increasingly important to a group of workers wanting to assert control of its occupation. Clegg (1972: 31) similarly argues that skill and craft used to be synonymous but that craft traditions can outlive the need for a high level of skill. 'A craft is a social institution based upon a set period and form of training, and the reservation of certain jobs for those who are undergoing or who have completed that training'.

For the most part, we will not be concerned here with assessing the technical skills held by workers or required by jobs, but there was a widespread view in our case study plant that the skills of the trade in question were much less substantial than they had been in the past. The 'craft' lay in the shaping of metal and the assembly of metal components into finished products. Improvements in techniques of pressing metal had meant that complex designs could be produced from power presses. Not only were fewer highly skilled workers needed, but the skills deployed by the remainder were more routine and limited than had been the case in the past. Most 'craftsmen' carried out only a small range of tasks. But the craft tradition remained powerful.

From the literature mentioned above, a key feature of the 'political' dimension of craft status appears to be the restriction of entry to the trade through apprenticeship rules. But some others can readily be listed. First, there is a claim to specialized knowledge of a practical sort, together with the view that this knowledge can be acquired only through long experience of the trade. Second, as the example of printers shows very clearly, craftsmen exhibit a high degree of solidarity within the craft, which is often enforced with powerful sanctions against those who step out of line. Going along with this is a strong sense of exclusiveness, and rigid separation from non-craft workers. Third, relations with management are dominated by a sense of being what Soffer (1960) has termed 'an autonomous workman'; craftsmen sell their abilities to employers but do not expect to be closely supervised when exercising them. The craft itself will decide appropriate rules of conduct for its members, and management has very little right to interfere with this self-regulation. In short, although recognizing the need for collective bargaining on issues of wages, craftsmen prefer unilateral control of the conduct of work itself: the allocation of jobs between workers, access to overtime, and so forth.

As noted above, 'job control' is not peculiar to craft workers. Each of the features just listed can, moreover, be exhibited by non-craftsmen. But the combination of all of them leads to a distinct craft tradition. The tradition does not just involve restrictions, for norms of high quality workmanship are also important. And, as against some interpretations, it is not static and unchanging but can exhibit considerable flexibility. It is a complex resource which has to be defined and maintained, and not a fixed set of attributes. In this chapter we analyse the operation of this tradition, paying particular emphasis to relations with management: just what kinds of job control were associated with it, how did they work, how did they change, and why did management tolerate them?

The Case Study
In many engineering factories workers claiming some kind of craft status are concentrated in non-production areas such as the toolroom or comprise only a fairly small proportion of the workforce (see Bélanger and Evans, pp. 157–81 this volume). In our factory, which we will call Premier Metals, the craft union covered all the main production jobs. It was, moreover, a particularly tightly-knit craft society. If strong restrictive practices with a direct effect on production

are to be found anywhere they should be apparent here. The factory is interesting not because it is in any way 'typical' of engineering but because of its atypicality.

We have to be vague about the details of the plant because we began to study it under guarantees of confidentiality. The results of that investigation are available elsewhere (Edwards and Scullion, 1982). Under these guarantees we called the plant the Small Metals Factory and referred to the main union as the 'ex-craft' union to underline the decline in technical skills mentioned above. For present purposes, 'Craft Union' is a better designation since a distinct craft identity was more apparent in the 1950s and since 'ex-craft' prejudges some of the issues that we analyse.

Apart from the vagueness and blandness of some of our descriptions, treating the plant under a pseudonym causes no real problems for the analysis. But we recognize that historians may need to know some of the details that we have hidden; a separate document describing the plant and our sources is available for *bona fide* researchers. Any limitations are balanced by the great benefit of being able to draw on observational data as well as historical records. We cite, for example, deep antagonisms between the Craft Union and what we will call the General Union, which emerged to challenge the former union's predominance. Our evidence is not just documents and recollections of the past but also observation of day-to-day relations between two unions. Similarly, we feel that our account of craft job controls is more firmly established than it would be if we were relying on a reconstruction of past events.

We began our investigation by carrying out a programme of interviewing and observation during 1979, with some follow-up visits during 1980. We spoke on numerous occasions to all levels of management, to stewards, and to shopfloor workers. Some management documents, which generally dated back to the early 1970s, were also consulted. We subsequently pursued the plant's history by making a detailed study of the minute books of the Craft Union's 'Central Committee', which were begun in 1954. This was backed up with interviews about the past with stewards from both unions, members of management, some former activists in the plant, and with officials of the Craft Union. This union's executive committee minutes were also consulted. Finally, we studied the firm's records, the most important of which are profit-and-loss accounts and minutes of board meetings.

The Company and the Unions

Premier Metals Ltd

The company was established in 1919 to produce and repair a range of metal products. The early involvement of the union is evidenced by a minute of 1920 stating that, as a result of a national wage increase, the salaries of the four directors would be raised in proportion, on the grounds that all four were 'practical' craft workers. In 1925 the man who was to dominate the firm for many years became a director; we will call him George Thornton. He was made chairman ten years later and remained in charge until 1962. By the 1950s Premier was operating three separate sites, employing about 1000 people.

The firm supplied components to other firms. In 1953 one of its main customers, 'Midland Steel Fabrication', made a takeover bid. This failed since Thornton's terms were felt to be excessive, but a 51 per cent share of Premier was purchased in 1957. The firm's managing director justified this to his board by stressing 'the importance of [Midland's] having its own Press Shop for the supply of [components] at competitive prices'. The new company did not survive long. In 1954 Midland had entered a long-term agreement with one of its main customers, 'Advance Engineering', to supply semi-finished products which Advance then completed. Advance felt the same pressures to secure supplies as did Midland, and took over the latter firm in 1958.

These changes might be expected to have signalled the demise of Premier as an independent entity, but it survived because of reorganizations then in train. Midland had two sites, and it leased one back to Premier for the establishment of the new press shop. A further site was bought with the help of Advance, but the latter firm's expansion plans were curtailed in the face of a serious crisis. The old Midland site was closed, and the new one was consolidated into the rest of Advance. New products were later developed, and the old Midland site was reopened and allocated to Premier. Far from being submerged within Midland, Premier not only survived but now occupied the two Midland factories. One contained the press shop and some associated assembly operations. The other assembled sub-components which were then shipped to other Advance factories.

Premier's labour relations arrangements were remarkably undisturbed by these events or by subsequent mergers in which Advance was involved. The plant was treated as a supplier factory to others in the group. It was not until the 1970s, for example, that any effort was made to integrate its payment systems into those of the larger firm. Continuity was strengthened by Thornton's remaining as managing director until 1962, four years after the takeover by Advance. Management documents continued to refer to the firm as Premier into the 1970s. The shape of shop steward organization also continued unchanged, and owed far more to craft traditions dating back to the 1940s or earlier than to any influences which might have been imported from the firm's new owners. Contacts with stewards from other plants remained rare and insignificant. It is true that Premier's fortunes depended on those of Advance and that particular aspects of its history, notably rapid fluctuations in demand, reflected its role as a supplier plant; but this would have been equally true had Premier remained an independent company.

The Unions: Tradition and Organization
The Craft Union was founded in the mid-nineteenth century. It covered only the Midlands. Until 1939 it had a membership of about 4000; with the growth of

engineering during the war it doubled in size. It organized only time-served men working at its specific trade, thus fitting closely the model of a closed craft union. Its small size, regional concentration, and homogeneity of membership encouraged the development of a feature common in such unions, namely very close contact between members and officials and the fostering of a strong democratic tradition.

Its mode of operation contained some familiar features and some that seem to be less usual. Among the former was the control of the supply of labour. There were rules governing the ratio of apprentices to time-served men which aimed to regulate the total supply of labour. The union also tried to determine supply to individual firms by operating a list of unemployed members and persuading firms seeking labour to recruit from this list. A type of control more specific to it was the earnings ceiling, or limit system as it was otherwise known. This was a strict limit on the amount a member could earn, with anyone going above the ceiling being subject to fines. A former district secretary recalls three benefits of the system: it protected those, such as older workers, who could not work as fast as others; it restrained the tendency, inherent under the piecework system used in many shops, to rush a job and thus to endanger quality; and it protected the rate against managerial efforts to cut prices. The earnings ceiling was expressed as an hourly rate. How strictly it was enforced depended on the state of relations with management. When imposed tightly it could limit the amount of work done per hour to a level set by the union. It was part of a powerful battery of job controls wherein the union claimed the right to determine how many of its members worked in a particular shop and how hard they should work.

We have little hard information on the union's role in Premier until the mid-1950s. But recruitment controls and the earnings ceiling seem to have been firmly in place by then. In 1979 the union's long-serving 'convenor' (a term that we use for convenience although, as noted below, the union itself did not employ it) told us that he had joined the firm in the 1950s and that recruitment through the union had already been in place for many years. A senior foreman who was recruited as a craftsman in 1937 recalled the pre-war organization as being highly disciplined, with tight controls of recruitment, earnings, overtime, and the mobility of labour. Premier was, of course, very unusual in this respect. Tolliday (1985) has pointed to the very low levels of union membership, and sophisticated organization, in many of the car firms. Croucher (1982: 19–45) charts the resurgence of organization in much of engineering during the late 1930s, but this was plainly from a very low base, and a tradition of craft job controls was rare.

At the start of the 1950s the Craft Unions's National Executive Committee made a concerted attempt to broaden the union's base by making provision for an auxiliary section comprising workers carrying out operations ancillary to the main trade. It appears that in several shops no real efforts were made. Many unionists felt that to extend membership would dilute the craft. Things were different at Premier, for which two reasons may be suggested. First, the union already had in membership a large proportion of the workforce. Exact figures are not available but as late as the 1970s half the union's members were in the top skilled trade to which membership was restricted until 1958; at that date the proportion must have been considerably higher. There was little fear of being 'swamped' by the semiskilled. Second, there was no other union in the plant, so that the union did not have to worry about competing organizational claims to the workers in question.

Even then, it took some time to have the idea of an auxiliary section accepted. The Central Committee proposed it in 1956 but the plan was defeated in a vote of shopfloor workers. It was adopted two years later, with workers possibly being influenced by the stewards' argument that the move to the new factory leased from Midland would give other unions the chance of establishing themselves if semiskilled workers were not admitted. Membership was now open to anyone performing direct production operations.

The danger of competition was not, however, avoided. At the end of the 1950s the General Union began to recruit those groups, notably labourers and truck drivers, excluded from the Craft Union. In addition to the wish to organize the unorganized there was a specific impetus at Premier. The firm had a system of promotion from unskilled to semiskilled jobs according to seniority. But the man at the top of the list could never be sure of promotion because the Craft Union insisted on the absolute right to determine who held one of its cards. Until 1958 this made no difference, since the semiskilled were, in any event, excluded. But opening the doors paradoxically increased the chance of competition since the boundary of the union's territory now extended to semiskilled production jobs.

The matter came to a head when a man in line for promotion was passed over. The Craft Union refused to accept him, and the General Union's members decided to abandon the up-grading system. As a former convenor of the General Union put it, when the craft convenor 'threw down the challenge, we accepted it'. His union decided that, instead of depending on the mercies of the Craft Union for access to semiskilled work, it would claim all new work coming into the factory. Although gaining certain jobs that the Craft Union still disdained, for example operating paint spraying equipment, it was largely unsuccessful in encroaching on that union's traditional spheres of influence.

Inter-union demarcations were particularly significant in the press shop. The Craft Union had been willing to take into its auxiliary section press 'operators', that is workers who placed pieces in presses and pushed the button to make a press work. But they drew the line at 'holders up', who removed pieces from presses at the end of an operation and moved them from one press to another. They were organized by the General Union. A rigid division between the two jobs grew up, with a set ratio being established between numbers of operators and holders up (who were later dignified with the title of press assistants). Different jobs required different proportions of the two grades, and it was difficult to plan operations so that there was work for all workers. Managers increasingly complained at the excess manning that they felt resulted, while for the unions the press shop was the front line of their demarcation struggles. Although it was admitted privately that assistants could operate presses perfectly well, the Craft Union could not acknowledge this because it would give the General Union a foothold on direct production work.

We may now examine the operation of shopfloor relations in more detail. We begin by analysing the craft tradition as it existed in the mid-1950s before turning to the role of management in the creation of the tradition. We then consider how it developed during the 1960s and 1970s.

The Craft Tradition

Work Organization

During the 1950s the plant employed about 1000 workers. By the early 1970s numbers had fallen to about 700, but the proportions represented by the two unions were much the same: two-thirds were in the Craft Union and one-third were members of the General Union. There was a small number of electricians who were represented by their own union, but all other skilled tradesmen, including groups such as fitters and toolmakers who are generally members of the Amalgamated Engineering Union, were covered by the Craft Union. This pattern of organization prevented disputes between craft unions and contributed to the authority of the Craft Union.

The payment system was piecework, using a 'pricing' and not a 'timing' basis: there was no system of timing jobs and setting allowed times for the calculation of piecework bonus, and instead stewards negotiated with foremen a cash price for each job. A management attempt in the 1960s to introduce a timing system was defeated, and there was no formal work study until the 1970s. Most jobs were performed on individual machines with workers working alone or in small teams. There was very little machine pacing of work. One shop had a moving assembly line, but this handled only the final assembly of parts made at individual work stations and workers employed on it each carried out a series of operations. Mechanization and task fragmentation were little in evidence.

A key feature of the plant's division of labour was its hierarchy of trades. At the top were the fully skilled craftsmen who shaped the metal. Then came welders, who were seen as less skilled but who qualified as full members of the union; several types of welder, such as gas and arc welder, were distinguished. The auxiliary section comprised several separate lower grades such as inspectors, press operators, and spot welders. As explained in more detail below, the significance of these divisions was that each trade was formally distinct. A worker was employed as, say, a gas welder and management had no right to ask him to work outside his trade. In practice, the union exercised some flexibility, but only in a downward direction: a skilled craftsman was deemed capable of any job, but other workers remained firmly within their own trades. Demarcations arose not from job territories staked out by craft unions but from divisions in semiskilled areas. The most visible of these was that between the unions, but within the Craft Union's territory there were also clear boundaries between trades. These were closely connected with the union's job controls.

Job Controls
We define job controls as all the means used by workers and their unions to influence the pace and timing of work, the balance between effort and reward, and the conditions impinging on the immediate effort bargain. They are not peculiar to craft workers. What is distinctive about craft controls is the use of methods that are rare elsewhere together with their interconnected nature which reflects the self-image of the independent craftsman. Different craft unions have different controls. Those employed by the Craft Union should be seen not as typifying all such controls but as exemplifying how they work.

The Craft Union saw itself as controlling the trade. Its members may have been employed by firms, but how hard they worked and how workplace discipline operated was for it to determine. A worker was a self-sufficient craftsman, not an employee to be subjected to close supervision by the employer. The earnings ceiling was important in this. The union tried to impose maximum hourly earnings throughout the trade although, as shown below, individual plants could sometimes set their own ceilings. Within Premier, the ceiling set by the stewards was absolute. The Central Committee's standing orders stated, 'pay slips will be scrutinized periodically: anyone found over-booking will reimburse the Shop Fund to double the amount'. The ceiling was raised periodically to allow for inflation and increases in real earnings. The stewards claimed total discretion here, sometimes rejecting a management request to allow increased output by raising it and sometimes insisting on increasing it against managerial opposition. The ceiling was not, of course, set at the whim of the stewards. They took into account earnings and the general condition of the trade elsewhere and the demand position of Premier itself. But in responding to these external conditions they saw themselves, and not management, as making the key decisions.

Allied to this was an absolute control of numbers recruited. Any new labour in the union's sphere of influence could be employed only after the Central Committee had considered the matter. The main influences on its decision were the level of employment in the trade as a whole and expected orders within Premier. If these did not merit an increase in the supply of labour, recruitment was banned. Control remained entirely centralized, an experiment in 1958, when stewards at shop level were given the right to agree to the recruitment of up to three workers, being soon abandoned.

In addition to determining numbers, the stewards had a considerable say in who was recruited. A potential employee was interviewed by a foreman and a steward, with the latter deciding on his suitability. A managerial complaint in 1957 at a refusal to admit an applicant, for example, led the steward concerned to explain that the man's health had looked poor; and the explanation was accepted. In addition to their effective veto over 'unsuitable' applicants, the stewards had a more positive role in the process. They submitted their own list of names to management. This practice did not really increase their control of recruitment, which was already considerable, but it enabled the stewards to secure jobs for particular individuals. A former district official told us of his disapproval of the practice, which could easily lead to abuse and which involved the stewards in activities which were properly the task of management; but there was little that the national union could do about it. As will be seen below, its consequences were perhaps more important when it was copied by the General Union than when it was limited to an already exclusive craft society.

Controlling recruitment means that total numbers employed are determined. The earnings ceiling sets how much work each worker will do per hour. The other main influence on the supply of labour is how many hours are worked. The stewards expected to negotiate on the use of overtime, and they could bar its use if they saw fit. In practice, they allowed it if they could see the need for it and, has been seen, sometimes saw it as preferable to 'setting on' new labour.

As well as influencing the supply of labour and its price, the stewards had a large role in the conduct of work itself. An important element was the allocation of workers to jobs. The stewards' minutes contain numerous references to mobility between one part of the factory and another. Movements within one's trade and between trades need to be distinguished. On the former, the stewards established the principle that management must first seek volunteers. They conceded the formal right of management to direct someone to move but they kept a very close watch on its exercise. One note records a steward's concern that management was using mobility to cut manning levels. In such instances the stewards could always oppose a movement of labour. A man who joined the firm in 1941 and who became the works manager recalls that directing workers to move was done occasionally but that it always created problems; managers were never free to move workers even within trades and had to rely on persuasion and cajolery. Movement between trades was more complex. As shown below, its main feature was that management had no rights at all. It was customary in some shops for skilled men to do semiskilled jobs but this was seen as a concession to be withdrawn at will.

Despite its exclusivity and the reluctant opening of its doors to ancillary workers, the Craft Union did not insist on earnings differentials between craftsmen and others. On the contrary, it used the same earnings ceiling for all members and thus enabled semiskilled workers to earn the same as craftsmen. In 1979, this was not seen as at all strange, and attempts to restore craft differentials which appeared in firms such as BL at the time (see Scullion, 1981) brought forth no sympathies. The documentary record is silent on possible resentments at the erosion of differentials during the 1950s, when the auxiliary section was founded. We can only presume that the craft ethic of equality, namely that any man is as good as any other once admitted into the craft, was sufficiently strong to be generalized to the ancillary workers. A condition permitting this was, of course, the relatively small number of semiskilled workers at Premier. Precise data for the 1950s are absent, but in the 1970s just over half the Craft Union's members (and a third of the plant's manual workers) were in the top skilled grade.

What sort of character did these controls give to relations with management? Many craft controls were institutionalized: they were established ways of dealing with earnings and mobility, they were not directly challenged by management (although there would, of course, be disputes about their application in particular cases), and they were largely taken for granted. The manager just mentioned felt that, when the plant was organized by just the Craft Union, labour relations were good: there were, for example, no strikes. Whether or not this is strictly correct we cannot say, although it is notable that the first mention of a domestic strike in the craft stewards' minute book comes in 1964. The overall picture is one of a cosy relationship in which overt conflict was rare. Craft controls appear to have been tolerated by management, and some managers found advantages in them, notably that they established rules of behaviour that were well understood and thus contributed to order and discipline on the shopfloor.

Stewards and Members

This discipline was supported by strong norms of direct democracy. Stewards had a considerable degree of authority, as the use of fines for exceeding the earnings ceiling illustrates. But they were not autocrats, and saw themselves as guardians of the union's traditions. Their links with their members were very close.

Elections were held frequently. Each shop elected a committee every quarter. The committees comprised several representatives from the top grade of craft workers, plus one from each of the other trades. The title 'shop steward' was reserved for the leader of the committee, who always came from the top grade and who was responsible for all matters in the shop. A press operator's representative, for example, could not do anything without the steward's approval. The Central Committee was chosen every six months; it comprised the three shop stewards and delegates from each trade. Its chairman led negotiations with management but the title of convenor was not used. There were also weekly meetings of members in each shop, where current issues were discussed. Attendance was compulsory; as the standing orders state, 'any member being absent from meeting without reasonable excuse will be fined'.

The stewards, by which term we mean all elected representatives, also stayed close to their members. They spent most of their time on the shopfloor. Although by the 1970s they had a union office, they preferred to be out on the floor whenever possible. Although the 'convenor' and the three leading stewards spent all their time on union business, they were generally to be found in their shops and were readily approachable by members.

The Central Committee acted to represent the interests of the union as a whole. It exerted strong discipline and in particular restrained independent action by sections of the work force. A minute of 1966, for example, records a steward's report that bad weather had caused many workers to arrive late and that management had allowed them their full day's earnings if they made up the lost output. The committee insisted that such arrangements required its permission. There was a strong emphasis on the collectivity as a whole, and a disapproval of local deals. This is one important part of the craft tradition. It is common in other factories for individual sections to bargain about pay and effort, and the stewards then have the difficult job of establishing common principles. In the Craft Union the basic principles were set at the top, and local deals were restrained. Most importantly, the earnings ceiling prevented fragmented effort bargaining and attempts by one section to 'leapfrog' over another. There was thus a strong sense of union discipline, allied to a belief in direct democracy and in stewards staying close to the membership.

Workplace and Union

The sense of craft identity was not limited to the individual factory: a craft tradition involves allegiance to a trade as a whole. The national union tried to regulate the trade. This led to some revealing disputes with the stewards at Premier, who were caught between their role as custodians of union policy and their desire to protect workers already in the firm. The disputes revolved around the issues of the earnings ceiling and the working of overtime, recruitment levels, and redundancy policy. All three issues were linked because they involved contrasting policies on employment security.

There were during the late 1950s and early 1960s several arguments between union officials and the stewards regarding increases in the ceiling: the officials felt that, rather than increase the ceiling, the stewards should permit the recruitment of unemployed workers on the union's books. Similarly, on overtime, the stewards could argue that any high amounts of overtime were only temporary and that the situation did not warrant recruitment. Redundancy policy was more contentious, and in 1958 the stewards were forced to fall into line with union policy after some acrimonious exchanges. The stewards had been using the 'last in, first out' principle. The union, however, refused to endorse this as the sole criterion, instead placing weight on capability in the trade and service to the union. A former district secretary explained that 'last in, first out' was felt to be unfair to apprentices and to make service with a particular firm too important as compared with a man's general competence in and commitment to the trade as a whole. He also felt that the Premier tradition of frequent shop meetings elevated the interests of members of each shop above those of the union: shopfloor involvement in decision-making forced stewards to accept resolutions that were contrary to union policy.

Here, then, we have an interesting case in which notions of the trade as a whole clashed with sectional interests. At the time, the former were powerful enough to prevail, with what were plainly seen as the rather selfish attitutdes of some workers at Premier being subordinated to the larger good. From the mid-1960s references to this kind of dispute disappear. It is not clear whether this means that redundancy policy was now accepted or whether the stewards were able to interpret it as they wished. A plausible interpretation is based on two developments. First, the craft in question covered two main areas, factories and the 'general trade' in which craftsmen moved from one job to another, for example in fitting piping and ducting into new buildings. The latter was declining in importance, and links with the individual employer tended to become more important than relations with the 'trade'. To a worker who had acquired his skills and experience solely within factories, notions of the trade and the craft must have appeared somewhat distant. Second, such a worker would have exercised a limited range of abilities, and might for this reason, too, find his allegiance to the craft slipping. It is thus likely that steward organizations came to have a less close link with the union than they had during the 1950s. A decline in the frequency of references to dealings with the union in the minutes of the central committee is consistent with this. And our observations in 1979 pointed to a distinct coolness between stewards and the union officials; in the course of a dispute that we observed (and that we describe elsewhere: Edwards and Scullion, 1982: 238—44) this coolness turned into open distrust, with stewards arguing that the district official did not understand the issues and was liable to make agreements behind their backs.

Conclusions

These aspects of the craft tradition were closely connected. Direct democracy, for example, encouraged an allegiance to the craft as a whole, while notions of exclusivity governed attitudes to the General Union and to management. If we have said little about demarcations and restricitve practices, this is because these aspects of craft regulation did not appear to loom large during the 1950s. They became more significant later, and are discussed below. But to see why they were not important at first we need to examine the position of management.

The Role of Management

Why did Premier managers tolerate craft controls? Various possible benefits have been identified. Hyman and Elger (1981: 135) cite the reduced levels of supervision permitted by any shopfloor controls (and not just craft controls) wherein workers organize the work process. Craft unions' recruitment controls have been claimed to ensure a high quality work force and to reduce the costs of screening applicants and training recruits (Allen, 1984). The problem is to find concrete evidence of management's endorsement, or even recognition, of such points. In the case of Premier we can certainly identify several positive features of craft control, although how far managers consciously recognized them is not clear. The strong tradition of self-discipline within the craft meant that close supervision was unnecessary. Recruitment through the union provided a supply of qualified workers, and there is some evidence that the Premier stewards included workmanship among their criteria for admission to the firm, although it is unclear how thoroughly they assessed it. The craft ethic of workmanship also contributed to ensuring high quality standards.

Such benefits were probably not consciously articulated by managers at the time when craft controls were being consolidated. It was not a matter of comparing costs and benefits, still less of considering alternative systems of work organization. Managers appear to have accommodated to things as they were, and did not deliberately embrace any particular system of work design. This accommodation may have been assisted by managers' immersion in the craft tradition. We have no information on the backgrounds of senior managers, although until the 1970s all foremen were recruited from the Craft Union, and managers up to departmental manager level were commonly ex-craftsmen. But senior managers too may have embraced craft assumptions. Certainly craft controls do not seem to have generated any specific problems for managers until the late 1950s. Product market conditions were crucial in this.

As noted above, Premier supplied components to several other firms, to which, in the conditions of buoyant market demand during the 1950s, a regular supply of good quality products was probably more important than the lowest possible price. The view that a high level of market demand enabled firms to pay little attention to price is often cited as a reason why they tolerated the growth of job controls. But in this case there is some detailed evidence to support it. The Managing Director of Midland Steel Fabrication, the Premier customer who in 1957 had purchased a 51% share of Premier, plainly implied that there was a cost-plus system of pricing in the most important aspects of the firm's business when he reported to his directors in 1958 that the firm had formerly operated on a profit margin based on a ten per cent mark-up on costs. It is reasonable to infer that Premier also operated on cost-plus contracts.

The Midland managing director returned to the question a year later. Contemplating a year of considerable turbulence, with several strikes, he assessed the situation in terms that are worth quoting in full:

> Labour relations have not been too satisfactory, and I attribute this to two causes. Firstly, bad practices in the past which were condoned by Management and which are now claimed as 'Custom and Practice' by the Unions. These practices were the inevitable outcome of our costing formula which was virtually a 'cost plus' basis. In other words, the higher the labour cost the more profit was made and a bigger return to overheads. Secondly, to the fact that labour has not taken kindly to the mechanization which has been installed.

Numerous commentators have inferred the role of cost-plus pricing. Here we have a valuable statement from someone close to the action.

In addition to not having to worry about labour costs, the system brought reasonable financial returns to firms such as Premier. Some relevant information is given in table 5.1. Turnover grew, albeit with some reverses, over the 1950s, with a rapid advance at the end of the period. Profits were generally healthy, and there is no evidence that wage costs were an increasing proportion of total costs: craft controls did not, apparently, mean a rise in wage costs or a squeeze on profits. To George Thornton the situation must have appeared highly satisfactory. Before the takeover by Midland all the shares of Premier were owned by him, his wife, and a director of the company who held shares in trust for Thornton's children. He had good trading relationships with his customers, he was

TABLE 5.1
Premier Metal Components: Financial Performance, 1951–1959

| Year Ending 30 June | Sales (£000) | | Profit as % Sales | Wages as % Sales |
	Current Prices	1951 Prices		
1951	474	474	5.2	41.4
1952	529	485	8.6	34.1
1953	333	296	2.2	34.8
1954	521	455	−0.3	38.2
1955	694	580	5.3	33.2
1956	701	558	7.2	39.9
1957	754	578	7.8	39.6
1958	1164	867	7.7	43.3
1959[a]	1465	1086	2.0	49.0

Source: Calculated from Company accounts.
Note: [a] Figures distorted by costs of new press facilities, which were as yet making little contribution to sales. Excluding these, profits were 9.9% of sales of £1,357,000, and wages were 44% of sales revenue.

earning a reasonable return, and he had few strikes or similar problems. What would have been the point of trying to root out firmly entrenched craft controls, when these were not causing him any specific difficulties?

This is not to suggest that craft controls were positively favoured by management. Even during the 1950s refusals to raise the earnings ceiling plainly caused difficulties. However, they were tolerable, and their restrictive side came to the fore only later, after they had become firmly established and hence very difficult for management to attack. It is common to see this as the result of changes in the product market, with increasing competition forcing firms to try to rationalize production methods, which in turn brought them into conflict with restrictive practices (Friedman, 1977). This was certainly the case at Premier, but in addition rivalries between the two unions were an independent force that strengthened the effects of these practices.

Struggles for Control, 1960–1975

Rise of the General Union

The General Union began its serious organizing efforts in 1958. These met with rapid success: a steward organization was built up, there was sufficient strength to carry out some strikes from 1959, and in 1964 the Craft Union recognized the position of the new union by agreeing to establish a Joint Union Committee which was to deal with all matters of common interest. An early activist recalls that within eighteen months control of recruitment similar to that practised by the Craft Union had been achieved. The reasons for this success are not hard to find. There was, as noted earlier, substantial discontent among those grades of worker that the Craft Union refused to organize because of the attitude of that union towards them. Management could not readily oppose organization when it accepted the position of the Craft Union. And there was a group of able and committed activists who were determined to raise the unorganized to a position of dignity in the firm. The activist just quoted recalls that the union's bargaining position was strong. Management could not increase output without the co-operation of groups such as drivers and materials handlers. Similarly, the Craft Union's members relied on members of the General Union to supply them with parts, and they could not increase their earning ceiling without the agreement of people whom they saw as mere 'labourers'. Once organized, the General Union could make even elitist craftsmen pay attention to it.

The union developed several means to consolidate its strength and then to make use of this strength. In an attempt to gain a foothold in production areas a policy was adopted of claiming all new work that came into the factory. Throughout the 1960s and 1970s there were demarcation disputes on the issue. The Craft Union argued local custom and practice regarding the jobs in question, generally semiskilled welding and press operation. The General Union cited practice in the engineering industry generally, and where relevant the fact that the particular jobs in dispute were being done by their members in the factories from which the work was being transferred. In broad terms, the former view prevailed, and direct production work remained in the hands of the Craft Union. In particular, the General Union made several attempts to gain access to press operations arguing that the duties of holder up and operator were substantially the same, except that the latter pushed the control button to operate the press. The Craft Union was adamant that operating the press was the responsibility of their own members, and the distinction between operator and assistant remained in force until 1980. But the General Union was able to gain control of several peripheral jobs such as operating spray painting equipment.

It was also able to improve the relative position of its members. There was a persistent campaign to raise basic wage rates. The gap between press operator and assistant, for example, was progressively narrowed and was finally eliminated in 1974. Other methods were used for other groups. Allowances for working in the cold or wet were negotiated for drivers and related groups. And a form of gang system was introduced from the mid-1960s throughout the factory. This was based on the formation of a 'pool' of labour in a given shop. If a member of the pool was absent no production would be lost and the remaining members would share between themselves a sum equivalent to 75 per cent of the absentee's wages. As a form of productivity deal, there were benefits to management as well as workers in this arrangement, and it does not seem to have been abused.

Several consequences of the rise of the General Union should be noted. First, there was a notable compression of wage differentials within the plant. As noted above, the Craft Union ensured that workers in its auxiliary section earned much the same as its craftsmen. The pressure on semiskilled and unskilled workers' wages from the General Union produced a further compression. The result was that, by the time that piecework was ended in 1975, the great majority of workers were on the same rate. This was recognized in the grade-rate structure in which all production workers were on the same grade, with lower grades being limited to groups such as drivers and store-keepers. Over two-thirds (69 per cent) of the plant's workers were in grade 1, 10 per cent were in grade 2, and 16 per cent in grade 3. The last of these earned 89 per cent of the grade 1 rate. A survey of all the company's plants in 1977 showed that, in terms of grade rates, the plant was quite high in the league table but not at the top. The compression of its earnings structure, however, meant that the weighted average of the earnings of all workers placed it at the top.[2] (Some further discussion of wages and their trends over time will be found below.)

Second, there was the creation of rigid demarcation lines and disputes around these boundaries. As a consequence, the company found itself having to deal with a new challenge over the frontier of control, as the General Union strove to carve out a place for itself. This challenge contributed to the turbulence of labour relations. A manager in the plant recalls that the General Union lacked the Craft Union's established way of going about things. Managers plainly found it difficult to cope, and responded by reaching agreement on many of the union's demands on such things as recruitment control and pool systems. Concessions no doubt seemed necessary. As late as 1979 our general impression of the way in which managers at shop level dealt with both unions was that the managers felt confused and powerless and unable to mount serious arguments against the views of the unions. They had little self-confidence or self-assurance. The effects of the General Union were also coming to the attention of more senior management. In January 1964 Advance, who had taken over from Midland in 1958, introduced a new cost control system into several plants, as part of its continuing programme of cutting losses. The general manager reported to the board that Premier was a difficult case 'in view of the rigid practices of labour which have grown up over the past years'. Reviewing the results of the exercise four months later, he reported that the position was improving and that the Craft Union was 'co-operating well'; 'the same could not be said', he went on, 'of the [General Union] who were a law unto themselves, ignoring both the Management and their own Union officials'.

Before analysing union—management relations during the 1960s in more detail, a final consequence of the pattern of union organization should be noted. Craft exclusivity is renowned for its preservation of privileged jobs for white male workers. Premier was no exception. Indeed, the Craft Union's rules forbade members from working alongside or assisting women. At one time Premier employed a small number of women in the press shop, and the question of their unionization arose at the time of the move to the new facilities in 1959. The Craft stewards argued that, as the work was transferred from the old sites, women's employment should be discontinued, and this was done. In 1979 the only women employees were clerical and catering staff. The General Union's emulation of the craft control of recruitment strengthened this pattern, and also led to the effective exclusion of black workers. Although the plant was located in an inner-city area with a large number of West Indian and Asian families, in 1979 there were very few black faces on the shopfloor. Our respondents disagreed as to the precise processes involved, and there was some reticence as to how deliberate the policy of racial exclusion was. We have no evidence of direct discrimination, but the indirect effects of the recruitment process, wherein the best way to obtain a job was to have a union card and to know a shop steward, must have been substantial.

The Market Environment and the Effort Bargain
Despite their obvious strengths, stewards did not find life easy after the takeover by Advance. The underlying problem was the company's inability to sell its products in sufficient volume to generate consistent profits. This had several effects on Premier. There was a continual threat to the survival of the plant, as successive crises hit the company. The lack of consistent sales led to sharp fluctuations in the plant's work load, which created cycles of overtime followed by short-time working and lay-offs. Plant management also made several attempts to end customary agreements. The story is complex and we will do no more than pick out some major themes, taking these three issues in reverse order.

Examples of managerial attacks on custom and practice seem to be concentrated in the period from 1963 to 1966, when Thornton had been replaced. The new management was perhaps less tolerant of restrictive practices, particularly when the profitability of the group as a whole was very low. In 1964 for example there were complaints about the excessive length of stewards' committee and shop meetings and an attempt was made to end the tea-break on Friday afternoons. In 1965 management tried to stop the customary arrangement of stopping work half an hour early on the day after a holiday. These cases illustrate the nature of management's approach, namely to concentrate on issues on the fringes of the unions' job controls. There may have been a hope that other concessions could be forced out of the stewards if victories were gained on these marginal issues. But the stewards were able to resist management without much difficulty. These episodes, together with similar later events, contributed to an atmosphere of distrust: stewards felt that managers attacked their traditions out of a mixture of malice and incompetence, for they would have been better engaged in dealing with real problems with the planning of production. The stewards' response was to defend themselves against what they saw as an irrational and unprovoked attack; managers saw this as clinging to tradition for its own sake. Mutual suspicion and distrust intensified.

Numerous cases of the application of sanctions are recorded in the Central Committee's minutes, and no doubt there were many others at shop level. The first recorded strike, in 1964, was a one-day stoppage initiated by another managerial attack on custom and practice, in this case the custom that on the day prior to a holiday pieceworkers booked and were paid eight hours for a seven-hour day. This was linked with what the minutes describe as an 'ultimatum' from management concerning the level of waiting time that would be paid. There was a complaint at management's 'dictatorial attitude' on the matter. In 1965 there was a two-day strike over the dismissal of a worker; the stewards were successful in having him reinstated.

Somewhat more co-operative approaches were evident on both sides concerning the instability of employment that affected the plant. An important extension of the frontier of control took place at the end of the 1960s when the stewards were able to secure what was termed an overtime buffer. This was an arrangement whereby the production schedules for the plant were planned in such a way that a certain level of overtime would be required to meet them. The idea was that reductions in demand would be met by cutting the size of the buffer, which would therefore protect workers from being laid off whenever there was a dip in demand.

Stewards also took an increasingly flexible approach toward the mobility of labour between trades. They would not accept any movement across the interunion demarcation line, of course, but mobility was increasingly granted between trades organized by the Craft Union. This took a downward form, so that a skilled man could do a range of semiskilled jobs, while movement in the opposite direction was still banned. For management, the rationale was simple: it was essential to have labour effectively employed and not standing around doing nothing. For the workers there were some immediate benefits. Thus a skilled man with nothing to do would be paid only waiting time, whereas if he 'went on mobility' he could earn his normal piecework earnings. More generally, there was an appreciation of the need to keep the plant competitive, without which it is doubtful whether any concessions on mobility would have been made. The Central Committee recognized that there were genuine problems with the balancing of labour. This was in part the result of the plant's size: a small number of absentees on one section could disrupt operations elsewhere very quickly. It also reflected the range of products that was made. One product might call for a large number of semiskilled workers while another called for more skilled men. If demand for the former was high while that for the latter was low there would be an imbalance in the supply of and demand for particular skills. Mobility was a way of balancing different operations.

Throughout the 1960s the stewards grappled with the problems arising from mobility. A central difficulty was reconciling the wishes of individual members, who resented being moved around from shop to shop, and the needs of production. In 1962, for example, three auxiliary members are recorded as having complained about excessive mobility: the Central Committee noted that if they insisted on returning to their own sections, an 'indent', that is the recruitment of labour from outside, would be required. To avoid this, the committee asked the relevant shop committee to prevail on the men to accept the need for mobility. Such issues continued to arise, but in general members seem to have been persuaded of the need for mobility. In 1970 it was recorded that a group of semiskilled welders and polishers had accepted 'semi-permanent' mobility in preference to lay-offs. In theory mobility remained strictly voluntary, but in practice the stewards operated rotas, with workers taking it in turns to move.

Although mobility eased management's problems in the short-run, it also put a powerful weapon in the stewards' hands, for they could withdraw it whenever they chose. On several occasions they used a ban on mobility as a bargaining lever, sometimes in a particular section and sometimes across the whole factory. It was not a weapon to be used lightly, for it brought with it the danger of the loss of piecework earnings and of lay-off. But it was a potentially powerful sanction. In any well-organized plant the withdrawal of normal co-operation is a useful means by which workers can put pressure on management (Batstone *et al.*, 1978: 41−2). All the many ways in which workers help to keep production running smoothly can suddenly disappear: a welding gun that was perfectly acceptable can now require adjustment, a floor which was clean enough is now a safety hazard until spilt oil is cleaned up, and so on. The stewards at Premier were skilled at the deployment of such tactics. But, in addition, their strong control of the allocation of labour provided them with weapons of a different order. 'Normal' co-operation is something that managements have a customary right to expect. It can never be guaranteed, but it sets a basic standard of behaviour. Workers may find it hard to think outside its parameters, and if they do step outside it management can argue that they are not fulfilling their contractual obligations. At Premier mobility may have been usual, but it was not normal in the sense of being something that management had the right to expect. A ban on mobility was a powerful reaffirmation of managerial dependence on the union's co-operation.

The major issue facing the stewards during the 1960s and 1970s was the threat of the closure of the plant. In 1961 the Central Committee approached management to express its concern and to ask what new work was being sought. Later that year the committee took up a refusal by management to pay full holiday pay to some workers who had been re-employed after a redundancy. It argued that this reflected a disregard for workers' interests when the committee itself was pressing members to do their utmost to save the firm. Management would have been better employed in looking to the future of the plant. For managers, costs had to be contained and concessions removed. Thus began a cycle of distrust that ran through industrial relations to the end of the 1970s.

The clash of perspectives was evident a year later. In the course of an argument about failures to meet schedules and piecework prices, the Central Committee sought a meeting with Thornton, but he refused, stating that he was disgusted at the over-pricing of jobs and that he intended to tell Advance that Premier could not remain solvent. Several meetings took place with national officials of the Craft Union, who argued that small subsidiaries such as Premier were often closed down, citing the recent fate of Midland as an example. The Central Committee agreed to recommend a reduction in piecework prices of ten per cent across the factory. This seems to have lifted the immediate threat of closure, but management continued to argue the need to run profitably.

Several re-organizations were taking place connected with the operation of the old Midland plant and the reallocation of work as old jobs were run down and new ones were introduced. In particular, Advance was developing a new product, a large part of the work for which was allocated to Premier. In connection with this, the Central Committee debated the future in 1963. They noted the praise for Premier's efforts from the managing director of Advance for getting the product from the design to the production stage in record time. The committee appealed to members to offer to their stewards any sensible reductions on price on the product, arguing that reducing the price could secure the plant's future. This is what happened. The product stayed in production until the early 1980s, and it provided the plant with a solid amount of work.

The future was never guaranteed, however, for it was always possible for new rationalization plans to call for the closure of Premier, which as a small supplier plant was in an exposed position should corporate managers decide that they had problems of over-capacity. Several threats of this nature appeared, with management arguing that labour efficiency had to be improved if new work was to be secured. The stewards came to feel that they had heard all this before: successive managements complained about work practices, but the plant stayed open. Although they were willing to respond to severe threats to the plant's future, they also felt that managements were not taking the appropriate action and in particular that the attempt to restrain custom and practice was misconceived. Distrust of management was increased by the lack of a steady programme of work and the speed with which the plant moved from short-time working to overtime and back again.

Managers obviously saw things rather differently and a number of the stewards' controls became the focus for concern. Apart from the control of recruitment, inter-union demarcation lines, particularly that in the press shop, were seen as causes of the inefficient use of labour. Perhaps more important than these fairly fixed aspects of union operation were the effects of the control of production on the introduction of new work. Some known degree of inflexibility could probably be tolerated, but what seems to have worried managers more was the unknown: when they wanted to bring in new work, they could not be sure that they would not be met with a demarcation dispute or other sources of delay. At the time when we observed the plant, a job that had come in relatively recently had been the subject of a demarcation dispute which had involved a strike by the General Union as part of a lengthy battle to control it. Even jobs which belonged unambiguously to the Craft Union could involve disputes about manning levels and other aspects of their operation. Thus one concern of the stewards was to establish 'maximum production on days', that is, to minimize the use of night-shift working. This policy seems to have been formulated in the late 1960s, but the dislike of night working can be traced back further: in the 1950s there were disputes with the national union over attempts by the stewards to make new employees work permanently on nights so that existing employees could retain work on days for themselves. (The union opposed this, on the grounds that craft workers were equals and should be treated as such.) Management saw the opposition to night shifts as simply a means of delaying change. It was, in their view, just one part of the stewards' inflexibility and traditionalism, wherein any proposed change was resisted and firm agreements were avoided.

A repeated managerial argument was that the plant was inefficient. But the assessment of efficiency was not as objective as might appear. Higher management deliberately used the prices paid to Premier by other plants to lower the plant's measured profitability; whether or not plant managers knew of this we cannot say. In 1966 the chief accountant of Advance reported to the board that Premier was making losses. Normal policy was what he called arms'-length trading (presumably meaning paying subsidiaries a market price for their products), but in the case of Premier he advocated retaining a different system. The minutes report him as saying that:

> although this aggravated the loss position it helped considerably in keeping down wage demands. He agreed with [a director] that this course was contrary to accepted financial policy, but if the labour position at [Premier] was to be contained there was no alternative.

In short, transfer prices were being set so as to promote a labour relations policy. How common this is, we cannot say, but here is a good example of a practice that is often suspected but rarely documented.

Conclusion: Rigidity and Flexibility

The ways in which craft controls were exercised appear to have been more subtle than managerial characterizations suggest. If managers had really struggled for twenty years against rigid craft controls and excessive manning levels, why was the plant not closed in one of the many rationalizations that took place over the period? How was it that the plant was successful in attracting new work? And how could an experienced manager write in 1980 that the plant 'has always been considered one of the most efficient in [the company] as measured by its off-standard performance'? 'Off-standard' refers to the number of hours of work that are additional to the standard hours prescribed by production planners; it includes mechanical breakdowns as well as labour-related problems such as manning levels above the standard level. Our own investigations confirm the manager's remark: at Premier off-standard hours added about ten per cent to standard hours, whereas in another plant that we studied (now owned by the same firm) the addition was 30 per cent, with some other plants being said to have figures of up to 200 per cent (Edwards and Scullion, 1982: 184).

The answer to these questions lies in the flexibility of the stewards' approach and also in the fact that labour problems were far from absent in the company's other plants. The stewards' willingness to take cuts in piecework prices, to increase the mobility of labour, and to co-operate in keeping the plant open suggest that they did not adopt a rigid or dogmatic approach. They took threats to the future of the plant very seriously. But it was not simply a matter of co-operation. The plant's labour relations became more brittle, with exchanges becoming more acrimonious and with the two sides adopting perspectives that became radically different. There was a curious balance between co-operation and hostility. By the 1970s there was a great deal of distrust, and this shaped the atmosphere of day-to-day industrial relations between senior plant managers and the shop stewards. But at the level of the shopfloor there was a greater degree of trust, based on shared understandings and patterns of accommodation that had been worked out over many years. The stewards felt that managers had spent years in unnecessarily attacking their organization. They also felt, understandably, that management did not know where it was going: at one time they were told that the plant's future was in jeopardy while at another they were led to believe that it was secure and that new work was planned. These uncertainties led them to doubt management's competence and good faith. They felt that they had to protect their craft traditions when they were attacked. Nevertheless, they also deployed their controls flexibly in the face of external threats, and underlying this flexibility was a strong commitment to production and a high standard of workmanship. The interactions of stewards and managers strengthened the conflictual elements of the relationship when major clashes occurred, but for much of the time there was sufficient co-operation to enable the plant to keep going, albeit with many issues unresolved.

Measured Daywork, Decline and Closure: 1975–1985

In 1975 piecework was ended. This did not reflect events at Premier, but instead depended on developments in the company as a whole, notably a wish to bring some order into payments systems that were felt to have decayed. Local managers at Premier were not keen on the measured daywork system, which in their view removed all incentives. For the stewards, MDW was a disaster: as well as removing incentives it precipitated a decline in the plant's standing in the local earnings league since workers could no longer raise earnings through their own efforts.

The negotiations to end piecework ran from 1972 to 1975. The stewards naturally bargained hard about the details of the new system, but the length of time taken reflects difficulties managers in other plants were having in implementing MDW. Its principles seem to have been accepted relatively easily at Premier, for which three reasons can be identified. First, the stewards' highly centralized and disciplined negotiating arrangements, together with the fact that most workers were already in the top grade, meant that they did not have to deal with the inter-sectional rivalries and the jockeying for position that characterized some other plants. The fear of the loss of bargaining leverage that affected other steward bodies was largely absent. Second, the new system promised important benefits, notably guaranteed lay-off pay: a degree of security in the face of rapidly fluctuating market demand was something that the stewards had long sought. Third, the stewards were confident that MDW would not disrupt their traditional controls.

This proved to be the case. The stewards retained their controls of the mobility and allocation of labour, and 'mutuality' continued to be a central feature of the plant's labour relations. There does not appear to have been any developed managerial policy to implement changes in shopfloor behaviour, and where there was such a policy it was not, by 1979, successful. The existing foremen, who were, as noted above, steeped in shopfloor traditions, were retained. There was no attempt to establish a more authoritative role for the first and second levels of management. Some efforts were made to introduce industrial engineering techniques, but these techniques were little in evidence on the shopfloor. Most of the jobs done in 1979 had been priced under piecework, and these were simply converted to new times; they were not subject to work study. Newer jobs were studied, but the exercises that we observed were carried out with such limited co-operation that the value of the results was questionable: stewards and workers used every means possible to prevent adequate timing from being carried out.

By 1979, therefore, many craft-like practices remained in place. They came under renewed challenge after that date. In contrast to the earlier piecemeal and half-hearted efforts, there was now a co-ordinated and widespread attack on existing working practices. With the onset of the recession, economic problems which had troubled the firm throughout the 1970s were increasingly apparent. The company was in such difficulties that there were fears that it might collapse. As part of its recovery programme management insisted on sweeping changes in labour relations, including the end of mutuality, increased mobility of labour, reductions in the number of shop stewards, and an increase in effort levels. We are not in a position to asess the detailed impact of this policy at Premier. This would require a detailed study of events between 1979 and 1985, and it would take us beyond our present concern with the nature of craft and craft-like practices. However, we do need to comment briefly on one question: did the job controls which looked so powerful in 1979 survive the new attack and, if not, were they really as powerful as they seemed?

The short answer to the first part of the question is that they certainly did not survive intact. The inter-union demarcation in the press shop was removed and a number of other changes in working practices were introduced. Management appears, however, to have been rather less aggressive in asserting its right to manage than it was elsewhere in the company. Speaking in 1982 an experienced General Union steward attributed this to a difference in managerial approach in different parts of the company. It is possible that in those parts where market competition was fiercest and where productivity was most critical, managers adopted a very tough line. Premier was now part of a division with a more secure product market, and the pressure on management may have been correspondingly weaker. In addition, a substantial reorganization was in progress, as old jobs were ended and new work was brought in. Part of this involved moving former Premier employees to the main site of the division to which it belonged. The Premier site was run down, and closed in 1985. There would have been little point in management's attacking existing work practices: the plant was only a small part of its activities, and the practices would disappear naturally as it was run down.

As for the stewards, they could see their counterparts in larger plants acquiescing in massive changes. There was little that they could do to defend their own position, and, in view of the impending closure of Premier, there seems to have been little heart in any resistance to management. The demarcation in the press shop, against which managers had railed for so long, was now seen as irrational, and making a stout defence of it cannot have seemed to be very important. A head-on managerial attack might have provoked a different response. As it was, a few controls were removed while the rest were allowed to fall away as the plant shrank.

Earnings Trends

Before drawing together the conclusions of the above analysis, one concomitant of job controls, namely earnings trends, must be described. Did craft control lead to high earnings, and how did earnings levels respond to the changing circumstances of the plant? We have already examined the structure of earnings in the plant, relating the very compressed pattern to the tradition of equality among craftsmen and to successful attempts by the General Union to push its members towards equality with the Craft Union. We now turn to the level of earnings.

Detailed data on earnings levels and trends are very scarce. For the period since 1975 there are the basic grade rates introduced along with measured day work, although for the period after 1980 even these are affected by bonus payments. Before then, there is no reliable series for the earnings of the great majority of the work force, namely those on piecework; wage sheets appear to have been destroyed some time ago. The best indication of earnings is the level of the earnings ceiling that is mentioned from time to time in the Craft Union's minute book and a few other sources. Increases and reductions in the ceiling are generally noted, but the amounts in question are not always clear. We cannot produce a continuous series of wage movements, and have fallen back on giving figures for a few specific years. The ceiling was plainly a maximum and not an average figure. The minute books contain several cases in which the Central Committee agreed with management that the ceiling had to be earned, with people booking the ceiling without earning it being rebuked. In addition, average earnings would be reduced to the extent that workers were on waiting time or day work (that is, paid a fixed sum per hour on jobs without piecework prices). Finally, overtime can increase weekly earnings, while short-time working can reduce them, often, as has been seen, by substantial amounts. Despite these problems, the earnings ceiling can be treated as the hourly rate that a worker could reasonably hope to attain. Trends in the ceiling can be compared with trends in other earnings figures to assess relative wage movements.

In table 5.2 the ceiling is compared with several earnings figures, in engineering as a whole and in the particular sector closest to Premier in terms of the types of work that Premier workers used as standards of comparison. The absolute level of the differential should not, for the reasons just given, be treated too seriously, since the ceiling does not measure actual earnings. As a rough guide

TABLE 5.2
Comparative Wage Data, Selected Years

	Premier Metals Earnings Ceiling as % of:				
	Average Hourly Male Manual Earnings in:		Hourly Earnings (Excluding Overtime Premia) of Men on PBR in:		
			Engineering		A Skilled Group in Another Industry[b]
	Engineering[a]	Another Industry[b]	Skilled	Semiskilled	
1957	118	110	na	na	na
1958	133	123	na	na	na
1960	148	125	na	na	na
1964	125	104	111	119	83
1968	114	95	101	112	79
1970	111	92	100	112	83
1975[c]	125	116	116	128	106
1979[c]	92	88	92	104	89

Sources: [a] Average hourly male manual earnings calculated from series of annual weekly earnings of manual men aged 21 and over, and from hours worked by this group. Hourly earnings of PBR workers taken from a survey of occupational wage levels, based on employers' returns which was begun in 1963. Data for both series up to 1968 are from British Labour Statistics, Historical Abstract 1886–1968 (HMSO, 1971). For later years they are from the DE Gazette, various editions: see, e.g. Gazette, November 1979, pp. 1137–47 for the 1979 occupational wage survey results.

Notes: [a] For 1957 and 1958, engineering, shipbuilding and electrical industries of 1948 SIC; for other years, mechanical engineering of 1958 SIC. Data not strictly comparable between 2 groups of years.
[b] Identity of skilled group and industry in question withheld to preserve anonymity.
[c] Earnings ceiling taken as grade 1 rate in new earnings structure.

someone on the ceiling of 7/6d an hour in 1958 would have earned £16/10/0 for a week of 44 hours (the standard week in the plant at the time). The average wage in engineering is given in the official figures as £13/9/4 for 47.6 hours. The size of the differential is not surprising in view of the location of Premier in an area with a fairly high general level of wages and of the 'skilled' character of its workforce. From 1963, comparisons with skilled trades are possible, and the differential is much smaller. The final column in the table is particularly revealing, since it suggests that, in relation to the closest comparator, workers in Premier were below the average. This is consistent with more qualitative evidence: Premier was not located in the very highest earning region of the country, and even within its own region there were some other groups with whom Premier workers compared their own position unfavourably. Premier workers were not wage leaders. The compression of the plant's earnings structure meant, however, that semiskilled employees were probably doing well in comparative terms (as the comparison between the ceiling and semiskilled rates suggests).

As for trends, table 5.2 points to two periods during which Premier workers were doing relatively badly, the 1960s and the late 1970s. On the former, cuts in the earnings ceiling were, as noted above, instituted at the start of the decade, and the threat of closure was ever-present. The rapid collapse of relative earnings in the late 1970s reflected the economic position that was affecting the company as a whole at the time; it confirms the universal view of shopfloor workers that their earnings had been sliding rapidly. Against this must be set the apparent improvement in the position from 1970 to 1975. This may be illusory in that the figures for 1975 and 1979 are not directly comparable to the earnings ceiling. But it may have some basis in fact: money was plainly attached to the introduction of measured day work, and management at the time may have been willing to make concessions on wage levels in order to establish a new pay structure.

The overall impression is certainly not one of craft controls being used to push up wages. In contrast to a sector such as the Fleet Street newspaper industry, where tight union controls on the shopfloor are widely linked to very high levels of earnings, earnings levels do not seem to have been raised very far above norms within the engineering industry as a whole. This is important in assessing the overall implications of craft control.

Conclusions: Consequences of Craft Control

The foregoing analysis has tried to identify some of the key features of craft controls. It has spoken of two traditions: the broad historical assessment of crafts and their place in British industrial relations, and the analysis of shopfloor relations in the post-war period. On the former, we hope that analysis at the level of the individual workplace can complement studies of whole industries or locations. On the latter, this case study, unlike others in this volume, does not directly bear on the interpretation of the timing and character of the growth of workplace union organization in engineering. It is interesting precisely because it is exceptional: here was a plant where a union had been strongly established for many years and where union controls of recruitment and work practices were firmly entrenched. In drawing out the implications of the analysis, we focus on three issues: links between craft and non-craft workers; the distinctiveness of craft controls; and the effects of the controls on management and on productivity.

Diffusion
Zeitlin (1980: 128) writes: 'where craftsmen adopted a hostile attitude toward the organization of the less skilled, the latter often found themselves compelled to imitate the tactics and organizational practices of the former in self-defence'. The Premier case plainly provides a good example of this process, with the General Union copying many of the Craft Union's practices. But we see it as an exceptional and not a typical situation. It is rare for craft workers to have such a dominant position in a factory as was the case here, for they are usually restricted to specific areas such as toolrooms. This would make opportunities for emulation much less common than was the case at Premier. We would also doubt the idea that non-craft workers directly copy craft practice. We have pointed out elsewhere that in other, arguably more 'typical', factories semiskilled workers operated without reference to craftsmen and developed their own forms of job control and union organization (Edwards and Scullion, 1982: 265–6), a point which is supported by numerous other studies (Beynon, 1973; Batstone *et al.*, 1977; Bélanger and Evans, this volume).

For Premier itself we have to ask why it took unskilled workers until the late 1950s to copy craft workers. There was no natural tendency to 'imitation'. The growth of organization among the unskilled depended on specific circumstances such as the stimulus of the formation of the Craft Union's auxiliary section, the perceived abuse of the upgrading system, and the presence of some determined union activists.

More generally, there is the question of how far similar practices reflected not direct copying but an adaptation to similar circumstances: were craft-like practices copied, or did they arise out of the work conditions facing semiskilled workers? We would argue that the latter is the more likely. Unlike their European counterparts, British workers have not found themselves in an environment in which many aspects of the effort bargain are determined away from the workplace; the emphasis on controlling the immediate effort bargain among oil refinery workers (who plainly have, at most, only an indirect link with craft traditions) in Britain contrasts sharply with much more limited developments among their French counterparts (Gallie, 1978). In America, bargaining at shop level has been more common, but it has been constrained by the law, employers' policy, and the behaviour of unions themselves (Edwards, 1983b). British workers have been placed in a situation in which the effort bargain at the point of production is much more open. In some circumstances they have tried to influence this bargain, and it is not surprising that their efforts have had parallels with the activities of craft unions. This leads to the question of whether there is anything distinctive about the craft tradition.

The Nature of a Craft

We began by noting a tendency to conflate job controls and craft controls. As just suggested, the practices of semiskilled workers cannot be seen as the continuation and diffusion of a craft tradition. To see all 'restrictive practices' as craft practices is to drain the notion of craft of any meaning. Thus Kilpatrick and Lawson (1980) use studies of the cotton industry (Lazonick, 1979) to argue that craft controls have retarded productivity even though Turner (1962) showed convincingly that the cotton unions could not be characterized as being 'craft' organizations.

A rigid distinction between craft and non-craft practices would be unwise. A specific practice such as controlling the amount of overtime to be worked or a broader philosophy of sectionalism can characterize non-craft groups. But a craft tradition, comprising notions of exclusivity, control of recruitment, equality of members of the craft, direct democracy, and the autonomous workman, can be identified. As noted above, writers as different as Clegg and Cockburn agree that the tradition can survive even when the skills on which it is based are in decay. The force of the tradition itself then becomes crucial, with the power to defend established rights depending on politics and not on 'objective' bases. At Premier, craft workers were successful in defending their craft for many years, against the claims of the General Union to do work that was 'really' only semiskilled, and against managerial efforts to break down the job controls that had been developed. Important here was the sense of solidarity among craft workers, which was assisted by their traditions of direct democracy, their numerical preponderance in the plant, the often half-hearted nature of managerial attacks together with the pro-craft sympathies of many supervisors and managers, and the very high degree of continuity of employment (in 1979, 60 per cent of the plant's workers had been employed for ten years or more, a figure far higher than that in other engineering factories: Edwards and Scullion, 1982: 64).

In view of the confusions about job control, this aspect of craft controls must be stressed. One important feature was the centralization of bargaining: job controls were not the outgrowth of individual work groups' struggles but were developed for the plant as a whole. Beynon (1973: 142), having documented the differing degrees of job control exercised by workers at Ford's Halewood factory, notes that 'by 1968 the shop stewards committee was in a position to establish a level of consistency in the job control exercised by each of its stewards'. At Premier, control was not carved out and then generalized but was established over the craft as a whole. Related to this was the refusal to tolerate written agreements. The Central Committee would regulate the trade according to its own principles: a written agreement either stated the obvious, and was thus redundant, or tried to specify that certain concessions, such as mobility across trades, were things that management had a right to expect, in which case it was anathema. This suspicion of committing themselves ran very deep in the stewards' consciousness. Management's job was to provide the work, but the stewards would then decide how it should be carried out. This strong sense of independence and of allegiance to the trade stands in contrast to the job control activities of semiskilled workers.

A more 'positive' aspect, from management's point of view, of the craft tradition was a strong commitment to production and to standards of workmanship. To quote Beynon (p. 140) again, 'trade unionism is about work and sometimes the lads just don't want to work'. Incidents of carelessness and a lack of interest in work obviously occurred at Premier, but the overall sense was of a place in which workers adhered to ideas that production was a good thing and that quality standards were important not just to satisfy customers but also because a craftsman took pride in his work. Instances of sabotage, for example, were, as far as we could discover, absent. The tradition of the autonomous and responsible craftsman again shows through.

A craft tradition is, then, distinct from job controls, but controlling the job was plainly an important aspect of the tradition. What effect did this have on productivity?

'Restrictive Practices' and Productivity

We need to look first at practices as they existed in the 1960s and 1970s before considering their origins. 'Efficiency' is very difficult to assess. Indeed, as shown above, higher management could manipulate measurement of profitability to suit itself. Whether the plant was deemed profitable depended on political processes. Productivity is better measured in terms of physical output per unit of labour input. The only comparative data bearing on this have been cited above: figures of 'off-standard' made the plant quite efficient compared with others in the firm. We have shown elsewhere that, over a six-year period, output in the main assembly shop was 97 per cent of target levels (Edwards and Scullion, 1982: 232). This does not, of course, demonstrate efficiency. As the plant manager put it, meeting targets was one thing, but they were too low and depended on excessive manning levels so that attaining a satisfactory level of output per worker was quite another. But the figures at least show that the plant was not grossly out of line with others, where craft controls were weaker. As shown above, moreover, craft controls did not lead to particularly high levels of earnings.

The main point, however, is not to treat job controls as fixed things interfering with a management which would, in their absence, manage 'efficiently'. As events during the 1960s showed clearly, stewards were willing and able to be flexible when the plant's future was endangered, sometimes exhorting members to 'get down to price'. And, as they stressed, the degree of mobility between trades that they offered was far greater than that enjoyed by managements elsewhere. Skilled craftsmen worked at a range of jobs, including such routine and boring activities as putting sheets of metal through guillotine presses. This co-operation was a direct product of the power of the Craft Union in the plant:

had semiskilled jobs been organized by other unions there would have been no working across inter-union demarcations. Another important characteristic of craftsmen at Premier was their commitment to workmanship. The Central Committee's minute books contain two references to complaints that management was sending out sub-standard work: hardly a reflection of a uniformly 'restrictivist' approach. The union also imposed penalties on workers for poor quality work, and our interview evidence points to a considerable commitment to quality standards. Norms of workmanship must have had some effect on product quality. More generally, the self-discipline of the craft contained benefits for management that went deeper than that of reducing the number of supervisors which we mentioned above. There was a strong sense of disciplined conduct, which was encouraged by the centralization of authority in the union. Management's problem was not the 'disorder' which was widely diagnosed at the time of the Donovan Commission (see Fox and Flanders, 1970). There was a very clear moral order on the shopfloor, in which discipline and self-regulation were central elements.

The role of management also has to be taken into account. We have shown that cost-plus pricing and the ability to sell all that the firm could produce encouraged Premier to tolerate craft controls up to the 1950s. These controls also brought the firm benefits on the shopfloor through the discipline that they engendered. One familiar point is thus that, when competitive conditions worsened, the controls that management had itself accepted came to have undesirable consequences. But two more subtle arguments can be made. First, at Premier it was not just the craft controls that came to be seen as constraints but also the demarcations between the unions. In 1979 managers regularly cited the demarcation in the press shop as a major problem, but this was not a deeply entrenched craft tradition but emerged with the rise of the General Union. Second, it should not be assumed that, in the absence of job controls, management would operate with maximum efficiency. It is not a question of managers wanting to do things and of their being prevented by recalcitrant shop stewards. Neither is it necessarily the case that what managers want to do is inherently rational.

To take the latter point first, we have shown that managers' wishes to recruit could be frustrated by the stewards, who argued that there was insufficient work to justify this. Since overtime generally seems to have been offered instead, the immediate needs of production will probably have been met. As for the longer term, there were several instances when short-time working followed soon after requests to recruit: the stewards were proved right. Their cautious approach to recruitment was arguably as 'rational', in keeping labour supply in line with long-term demand and in avoiding the costs of recruitment and redundancy, as was management's policy. This example also illustrates the stewards' general commitment to the goal of production: they were as concerned as were managers to meet customers' demands, and they differed only over the means to achieve this end. Their controls were not deliberate restrictions, but they grew out of particular circumstances and had complex and contradictory consequences.

Quite often, moreover, management did not seem to have any clear idea of what it wanted to do. Craft controls could be a useful excuse for managerial failures; certainly by 1979 a number of managers seemed almost to enjoy reciting a litany of how they were powerless to act. Indeed, a series of piecemeal and half-hearted efforts merely convinced the stewards that managers were driven by spite against themselves, that managers were incompetent, and that their own interests would be best served by defending traditional practice.

Shopfloor control was, moreover, only one part of management's problems. For Advance in general an appropriate investment, marketing, and product design strategy to secure the firm's long-term future proved elusive. For Premier in particular, attracting a supply of new work was a persistent problem. Writers such as Williams *et al.* (1983) have described at length the marketing and other weaknesses of British manufacturing firms. We mention the problems here to stress that shopfloor control was far from being the only, or indeed, major problem for management. But we do not follow Williams *et al.* in denying shopfloor relations any role in productivity. It is true that these relations cannot be reduced to 'restrictive practices' and that they were one among a set of influences. But at Premier, and, we would argue, in other firms too, they had distinct consequences which interacted with other parts of the firm's operations. Critics and defenders of the shopfloor record have tended to treat it as separate from other parts of companies' activities. They need to be examined together. Thus at Premier managerial efforts to develop a production policy in the face of continual crises led to rapid changes of direction as new approaches were tried out. This contributed to a sense of insecurity on the shopfloor, to the stewards' conviction that managers were incompetent, and to a cycle of distrust. The result was that the firm found it very hard to bring in new products quickly. It was an outcome that the stewards, no less than managers, wanted to avoid. But it was a result which the interaction of the two sides on the shopfloor had helped to create and from which they found it increasingly difficult to escape.

This is one example of the wider point that shopfloor relations are not a separate part of the development of productivity. This is not the place to enlarge on the point. We have considered in detail how craft controls work and have tried to draw out their implications for productivity. These implications are not simple, for some parts of the controls can help productivity while others can hinder it, and how far either effect is present depends crucially on managerial behaviour. The concluding chapter of this volume takes up some of the larger issues, in particular whether it was inevitable that craft controls had the impact that they did.

Notes

We owe a large debt to the managers, stewards, and workers at 'Premier Metals' for allowing very open access to the plant; a brief and anonymous acknowledgement is a scant reflection of what was learned from them. We are also grateful to union officials outside the plant for access to records and for discussion, and to the archivists who now hold the firm's records.

1. Since craft workers are predominantly men, and in our plant all such workers were men, we use 'craftsman' and 'craft worker' as synonymous.
2. In their study of the motor industry Turner *et al.* (1967: 153) note that otherwise similar plants can have very different earnings structures. They have no explanation of this, other than to invoke history. We have been able to explain the peculiar pattern at Premier by exploring the relevant history.

6

Job Controls and Shop Steward Leadership among Semiskilled Engineering Workers

Jacques Bélanger and Stephen Evans

Editors' Foreword

In this chapter Bélanger and Evans examine the development of shopfloor bargaining in a Coventry factory with some of the characteristic features of engineering: piecework, a large number of male semiskilled workers, and a management more given to reacting to events than to developing a long-term production strategy. Although not necessarily 'typical', events here can be taken as indicative of developments more generally.

The authors lack the material to reconstruct the detailed history of shopfloor relations before the late 1950s. But they can analyse very closely an issue which, as they point out, has remained obscure: just what were the processes through which bargaining over effort became established? How did shop stewards and workers build up their job controls, and how did these work? Stewards and workers are presented as active agents and not just as the passive recipients of the 'logic' of product and labour market conditions, an approach which underlies several of the other contributions in this book but which is developed particularly thoroughly by Bélanger and Evans.

A related theme is the nature of shop stewards' links with their members and with management. In the present case, the stewards' authority rested on their ability to represent workers. They were capable of acting on their own and had some room for manoeuvre. But they were not shopfloor bureaucrats and they ultimately relied on workers' acceptance of their policies which were closely tied up with the demands of the membership. The authors' account of the complex forces affecting the stewards thus throws considerable light on questions of workplace union democracy.

It is also often assumed that stewards will defend informality and custom and practice against managerial attempts to formalize industrial relations. In this case, the stewards valued formalization because it would institutionalize arrangements that had only a precarious and covert existence. This is likely to have been a fairly general phenomenon. If this is so, the opposition between managerial formalization and stewards' informality is thrown into question. As the authors argue, such arguments also cast doubt on some ideas associated with the thesis of the bureaucratization of shop stewards. These ideas suggest that managers wish to promote 'orderly' industrial relations by buttressing the authority of senior shop stewards. Bélanger and Evans argue that formality is a desire not just of management but also of shop stewards. In this case, however, the stewards' ability to pursue it was limited by their dependence on the shopfloor workers for agreement; this agreement was not forthcoming.

The picture painted is not one of powerful stewards imposing their will on management. It is one of weakness and uncertainty among all parties: unity among the stewards was always limited and precarious; managers were struggling with difficult external conditions as well as trying to secure some workable accommodation on the shopfloor; and the workers, although able to frustrate efforts at reform, found their own interests in job security and better conditions endangered as the firm went from crisis to crisis. It was not a matter of 'excessive' power being held by any one group but of no party having the ability to pursue long-term strategic goals.

Tolliday (1986: 228) notes that 'factory micro-histories invariably reveal a handful of now mythical figures who took it on their shoulders to "go union mad". . . . Less is known, however, about the sociology of various shop floors and their labour traditions that may have made such catalytic action possible'. This chapter is a rare attempt to deal with both these points, analysing the nature of shopfloor activism (and the constraints on it) and relating it to the material conditions of the production process.

Introduction

Arguably, what distinguishes British workplace relations in the period since 1945 is not so much the durable influence of craft union controls as the extent of job controls among semiskilled workers, in the engineering industry in particular. Explanations of how these job controls developed have conventionally emphasised institutional and economic factors. Tolliday (1985: 108) has characterized the argument thus:

In the postwar period the car firms found themselves facing a soft sellers' market, particularly in Europe, and a tight labour supply at home. In order to achieve continuous and expanding output, they conceded high wages and a considerable measure of job control to powerful shop steward organizations. By the time that international competition began to intensify in the mid-1950s, they had largely lost control of the shopfloor and were unable to dislodge the deeply entrenched shop steward organizations that faced them.

This line of analysis underpinned studies by Flanders (1970) and Turner, Clack and Roberts (1967), and gained pre-eminence with its adoption by the Donovan Commission (1968). More recently, it has been criticized for presenting a 'highly misleading' view of the general scope of the phenomenon, derived largely from some atypical Coventry factories; mistaking the period in which steward organization actually established itself (Tolliday, 1985: 108); lacking a historical perspective; and failing to appreciate that traditions of worker resistance 'cannot be regarded as the product of purely instrumental factors such as incomplete bargaining systems, or the sense of security that derived from post-war affluence' (Price, 1982: 197).

Drawing on evidence from a firm which we will call Presswork, a large Coventry motor components factory, this chapter examines the origins and growth of semiskilled workers' job controls, and the role of shop steward organization in their development. Presswork shared many of the features of post-war motor industry job controls described by Hyman and Elger (1981). Piecework bargaining became the setting for workers to win improvements in both pay and work pace and, even as economic performance deteriorated in the 1970s and measured daywork supplanted piecework, well-entrenched shopfloor organization was still able for a time at least to negotiate impressive wage gains and relaxation of work intensity. Nevertheless, as those authors point out but do not really explain, these bargained and parochial job controls were precarious and the 'scope for deals' with management was more restricted in some firms than others (1981: 136). Presswork was a good example of managerial ambivalence towards the institutionalization of job controls, and thus provides some insights into this question.

In most accounts, however, the origins and development of job controls among semiskilled workers, as opposed to the objects of control, remain obscure. By suggesting that 'elements of the craft tradition were generalized', albeit with the rider 'though they had to be pursued in new ways appropriate to these new conditions', Hyman and Elger (1981: 135) only imply what others (for example Zeitlin, 1980) claim more explicitly, namely the diffusion of craft controls by some unspecified process from craft to non-craft unions. Hyman and Elger's reference to 'steward-led workplace organization' (1981: 136) bears a similar implicit assumption of the leading role of the stewards in the formation of job controls. This contrasts with, but manages to evade the issue of, the stewards' ambiguous relationship to workers' self-activity as suggested in the Donovan Commission's view that stewards rarely pushed workers into un-constitutional action and generally restrained their members 'in conditions which promote disorder' (1968: 29). It is unclear, for instance, to what extent and on what issues stewards led rather than followed their members, or how much and why they should either want to, or be allowed to lead, not just by management but by the workers and the 'outside' union. Again, Presswork provides some valuable evidence on this.

The method of analysis in this chapter acknowledges the influence of institutional and economic factors on the growth of job controls, but insists that these represented only favourable conditions for their development. It confirms that they shared certain characteristics with craft union controls, but these were not borrowed or inherited from craft workers. They were an expression of worker adaptation to a specific labour process and pattern of managerial control. They were actively created by the workers themselves, largely independently of the union. Their extension from means of increasing piecework earnings to consolidating workers' control over their working time, and their successful defence over time, depended crucially on the stability and strength of shop steward organization. In this, the conscious activity and 'strategic' thinking of 'key' steward leaders was absolutely vital (Tolliday, 1986: 228). But, the relationship of the stewards to the job controls was ambiguous. For in pursuing stability and an enhanced bargaining role, the steward organization discovered its own separate interests and dependencies on management. In this way, autonomous job controls became a potential subject for 'expropriation' into more institutionalized bargaining. Contrary to various conventional wisdoms, however (Sisson and Brown, 1983: 152; Tolliday, 1985: 132–40), it was the stewards and not management who expressed the greater interest in institutional reform, to discipline arbitrary management behaviour. Management continued to resist any permanent accommodation with militant semiskilled unionism until a profits crisis created by wide-scale strike militancy in defence of job controls in 1970 induced industrial relations reforms on the lines of the Donovan proposals. These only consolidated the well-established steward organization and thereby reinforced the job controls and caused further deterioration in productivity.

For their part, despite the strengthened bargaining relations in the 1970s, the different union organizations in the factory were similarly constrained from providing any broader collective response to the crisis of mass redundancies and short-time working in the 1970s. This was due largely to the enduring tradition of sectional bargaining and autonomous job controls which undermined the development and stability of any authoritative leadership at the centre, either of the largest union, the Transport and General Workers Union (TGWU) which represented all the semiskilled workers, or of the all-union Joint Shop Stewards Committee (JSSC) which was riven by inter-union rivalry.

The chapter explores the material and social bases for the job controls and the stewards' roles in their development within the evolving social organization of the firm. Evidence is drawn from a longitudinal study of the factory from 1960 up to its sale in 1980. The first section presents an outline of Presswork's production activities and operating environment, and the structure of union organization in the factory. This is followed by an examination of the nature and growth of the job controls among the press operators, the largest and key group of semiskilled workers, which shows how, for more than 20 years, the pattern of conflict focused largely around the effort bargain. The third section looks at the role of the semiskilled stewards and the difficulties experienced in their organizational development. This is dealt with in two phases, an 'early' one dating from 1960—70, and a 'mature' one from 1970 onwards. The chapter concludes by considering the experience of Presswork against existing accounts of the origins of semiskilled job controls, how they compared with craft controls and the role and scope for independent shop steward organization.

The research data were collected by a quite distinctive method. Various classifications of participant observation have been proposed and their respective merits discussed, ranging from the 'complete observer' to the 'complete participant' (Roy, 1970; Burgess, 1984: 80—5). Our research does not fit any of these categories. The nature of the collaboration of the co-authors may be unique. Independently of each other, both carried out research in the same factory. One gained an intimate knowledge of the plant, being employed there as a power press operator from 1972 to 1979. He was a shop steward of the TGWU for five years, of which nearly four were spent as secretary of the TGWU shop stewards committee and delegate to the JSSC. During these years, he was not engaged in any kind of research. But he subsequently wrote a detailed case study of the factory organization, drawing on personal experience, shop stewards' shift and committee minutes books, and 20 extended interviews with senior managers and shop stewards (Evans, 1980). The other studied Presswork as part of his doctoral research (Bélanger, 1985). This was based on studies of management files and shop stewards' minutes books, together with a six-month period of systematic observation on the shopfloor in 1979 and a short follow-up visit in 1980. This non-participant observation had the full co-operation of management and unions to move freely and talk to people in the factory and attend labour—management meetings. Information collected through informal interviewing and observation was supplemented by 34 structured interviews with shop stewards, foremen, and production and industrial relations managers.

Production Activities and Union Structure

Product Markets

Presswork was formed in 1926 out of the merger of two companies, one fabricating radiators and the other specializing in steel pressings. It moved to its present site in Coventry in 1930 and concentrated outlying presswork activities there in 1950. It became a public company in 1953, and from 1955 belonged to a British engineering multinational. It supplied a wide range of components to the motor industry, including radiators, clutch and brake sub-assemblies, chassis pieces and bright trim (polished chrome) parts.

In its brass radiator and bright trim operations, the company was a direct supplier to motor vehicle manufacturers; pressed steel components were mostly supplied part-finished to other component manufacturers who in turn supplied finished components to the motor vehicle assemblers. Like 'Premier Metals' (Scullion and Edwards, this volume), Presswork's subcontracting role made it vulnerable to instability arising from both long-run cycles of demand in the industry and short-run cycles of 'production to orders' in which production was organized to satisfy specific, characteristically irregular, customer requirements. The company developed strongly in the inter-war years as part of the general growth in mass production vehicle building, and this pattern continued into the mid-1960s when the labour force exceeded 2000.

Expansion of the domestic industry began to falter in the face of growing competition in overseas markets and, more immediately, a combination of deflationary government economic measures and industrial disputes at vehicle assembly factories. These developments had an 'unpalatable effect on the company's operations' (Parent Group's Annual Report, 1967) and Presswork's performance and financial difficulties attracted increasing concern from the parent board.

These problems tended to exacerbate the uncertainties deriving from customer requirements to provide a wide range of product specifications in batches, or production runs, of varying size. The organization of production thus needed the ability to diversify products and respond to customer demand with flexibility. By the mid-1960s, the emphasis in Presswork's product range had already begun to shift from the relatively profitable and larger production runs of brass and chrome components to heavier steel pressings. Over the longer term, production became increasingly dependent on and vulnerable to unstable patterns of demand from a declining number of large component manufacturers. By the late 1970s, this trend had developed to a point where more than 80 per cent of presswork output was sold to three leading motor industry component assemblers.

In 1967, these increased market pressures led management to seek measures to improve performance. Because of the centrality of the presswork operations to all the production processes, this meant focusing effort on raising productivity in the press shops. The objective was to increase turnover by lowering unit costs and component prices. This required tighter managerial control over the effort and earnings of the semiskilled press operators who formed the largest single group of workers in the plant and who were central to presswork production. Their position was also strategic because the rates of pay of the large numbers of other, related non-production (ancillary) workers were guaranteed as a fixed percentage of the operators' average piecework earnings (APE). Management consultants were brought in and recommended a new incentive scheme for the press shops. At the same time, the managing director was replaced, a redundancy of 300 workers was carried through, and the new management team gave early notice of termination of the established piecework scheme. Following the exhaustion of the engineering industry's national disputes procedure, the new scheme was imposed in 1968.

Management became locked into a very difficult position. The press operators had already begun to demonstrate a significant degree of confidence and a capacity for sectional militancy in bargaining over piecework effort and earnings. As Presswork's market position deteriorated, its vulnerability both to customer demand and worker pressure intensified. Just when management set out to strengthen their control over labour costs and reassert their domination of the labour process, production stoppages could have proved particularly damaging to long-term customer relations.

These new measures did, indeed, lead to intensified struggle over the effort bargain and to a situation of deep crisis in the press shops, the most visible expression of which was the escalation of strikes and production losses. Evidence will be presented which shows the intensity of the conflict, especially in 1969. A major six-week strike by press operators, starting in November of that year, marked the peak of overt conflict, but its outcome was inconclusive. The malaise of labour relations persisted for several months more, and included many stoppages by skilled and ancillary workers seeking through fractional bargaining to re-establish their respective positions in the 'pecking order'.

Closure of the factory was contemplated but rejected by the parent board because of the scale of their assets in the company and because of the anticipated ramifications for their other business activities. Closure, at that time, would have halted operations in significant parts of the motor industry, and the group would not easily have withstood the pressures from its larger customers. But since they regarded Presswork as a liability, the parent board restricted credits for capital investment throughout the 1970s. Notably, no new technology was introduced in the press shops where it might have contributed to removing some of the basis for the press operators' job controls and militancy. But the company appeared equally unattractive to prospective buyers when efforts were made to sell it in 1971, 1975, and 1978. It was eventually sold at a 'knock down price' in 1980.

In 1970, another new management team was brought in with a mandate to implement a survival programme. They adopted a strategy of cutting labour costs with 400 redundancies, controlling more tightly shopfloor pressures on the wage-effort bargain, and reducing the relative importance of presswork by diversifying the product base. One aspect of this involved alleviating dependency over the long term on the outmoded, craft-dominated labour process in radiator assembly, and developing new products from different materials using technologies based on automated machinery and semiskilled labour. £4 million was invested in research and development of an aluminium radiator, but it failed to get into production. Radiator manufacture remained labour intensive with high material costs, which became increasingly uncompetitive in the contracting markets of volume passenger cars. As noted above, closure of radiator production was not feasible, and efforts were then concentrated on low volume, high profit margin, commercial vehicle and specialist replacement markets.

More resolutely, the emphasis of production was shifted to large industrial heat transfer equipment for power generation. This change in product market strategy was based on a belief that 'future growth lies mainly in the field of heat transfer technology, particularly industrial heat exchangers, space and process heating . . . and concentrating the presswork activities into those specialist areas where the company has particular expertise' (Parent Group's Annual Report, 1972). In the early 1970s, the market for industrial heat transfer seemed very bright, but the first oil shock intervened and by the end of the decade production had fallen to a very low level. In addition to the questionable basis of this strategic reorientation, the way in which management proceeded to apply it to presswork contributed to a further and continuing erosion of the company's share of the market for pressed steel components. Dramatic price increases on many components were imposed on customers, and it was only a matter of time before they turned to alternative suppliers. Nevertheless, compared with heat transfer, presswork demand remained relatively stable, although there was a lower aggregate level of activity as a result of the deepening recession in the domestic motor industry.

Product market changes were complemented by reform of industrial relations institutions. Wishing to avoid costly confrontation with a 'proven' shopfloor organization, the new management in 1970 elected not to attempt major, unilateral change which would, moreover, have been inconsistent with their philosophy of sharing information, consulting and negotiating with workers' representatives. Their strategy fitted well with the spirit and substance of the Donovan Commission's recommendations. As shown in more detail elsewhere (Bélanger, 1987), it included the creation of a new, reformulated Joint Shop Stewards Committee, a recognized disputes procedure based on mutuality, a revised wage structure and annual negotiation of a comprehensive wages and conditions agreement.

Labour Processes and Union Organization

The division of labour based on the different production processes was essentially unchanged in the 1970s from when the various operations were brought under the same roof in 1950. Radiator assembly and bright trim used hand-tool technologies, assembling and finishing parts manufactured in the press shops. The bulk of this work was undertaken by craft workers, with only a low proportion of ancillary labour, as was the case in the toolroom where tools and dies were made and repaired for the presses. The majority of the remaining workforce was in presswork. Some of the non-craft workers in this area, such as press toolsetters and inspectors, were classified by management as skilled. But, while the skilled status of the craft workers was generally conceded by other workers, the claims of these non-craft 'skilled' were more commonly contested by their fellow workers in craft and semi and unskilled areas. Perhaps this was because their work was more immediately observable to the latter who often worked alongside them, and because they required no formal apprenticeship but only on-the-job training. Furthermore, many of these 'skilled' workers had themselves risen from the ranks of the semiskilled.

These divisions among the labour force continued to contribute to the lack of coherence in union organization throughout the period of study, both among the different unions and within the largest union, the Transport and General Workers' Union (TGWU), which represented the bulk of semiskilled and unskilled workers. Most labour in the press shops was in fact of this kind, of whom the largest single group was the press operators, with smaller groups of production workers and a large number of ancillary workers servicing the main pressing processes.

The craft workers. The work of the three main groups of craftsmen, toolmakers, tinsmiths and polishers, was highly regulated by long-standing arrangements enforced by their respective unions. Insufficient data were available to establish when or how these craftsmen established union organization at Presswork. However, by the late 1950s all three had pre-entry closed shops. In contrast with the territory of the TGWU, these areas were single union shops. The National Union of Sheet Metal Workers (NUSMW) organized all tinsmiths but excluded ancillary workers in their shop, while the National Society of Metal Mechanics (NSMM) organized craft and non-craft alike in the bright trim polishing section. NUSMW membership fell from 200 to 100 between 1959 and 1969, and to 34 in 1979; the NSMM was reduced from 150-plus to under 100, and then to fewer than 10 over the same periods. The Amalgamated Engineering Union (AEU), as it then was, organized the toolroom which was large: as many as 93 toolmakers were still employed in 1979. Each of these unions was accredited one shop steward who was elected annually. They were supported by elected shop committees which were recognized by management and provided deputy stewards.

By the late 1950s, the conditions of employment of these workers and their union organizations had achieved a stability and permanency which distinguished them from the semiskilled workers. The toolmakers came under the Coventry Toolroom Agreement, whereby their earnings were equated with the average earnings of skilled fitters, turners and machinists in firms federated to the Coventry and District Engineering Employers' Association. The tinsmiths and polishers continued to work under a traditional piecework system throughout the period studied. There was no work study of any kind. A provisional price per piece was offered by the shop manager, and the job was tried for its yield by a number of workers and then discussed by them with the shop steward and shop committee before acceptance. Individual earnings were subject to a 'ceiling' imposed by local union policy. If workers wanted to speed up and earn more, they had to reach agreement to increase the 'striking rate' not only among the members in the shop but also those in the local branch. Enforcement of union policy required a high degree of collective discipline in the shop. It meant, for instance, that the tinsmiths had to spread effort over the whole shift, and any member making the price look too high might have to answer for his behaviour. The shop steward also checked individuals' piecework cards, and overbooking or excessive use of the practice of holding piecework bookings in reserve once work was completed (known as recording output 'in the back of the book', the aim being to even out earnings), were matters for discipline by the shop committee.

As well as enforcing discipline among its members, the NUSMW assured management of skilled labour and high quality and productive work. Nevertheless, it is worth speculating briefly on why these controls persisted in radiator assembly. Clearly, the existing technology and craft union controls through the external labour market were mutually reinforcing. Under the favourable conditions of extended production runs, these combined to make the piecework scheme under craft control a relatively efficient mode of organization and administration of resources. In this sense, they resembled similar processes of craft labour market formation and production organization supporting the relative autonomy of craft workers from direct management supervision in industries like printing and construction (Jackson, 1984; Stinchcombe, 1959). They survived intact at Presswork 'like the last of the dinosaurs' in the words of the managing director of the 1970s, until 1980 when market forces finally dictated complete withdrawal from radiator assembly and the closure of the department.

The semiskilled workers. Most workers in the press shops began employment as press operators or operators' mates handling materials for the press lines. There were a few female operators, concentrated on the lighter machines, but press operating was overwhelmingly a male occupation. Work on the presses was physically arduous, noisy and repetitive. Management discipline before the 1970s could be harsh. 'Crunches', component mislocations leading to tool damage, for instance, could bring summary dismissal. Labour turnover was high, caused by transferring to lighter work in other production or ancillary jobs, or by quitting. In addition, the operators were more prone than others in the factory to seasonal lay-off, an insecurity exacerbated by the development of a (limited) form of protection from lay-off for some through a seniority system involving the bumping of operators by press toolsetters claiming the right to return to their former operating roles at such times.

Each of the twelve production groups in the press shops was paid on different payment by results (PBR) schemes. Until 1974, 38 groups of ancillary workers were paid according to their ranking on a scale based on the press operators' APE. Because of the latters' linch-pin position within this payment system, it was upon their work performance that management focused closest attention and effort to assert control. It was also the source of considerable tension between work groups. Press operators begrudged 'having to earn everyone else's money', whether through 'grafting' on the presses, 'haggling for ha'pennies', or having 'downers' to press their claims in piecework bargaining. Differentials between different piecework groups, and between skilled and semiskilled generally, were also unstable because of the variable opportunities to improve earnings through fractional bargaining.

There is no evidence available to determine exactly when or how the press operators and other semiskilled workers first began to develop the forms of job control and union organization which are the subject of this study. But discussion below will show how they appear to have been underdeveloped until the late 1950s, and how they evolved later.

The semiskilled grades were represented by the TGWU. It is possible that the

TGWU had secured this position before the various presswork activities were brought together from other establishments to join radiator assembly in new workshops built in 1950. It is not known when the TGWU won its post-entry closed shop, but it seems likely that this pre-dated the early 1960s, since the closed shop had already been conceded to all other unions on site, including the Draghtsmen and Allied Technicians Association (DATA). However, this level of union membership did not equate, in the TGWU's case, with the highly developed organization and job controls of the craft unions on the site. Shop steward organization developed more spasmodically through the 1960s. By the end of that decade and well into the next, though, it was well entrenched and brimming with confidence, coming into sharp conflict not only with management, but also with the craft unions.

It is clear from the sketchy evidence of the early post-war years that the press operators had developed a capacity to challenge standards of effort and reward in the piecework bargain. They used opportunities presented within agreed bargaining procedures, adopting go-slow tactics by working at the lowest level of effort allowed in the piecework scheme, and they used the strike, or more often the judicious threat of strike, to press their claims at critical moments in production schedules.

The underdevelopment of steward organization among the semiskilled workers in the 1950s and early 1960s is all the more striking when set against the highly developed individual and work group effort bargaining. This raises a question of whether the press operators actually needed a union to bargain for them, and indeed what relevance, if any, union membership had to them. We argue that while the press operators were able to establish these controls, they were weaker than those of the craft unions at this time and applied less uniformly. Furthermore, they were more unstable and vulnerable to erosion by a combination of variable product demand, labour turnover, management opposition and, crucially, the precariousness of shop steward organization.

The evidence suggests that comparatively rudimentary forms of job control had developed in the press shops, largely out of the operators' own responses to the immediate technical organization of production. But these controls were structurally limited by the underdevelopment of more cohesive social relations among the operators, certainly by comparison with those achieved by the craft unions. What influence, if any, union organization and shop stewards had over this early evolution of job controls is not known. One of their roles, however, was to make sense of the inchoate processes of evolution of these work relations, to the workers themselves and to management. Stewards' increasing success in doing so provided a legitimacy and stimulus to their further development. What is beyond doubt is that shop steward organization became critical to the elaboration, stabilization, more uniform application and wider dispersal of job controls in the period 1960—80.

There is no evidence for the view expressed by Zeitlin (1980) that semiskilled job controls were passed down by one generation of mature, craft unions to the next generation of eager, semiskilled student unionists. With the exception of the polishers, none of the craft unions seems to have tried to organize the semiskilled, even those most clearly associated with their own work. It seems more likely that the sphere of semiskilled union, i.e. TGWU, influence was already effectively marked out before presswork was fully concentrated on the new site. The tinsmiths serve as a representative example of the exclusivist or closed recruitment strategies pursued by craft unions (Ulman, 1955), leaving the TGWU to recruit the ancillary labour in the radiator assembly and related areas. Significantly, the tinsmiths declined to force any claim to the new aluminium radiator work introduced in the 1971 recovery programme. Moreover, this exclusivism was also expressed by a disdain for less skilled workers, to the point where the latter were restricted from entry into craft areas, and engagement between the different workers was discouraged. There was, therefore, neither the inclination among the craft unions to help the semiskilled establish similar detailed job controls, nor much opportunity afforded the latter to learn the secrets of those controls.

That any such diffusion of control was a most unlikely path of development is further demonstrated by the stunted evolution of factory-wide, multi-union shop steward organization. Little is known of the JSSC before 1960, but, by then it had a constitution which allowed for one delegate per 100 members from each of the five manual unions on the site. Since the TGWU had a built-in majority, the craft unions insisted on retaining autonomy of action within the JSSC framework. In practice, however, the unstable numbers and irregular attendance of TGWU stewards, combined with the perceived irrelevance of the JSSC to much routine shop steward bargaining activity, left effective control of it in the hands of the senior stewards from each union.

The JSSC really cohered only when TGWU convenors secured some autonomy for themselves from the TGWU steward organization. This was invariably achieved only during periods when managerial control of the labour process was less coercive. By contrast, when the level of conflict on the presses intensified, it became clear that this autonomy derived less from any credible authority of leadership, and more from a relaxation of the press operators' insistence on the accountability of their stewards. Whenever the TGWU stewards, under these conditions, attempted to press the JSSC to give priority to semiskilled workers' claims the craft unions resisted, to the point where the JSSC broke up on several occasions in the 1960s. It was only as a result of management intervention in the course of the 1970 reform of labour relations that the Joint Shop Stewards Committee (JSSC) became a permanent institution. Yet, because of the long-standing antipathy and rivalry between the unions, the JSSC had a fragile existence and it lacked authority over constituent unions, each of which retained its own autonomy.

Job Controls among Press Operators

Although the press operators developed certain job controls at an early date, their extent and stability fluctuated over time. This tended to follow the ebb and flow of their shop stewards' efforts to intervene in this largely autonomous sphere of work group bargaining and extend the scope of the union's bargaining role. Presswork offers an interesting example of how controls exercised primarily at the level of the work group can develop into union bargaining and a more organized struggle around the frontier of control. We begin by considering the job controls, which focused mainly on three areas, work allocation, labour mobility and, crucially, the wage-effort bargain. We then show how they merged into union bargaining and struggles over the frontier of control.

Work Allocation

Variable batch production required setting up and stripping out tools from the presses for each run, and this involved frequent allocation of operators to presses as work demanded and became available. Before the evolution of rules governing work allocation in the early 1960s, operators would be allocated by the foreman to a press or particular operation in a line of presses at the beginning of a shift or when beginning a new job in mid-shift. Their earnings were vulnerable to fluctuations both because of the uneven availability of jobs for all workers at any one time and because of the discretionary power of foremen to allocate workers to 'good' or 'bad' jobs. Rules to control these uncertainties gradually developed.

A system was first devised between the operators and supervisors of one of the four press shops whereby the foreman drew out, in the workers' presence, each operators's piecework booking card from the pack and allocated work from the list of available jobs. Once this was established, it allowed a greater cohesiveness to develop among the operators who began to share out the different conditions still more by swapping from one station to the next after an agreed number of components. In other press shops, working methods were less homogenous. Rules developed in one shop which allocated each operator a specific press on which he worked whenever work was available for it; in another shop, operators were allocated to a specific group of presses on a more or less permanent basis, and they drew cards each day for particular jobs on those presses.

For the most part, management came to tolerate and even encourage this form of regulation. They recognized that the rules in themselves presented no insurmountable constraints on the efficient deployment of labour. They also learned to appreciate the benefits of improved motivation and intra-work group self-discipline, which in turn alleviated some of the costs associated with controlling performance through direct supervision and authoritarian hiring and firing (Friedman, 1977).

However, it would be quite wrong to imply that these controls were unambiguously favourable to managerial objectives. In a kind of symbiosis, management's pragmatic encouragement of them was mirrored by and contributed to the cohesion of the social organization among the operators and subsequently the wider semiskilled workforce. For instance, in some shops, the toleration of the shop stewards taking over card-drawing entirely was just one tangible illustration of how management behaviour helped foster a more deeply entrenched role for stewards and thereby generated further pressures which did come to undermine managerial authority and control.

Labour Mobility

Restrictions over labour mobility between different shops and jobs were a source of contention only intermittently before 1970. Management occasionally tried to cope with variable demand by moving operators between press shops, but they rarely pressed hard for such mobility. Sometimes this was because either the 'host' or 'guest' operators objected to the transfer, and sometimes because management preferred to avoid the almost inevitable arguments by rearranging work schedules and, where feasible, reallocating the work rather than the operators. The operators resisted mobility for fear it would deplete the available workload and destabilize earnings, and not infrequently from 'sheer bloodymindedness'.

However, the same principles and traditions of resistance became more problematic for management when adopted more widely by all kinds of semiskilled workers in the context of the production reorganization after 1970. The 1975 collective agreement included a clause on labour mobility which appeared to give management considerable flexibility over transfers. However, it also made the issue subject to the mutuality clause in the 1972 disputes procedure. In practice, whenever a group of workers objected to a proposal to transfer labour from one section to another they invoked this clause. Some temporary transfers did take place among the new 'daywork' production sections. But these were usually subject to delay on account of procedural review, and in the press shops management completely lost the freedom to transfer operators between sections.

Management now identified this veto as the most serious obstacle to a more flexible response to customer demand. Because of the nature of production schedules, the demand for more labour in a particular department had very often dissipated by the time temporary transfers had actually been negotiated. It deterred managers from matching labour to production requirements and, consequently, contributed to what managers called 'unrealistic' manning levels. When shop stewards pressed a claim for a lay-off pay agreement in 1978, management insisted that any concession would depend on union compromise on mobility. Again, in management's 1979 pay proposals funding for part of the deal was intended to come through productivity improvements which included withdrawing mobility from the scope of the mutuality clause. Many stewards conceded the need for greater flexibility. But a large majority of the workers rejected the proposal and management was forced to drop it.

This experience demonstrated the ambiguous nature of the relationship between the work groups and steward organization, for each of whom the meaning and importance of the job controls were somewhat different. The stewards, as suggested earlier, had twin perspectives in intervening to claim rights of guardianship over them, so to speak. One was to defend the operators' own autonomous work practices, the other was to promote the organizational stability of the union itself as an agent in shaping those practices and the wider work relations in the factory. For their part, the operators regarded the controls as their own creation. Even though they could now call on the support of a formal disputes procedure with union representation to give defence of their practices wider legitimacy, the operators were not readily amenable to handing over completely to the stewards their 'property rights' in those controls.

Effort Bargaining

The effort bargain lay at the heart of the struggle for control over the labour process. The technical conditions underlying the operators' high degree of control were located in the machinery on which they worked, and the organization of production more generally. Each press shop had a large number of presses and used a variety of operating methods. Typically, each press performed a single operation. Most presses were non-automatic. The operator had to locate the component on the die of the tool, start the machine cycle by pressing a button or pulling a safety guard, and on completion of the machine cycle remove the component for transfer to the next work station before commencing the operation again, thousands of times each shift. Each machine had a maximum cycle speed. But with the exception of automatic presses, the speed of the actual work cycle was determined by the speed and efficiency of the operator's intervention on completion of the machine cycle. While standardization of the machinery and operations encouraged a form of work measurement based on quantifiable operating times, this dependency on the intervention of the operator at each completed cycle to reduce these times ensured that management was obliged to negotiate rather than impose levels of speed and effort.

Until the mid-1960s, the operators' piecework scheme was similar to that of the tinsmiths'. Operating time was observed by a rate fixer and a price per piece offered and negotiated over. 'Effort' was based on custom and practice. Bargaining involved deals struck between rate fixers and individual operators and/or work groups, independently of the union. Following considerable success by the stewards in the early 1960s in securing an enhanced role for themselves in bargaining under the old piecework scheme, a new scheme was conceived in 1967 to reward high output with an incentive bonus for production above a 'traditional piecework level'.

In the early days of these evolving job controls, 'making the job pay' was the operators' single, overriding preoccupation. Piecework performance was improved by three main means: 'fiddling', 'having downers', and bargaining within the system. 'Fiddling' took many ingenious forms, with the single aim of reducing the time booked on piecework sufficiently to increase the average yield (output against piecework hours) and thereby raise overall earnings. These included booking more components than actually produced, or more often extending the time entered on the operator's piecework card for 'downtime', which was paid at daywork rate, while actually working on the machine and earning piecework money as well (Burawoy, 1979: 58–9). These practices, however, tended to undermine the credibility of operators' claims that the price was too tight and the job could not pay (Brown, 1973). One common tactic was to 'let the job stand' by refusing to start work on it. But that required confidence and collective protection. 'Downers', or more commonly just the threat of a strike, were frequently judiciously used to press a claim. According to one manager:

> They would come along at 3 o'clock threatening to go home if they didn't get the price they wanted, knowing the night shift would back them up. We'd have a whole night shift to find new jobs for, and that job was probably promised to the customer for the next day.

Before the 1960s, these tactics remained more or less *ad hoc* and outside any systematic form of organization. Union, and particularly shop steward, involvement in their shaping was still marginal and underdeveloped. In a further suggestion of the ambiguous relationship between the press operators and their stewards, even after the growth of more stable steward organization in the press shops many operators continued to prefer the quick solution offered by the 'downer'.

Piecework performance figures for the 1960s are unavailable, but data from 1978–9 show how extensive an impact was made by operators' controls. The expected yield on piecework was typically three times the standard price agreed through work study, and operators were booked on daywork for between 43 per cent and 46 per cent of their working time. These figures are undoubtedly higher than would have been the case in the 1960s, if only because they were enhanced by a higher daywork rate for downtime negotiated in 1974. They also reflect management's considerably weaker control over the scheme in the 1970s. Nevertheless, the situation on the presses in the 1960s was different only by degree. In addition to the varying tightness of piecework prices, the technical conditions of production, changes in work schedules, movement between jobs, and innumerable interruptions to production assisted operators in exploiting legitimate downtime to boost piecework earnings. There is also evidence from this period of some collusion between foremen and operators to secure the desired flexibility of matching labour deployment to production demands, with foremen sometimes 'chasing' ancillary workers to maintain service of the presses, thus assisting operators in 'making the job pay'.

Of course, one could point to the positive contribution this mutual interest in high piecework earnings made to productivity (Lupton, 1963; Burawoy, 1979). But management faced two problems over the period of study. First, the operators developed these controls to the stage where their overriding preoccupation shifted from 'making it pay' to 'getting the day in', or managing their working time. Building on their control over the immediate intensity of effort, they were able to consolidate high levels of effort and production over several hours to accumulate a substantial reserve of time off within the duration of the shift. Once they had got their day in, they would stop work and retire to their rest area until the end of the shift. The length of these leisure periods varied depending on work availability and between individuals and work groups, but typically ranged from one to three hours each day (Bélanger, 1987).

This phenomenon has also been noted by Roy (1954) in his study of a factory in the United States, but Presswork marks a significant advance on what in Roy's case was essentially sporadic effort bargaining by workers themselves. In Presswork, effort bargaining became institutionalized through union practice as certain key stewards consciously strove, with increasing success, to negotiate favourable procedural rules for piecework bargaining which would enhance their own authority, albeit at some potential cost to the operators' own immediate control.

Nevertheless, the variable and unstable conditions of production across the different press shops meant that the job controls remained spasmodic and uneven in the early 1960s. They developed not only from the production technologies and payment system, but also, crucially, from the social organization fostered among the operators. Necessary forms of social control over individual discretion and of protection for individuals when challenging prices and other expressions of managerial authority were slow to develop. The cohesiveness of work groups and their identification of collective interests depended on stability which, in turn, required, so it turned out, the conscious intervention and activity of trade unionism.

Cohesion was assisted by 'working in line', when presses were linked in sequences of operations by conveyor belts, automatic 'catchers' and shutes. Under this arrangement, piecework prices applied to the line and were governed by the slowest operation in the line. This had a number of effects. It helped raise output on the slower operations closer to maximum. But it also reduced overall expenditure of effort by slowing the others, and allowed a more equitable sharing of workload by means of operators swapping from station to station. This facilitated closer observation of each other, and made group discipline less overt. But there was still considerable variation in both the opportunities for and achievement of a sense of collectivism among the different operator groups. The difficulties of enforcing 'ceilings' on piecework booking illustrates this well. By comparison with the example of the tinsmiths, this was a widespread problem, especially among the operators in no.1 press shop which had the most heterogeneous composition of presses and work practices. It persisted throughout the 1960s, despite the strengthening of collectivism under the shop stewards of that period, as shown in this entry in the press shop stewards' shift book in 1962:

> Re 5—3. H. . . . tried all Tuesday night for an extra 1d on the job. I had a lot of arguing to do before I convinced L. [the ratefixer]. C. . . . on days goes and f . . . s it up by booking 9/8d per hour, can you beat that my old fruit. Will you point out to C. . . . that we can't fight for better prices that way.

There are no records of strikes over fellow workers refusing to recognize ceilings in the early period in any of the shops. But these became more frequent, though still relatively uncommon, in no.1 shop where there was perhaps the lowest level of cohesion among the operators. Social ostracism, it seems, was the more usual weapon against this type of behaviour, as suggested by this entry from the same stewards' shift book in 1962:

> I discovered that some operators earned more than 6/- last night and I
> warned them that if any more of this goes on I will name the men
> concerned.

Beyond this, it depended on the scale of collective resistance that could be
organized against an intransigent management who ultimately had it in their
power to improve an offered price. Organization of that kind was the task of the
stewards, as the above quotation implies.

Union Bargaining

The turning point, or 'catalyst' (Tolliday, 1986: 228) in consolidating operators'
controls over the effort bargain was the successful conclusion to a lengthy
dispute in 1963 over their right to go-slow on disputed piecework jobs. When
no price was agreed on a provisional job, which could apply to a new untimed
job or to a timed job under changed conditions, stewards would refuse to
negotiate until an acceptable offer was made and the whole shop would go-slow,
dropping their effort to the level required to earn 6/- per hour. The effects of
this were not lost on management who estimated that production fell to one third
of normal. They would react to this with disciplinary sanctions, introducing a
system of coloured dockets for 'working below piecework effort'. When a go-
slow was on, the foreman would stand behind the weakest man in the shop and
time his performance. 'Crunches' received automatic dismissal.

This particular go-slow had lasted for six weeks when the stewards 'got wind
some of the lads were ready to jack it in'. They held a meeting of all the operators where they persuaded them to drop their output to 3/- per hour. In view
of the lack of sustained cohesion hitherto among the operators' ranks, their decision marked an impressive display of semiskilled union solidarity, and suggested
the considerable progress of the stewards in implanting themselves in the
bargaining process. After three days management conceded an agreement allowing them to reduce their effort to the equivalent needed to earn 6/- piecework
bonus per hour.

The 'six bob agreement' of 1963 represented a concession of such significance
that it allowed the job controls discussed above to become more firmly established. There had not, however, been any substantial insititutional changes in its
wake, and the pattern of bargaining persisted. There were still large numbers
of ancillary workers tied to the performance of the operators whose growing
success in raising their own earnings only added to the commerical pressures on
management to reassert control. By 1967, the space the operators had opened
up for themselves caused management to bring in a new piecework scheme.

Frontier of Control

The new scheme imposed in 1968 tried to remove the principal sanction
(go-slow) over management's unilateral fixing of job prices. Traditional
methods of work measurement were replaced by a 'standard' rate of output bas-

ed on 'effort rating' with a level of piecework effort built in even before any bonus could be earned. When measurement was incomplete or not feasible, special rates would apply, and seven days were allowed for appeal through procedure before sanctions could be invoked.

Initially the scheme 'gave the blokes more'. But it failed to remove the 'constant arguments over prices'. By obliging the operators to work on through procedure at an incentive level, it restored to management some control over output. However, the operators continued to impose a ceiling of 8/- per hour on disputed work. 'Working to standard' was still legitimate under the new scheme, and over the next months it became clogged up with procedural references over disputed prices. Protracted negotiations failed to secure for management the concessions on mutuality which they sought.

Through 1968—9 conflict intensified. In the first eleven months of 1969, there were 114 work stoppages on 81 days. A company dossier on industrial relations in the press shops registered 99 stoppages in a ten-month period. Table 6.1 classifies the issues resulting in these stoppages, the shop or shops in which they occurred, and the scale of disruption. It shows that 25 of the 99 stoppages lasted less than one hour, 29 between one and four hours, and 45 more than four hours (many stretching over more than one shift). Most involved directly only one work group or, more usually, shop. Half of all disputes originated over piecework standards. More generally, most issues leading to stoppages related to the effort bargain.

Disputes of this kind finally escalated into a 6½-week strike beginning in mid-November 1969. At first, it seemed to resemble a typical dispute on the presses, although more serious since it was triggered by the suspension of seven operators for going-slow. Nobody in fact had been suspended for this since a strike over two operators two years earlier. Over the next days, operators from different shifts and shops were in and out, awaiting the outcome of talks which made no headway, amid conjecture that management was sticking firm to stop the newly elected convenor 'scoring an early goal'. This convenor was a press operators' steward who had led the campaign to defend the 'six bob agreement' and remove the previous 'moderate' convenor from office. He was regarded by management as a 'militant'.

On the basis of this belief, the ancillaries in the press shops joined the strike. When talks broke down over management's insistence on a promise of normal working in return for re-engagement of the seven men, the operators sent the ancillaries back to work to avoid dilution of their cohesiveness. The stewards were far from confident of success: 'neither side could afford to lose ... our jobs were on the line'. The strike continued until two days before Christmas. It was starting to have an effect on the motor industry, with lay-offs announced at a large factory nearby. During a mass meeting, the full-time union official contacted management to advise them that the men were not planning to meet for another month. Management immediately announced that they were prepared to 'turn a blind eye' to operators working to standard if they returned to work to allow a works conference to take place, under the national engineering agreement.

TABLE 6.1

Recorded Stoppages in the Press Shops, 12 January–12 November 1969 by Nature of the Issue and Location of the Disputes

	Standard Quantity	Incentive Scheme (General)	Objection to Work Study	Operators Refusing to Go-Slow	Work Allocation	Issue About Trainee Setter	Issue About Gloves	Sympathy Action	Attend Meetings	Unspecified	Total
Press shop no.1	33 (3590)[a]		1 (54)	1 (15)	6 (487)		1 (32)	2 (350)	3 (34)	1 (7)	48 (4569)
Press shop no.3								6 (477)	1 (24)		7 (501)
Press shop no.4	6 (516)		1 (63)					4 (148)	3 (39)	1 (42)	15 (808)
Brake shoe section	13 (623)					4 (241)		1 (68)	1 (3)		19 (935)
more than one section	2 (327)	2 (920)					2 (1504)	3 (1323)	1 (29)		10 (4103)
Total	54 (5056)	2 (920)	2 (117)	1 (15)	6 (487)	4 (241)	3 (1536)	16 (2366)	9 (129)	2 (49)	99 (10,916)

Source: Company dossier on industrial relations in the press shops, 1969–70.
Note: [a] Figures in brackets give total number of production hours lost.

The strike settled nothing. There were 22 further stoppages, including many piecework disputes, in the three months before the conference. The settlement reached was regarded on all sides as management 'capitulation'. The operators were conceded the right when working on disputed jobs to reduce their output to the equivalent of 135R (100R being the minimum piecework effort, and 200R the then current average yield). This made necessary a complete round of wage negotiations which produced a further 25 stoppages over six months, many of them involving skilled and ancillary workers seeking to restore their differentials.

On the presses, operators and their stewards continued to exploit their advantage. Management certainly believed they had lost control and had no reliable union lifeline of support. There were daily discussions with the TGWU convenor over disputed standards, walk-outs in breach of procedure, restrictions on mobility and changes in work practices, limits on piecework bookings and sending home of operators who exceeded them. The convenor was generally unsympathetic to these overtures. Each time that there was 'unconstitutional action' a letter was sent through the Engineering Employers' Association to the TGWU district official, a total of ten times between 18 August and 29 September 1970. But there was little the outside union could do until management made a genuine accommodation with the press shop stewards who had begun to acquire a new authority with the wider TGWU membership beyond the presses.

After the 'crisis' of near-closure in 1970−1, which these events helped to engender, conditions for the operators were improved by a number of changes in the piecework scheme. In the long run, these undermined the impact of the institutional reforms described below, giving operators further space to control the effort bargain and lowering productivity drastically. From 1971 onwards, the coercive pressures within the piecework scheme were gradually relaxed. The proportion of guaranteed against incentive earnings was increased, relaxation allowances were extended, and time study techniques were applied less often and less rigorously. Any benefits derived by management from the 'tough' stance of the 1968 agreement to work through procedure were lost between 1971 and 1973 when they failed to withstand pressure on standards. In 1972, all time study sheets were declared obsolete, and new, more detailed recordings made. But lack of managerial competence and confidence ensured that the opportunities from widespread retiming of jobs were almost entirely exploited by the operators to improve 'bad jobs'. Shopfloor supervision now lacked the authority to impose discipline as this was centralized in higher management and, as one senior manager noted, commercial pressures made the firm even more vulnerable to lost production although profit margins remained sufficient to provide 'just enough room for manoeuvre to avoid a head-on clash'.

Over the 1970s, as production schedules grew even shorter and more unpredictable, the new relaxed regime used the provisional price more often again. This further weakened the incentive to produce, and piecework bonus yield rose while output fell proportionately. The introduction of new daywork production processes allowed many older operators to transfer from the presses, and the new younger intake was immediately antagonistic to the heaviest presswork. 'They didn't want to know . . . it was anarchy down there', and production stoppages increased again. 'Just to get an unspecified quantity out', as one manager put it, very heavy work was paid at 'agreed daywork' or 197R, very close to the then current average piecework bonus. This reduced stoppages but raised costs per component enormously. 197R came to be sought, and often conceded, when operators could not make other jobs pay. It also stimulated operator pressure for higher yield on genuine piecework, simultaneously compressing profit margins and eroding work group cohesiveness through 'fiddling' and demands that piecework ceilings be lifted.

Summary
From at least 1960 until the sale of Presswork in 1980, conflict always centred very much on effort and reward. Job controls over effort grew and stabilized in the first half of the 1960s, but remained vulnerable to market fluctuations. Under increased product market pressures, around 1967, management tried to reassert control over output levels and costs but conflict intensified into a major industrial relations crisis. Labour relations reform from 1971 to 1974 fostered an appeasement of overt conflict but only contributed to a consolidation of job control. Under the appearance of relative industrial peace, weak management control over the labour process ensured deteriorating productivity. In 1979–80, management concluded that this pattern of conflict, while unacceptable, could be significantly changed only through restructuring production processes and, critically, through a profound transformation of social relations in the factory. The latter remained the major influence over the maintenance of job controls, and central to this were the shop stewards in taking individual effort bargains and building them into a frontier of collective control. The next section examines the growth, role and influence of the semiskilled shop steward organization.

Shop Steward Organization

Early Shop Steward Organization
Early difficulties in sustaining shop steward organization among the semiskilled were due largely to the unstable conditions of employment in the press shops and to management reluctance to accommodate a high level of union activity. Two common difficulties were encountered: communication and co-ordination. It is not known when TGWU stewards first won recognition, but by the end of the 1950s there were some stewards in all the press shops. Without any agreed means of discussing union business, however, communication was a problem. The wide geographical spread of TGWU constituencies, as well as the built-in constraints from pieceworking and shift patterns, together with overt management opposition to steward mobility around the factory, obliged stewards to meet once a week by the clocking-in station for ten minutes at the end of the lunch-break.

Moreover, the effect of shift patterns, and the varying characteristics of worker relations on different shifts, made communication between them essential to developing coherent action, even over piecework prices, if management were not to play one shift against another. Night shift workers, especially, complained of being 'kept in the dark'. The stewards' shift books were introduced in 1961 in response to this and were used to pass on information about piecework bargaining, and to stimulate ideas and action of a more collective kind, as this entry from 1962 shows:

> On Friday a lot of the lads were talking about stopping. ... I held a meeting tonight to get clear what we are actually doing. First 6/- to be earned in every operating hour, this doesn't include breaks. The go-slow is also used on all studies (this was voted for).

Co-ordination was hampered by the instability in the stewards' ranks. Like their members, the press operators' stewards were pieceworkers. When they went on 'union business' they fell back to the basic rate of pay. Lost earnings were made up from a stewards' fund raised by weekly collections, but these rarely covered their losses. Stewards were thus particularly susceptible to being 'bought off' by promotion to toolsetter, foreman, or ratefixer.

There was considerable variation between the different shops and shifts, but it seems that turnover was a particular problem among the press operators' stewards and only began to settle down once their job controls began to be consolidated. In the largest press shop, for instance, there was no steward on one of the shifts for several months at the height of the conflict in 1968. In another press shop, as late as 1969−72, one shift retained the same steward while the other saw three changes, including one removal from office by a vote of 'no confidence' for accepting a bad price. Such removal was rare. More often, turnover was voluntary, due to 'war weariness', financial circumstances or redundancy. The different characteristics of the shifts − variety of operating conditions, strike-proneness of no.1 shop, differentials between the shops, and 'A' shift in no.3 shop being traditionally solid while 'B' shift was 'anarchic' so that 'you needed A's support to win' (Monk, 1969) − also made co-ordination difficult. In addition, the spontaneous character of the disputes on the presses and their sectional nature required quick responses from the stewards. Prior to 1971, the only factory-wide stoppage was the strike over the two suspended operators, in 1967. Stoppages in one shop would often see the steward seeking advice and assistance from those in the other shops. One no.3 shop steward commented how 'we used to spend half the time up in no.1 sorting their mess out'.

There are no records of victimization of stewards in the early days, but in 1967, there was a strike when two operators, one of them a steward, were disciplined for going slow, an action regarded by the strikers as a signal of management's attack on the operators' organization. Later that year, a TGWU steward was sacked for timekeeping offences, which was again interpreted as managerial provocation. The same year, a leading press operators' steward had his credentials removed by the union following complaints from management, only to be reinstated after the entire press operators' shift had marched on the union office. On the whole, these were exceptional incidents. It was more normal for management to make life hard for militant stewards rather than resort to actual discipline or dismissal (*cf.* Edwards, 1986: 190).

Looking more closely at the structure of the semiskilled shop stewards' organization, it is worth noting that in the early years the stewards came mostly from the ranks of the press operators and the tool-setters. There were relatively few from the smaller ancillary groups who relied on the press operators' stewards to represent their interests which were largely dependent on the APE scheme, and to provide the TGWU convenor and delegates to the JSSC. It was not until the mid-1960s when a moderate TGWU convenor, himself a press operators' steward, came under increasing attack from the other operators' stewards for failing to defend their interests against management's efforts to introduce the new incentive scheme, that there were more TGWU shop steward constituencies beyond the presses. In an attempt to retain his majority among the TGWU stewards, the convenor persuaded numerous ancillary groups to elect stewards of their own. Despite his subsequent defeat, the numbers and 'depth' of steward representation persisted right through to 1980. Indeed, the minute books of the TGWU shop stewards committee show that the number of TGWU stewards remained very stable throughout the 1970s in spite of the decline in the workforce. In 1979, there were 42 TGWU stewards out of a total of 50 accredited stewards in the factory. The average constituency size was then just 17 workers.

Besides the decline in the workforce, two factors contributed to such a high density of stewards. First, until 1980 management did not intervene on the issue, on the grounds that it was a matter for the unions. Second, a major feature of shop steward representation among non-craft workers in the factory was the narrow definition given to the stewards' sections. The steward was elected by a group of workers performing a specific task, usually within the same shop and shift. The constituencies thus followed the contours of the technical division, or 'decomposition' (Dubois 1980: 263), of labour and there were often many steward constituencies within a single shop. In the case of the largest press shop, for instance, there were ten different constituencies on each of two shifts. This ensured that, although the stewards were well placed to defend the job controls of their particular constituents, the many demarcations between different types of work were reproduced and sectionalism was encouraged.

In such a pattern of representation the strength of workers' organization was not due to the shop stewards themselves. They were genuinely subject to a direct democracy where decisions were taken by all constituents at shopfloor level. In most cases the stewards were not the initiators of issues, and they were frequently overruled by their sections. For a majority, their function consisted in monitoring shopfloor organization and stimulating cohesiveness within and between work groups in their own constituency. They were accountable to their sections before calling strikes, even though the normal challenge came when members voted with their feet. Removal from office was rare, but that it did occasionally occur in each of the press shops (usually for lack of rather than too much aggression), illustrates the residual strength of the tradition of direct accountability. It is noteworthy that this power remained relatively free at this stage from formal control by any union body, inside or outside the factory. Before the 1970s no rules had been developed among the stewards governing the rights and duties of sections and stewards.

Nevertheless, it still required the conscious intervention of 'key' stewards and activists to consolidate the gains from individual bargaining and build collective defences around them (*cf.* Tolliday, 1986: 228). These workers demonstrated vital attributes through which trade union regulation was made relevant to the press operators, and subsequently to other semiskilled workers. Of course, they had continually to re-establish their authority with their members through successful piecework 'haggling'. But, more than this, they were able to interpret and articulate the varied demands and sentiments of the workers. They took this further still by thinking more strategically about how the routine hassle of bargaining could be mitigated and the gains from workers' own bargaining protected through union organization. They came to understand how this depended on the stability of their own steward organization and that, in addition to the interests they shared with the workers, they had interests of their own. Principally these involved persuading management to reform itself, entertain a higher degree of trust towards the stewards, and appreciate the mutual benefits of greater predictability that would ensue from allowing them an enhanced bargaining role. The stewards understood that their mediating role between management and operators gave them a weapon with which to bargain for this, as was demonstrated by their initial conception and subsequent use of the 'six bob agreement' in 1963.

By 1967, the agreement was under attack from management. Its short life was indicative both of the operators' successful enforcement of its provisions and of management's continuing reluctance to entertain 'strong bargaining' or 'high trust' relations with the militant operators' stewards. There were several reasons for this. First, the commercial markets were increasingly competitive and unstable. Second, the rising levels of strike militancy among the operators, often against the recommendations of their stewards, helped dissuade management from believing in the stewards' ability to manage discontent, and thus deterred them from pursuing any further institutional reforms at this time. Third, the management organization for dealing with labour remained rudimentary and devolved. The personnel department was staffed by one officer each for Labour (recruitment), Training, and Industrial Relations. Authority to fix piece rates rested with the ratefixers and, in contrast to the situation after the 1970 reforms, power to discipline lay with the foremen who were 'gods'. In the event of a grievance 'you saw the foreman (or ratefixer) and Blondie (shop superintendent) – you couldn't get beyond him'. As a result, management preferred to respond with a 'take it or leave it' ultimatum when jobs were disputed, and the stewards continued to find themselves caught between the twin roles identified by Donovan (1968), alternately 'lubricating' the bargaining relationship by 'advising the lads to carry on working to standard', and 'irritating' it by 'getting them out'.

Despite this, their desire for a more stable environment led the operators' stewards to continue their pursuit of a more systematic method of regulating piecework bargaining, and one which enhanced their own contribution. In the wake of the new scheme in 1967, as a number of disputes were put through procedure, they seized the opportunity to propose changes aimed at improving bad standards by linking them with good ones through 'blueprinting', or grouping jobs of a similar kind. By removing the process from individual bargaining, it certainly meant an enhancement of the stewards' bargaining authority at the possible expense of the operators' immediate control over the effort bargain. However, the job controls remained sufficiently the property of the operators to ensure the stewards' continuing accountability to them.

This rudimentary character of the TGWU steward organization, even at the end of the 1960s, was also reflected in the absence of any formal constitution or rules governing either the stewards' committee or its relationship with the TGWU 'factory' branch outside. The lack of any reference to shop steward committees in the national union constitution frustrated the appeals of the 'new' leadership to the union branch in 1969 when they sought confirmation of their authority to depose the defiant if discredited convenor. The problem was lack of any standing orders for the TGWU stewards' committee. This was finally resolved after the endorsement of orders copied from those of another steward organization in a nearby factory.

The 'Maturing' of Shop Steward Organization

The development of strong bargaining relations had to await the production reorganization and institutional reforms after 1971. Management's strategy for labour relations reform was articulated around two main changes. One was the encouragement of a central, authoritative shop steward body to represent the whole manual workforce and be responsible for bargaining and consultation over a wider range of issues. Second, so as to reduce the frequency of spontaneous conflict, a comprehensive disputes procedure was agreed in 1972. Of the two, the former gave the appearance of a 'maturing' of the shop stewards' organization, but it was the latter which had the greater impact. In view of the long tradition of union and sectional autonomy, the senior stewards lacked the will and confidence systematically to concentrate power at the centre and develop an authoritative leadership at factory level. The concession of mutuality, well in advance of that in the national engineering agreement which did not come until 1972, reinforced the localized job controls which it was intended to alleviate.

In October 1970, the company publicly threatened to close down the factory, citing union rivalry as one of the main reasons. This forced the calling of two joint union conferences under national and local union officials, the second resulting in an agreement in January 1971. The new JSSC was to be the representative body on factory-wide issues, each union retaining its autonomy over its own jurisdictional affairs. The fears of craft and semiskilled stewards that one side could outvote the other were dealt with, if not resolved, by giving the craft unions the same number of seats on the JSSC as the TGWU had.

The stability of the JSSC over the next decade, its limited turnover of membership, and its regular participation in joint consultation and negotiation with management were manifestations of a 'maturing' of the shop steward organization. For various reasons, however, management only partially achieved their objective of reinforcing the authority of the senior stewards over section stewards and members. Continuing product market instability, as well as the pattern of steward representation described above, were unfavourable conditions for this managerial 'sponsorship', and likewise for any independent, alternative inter- and intra-union strategies.

Joint commitment to dispute procedures and procedural consensus had more profound implications for the stabilization of the stewards' organization. The core of the 1972 disputes procedure was the concession of mutuality over all matters, including discipline. The inclusion of a clause that there should be no industrial action before the procedure was exhausted was also to become important. The relaxation of coercive pressures within the labour process and the removal of disciplinary powers from shopfloor supervision on which the new mutuality-based proceduralism was predicated, combined to foster the strong bargaining relations sought by the stewards. They also, in turn, reinforced not only the press operators' job controls but those of the other semiskilled workers engaged on the newer production processes.

Through the 1970s the interests of operators and line management increasingly converged on a day-to-day basis as 'getting the day in' was tolerated in order to achieve required output within the tighter production schedules. The result was the further decline in competitiveness discussed above. For the moment, though, the limited accommodation on the shopfloor masked these deeper tensions. Under these conditions, the formal distinction between managers and managed was also obscured. As the gap between earnings and output widened, the stewards came to assume a higher profile in the organization of production lines, work allocation and the regulation of piecework. Foremen had little option but to go along with this, working more as ancillaries facilitating production.

Enforcement of piecework ceilings came to rely more on stewards' improved relations with line managers and ratefixers and less on intra-work group or shop sanctions. The close surveillance of individual earnings practised by the tinsmiths, where all piecework bookings were entered by their steward, was never feasible in the more heterogeneous operations on the presses. Instead, four of the operators' stewards in the mid-1970s reached 'understandings' with the ratefixers, after agreement with their members, that they would be informed of any operator breaking the ceiling. One steward had authority, after notifying the individual concerned, to change any excess booking.

Similar though less pronounced patterns of behaviour developed in management—worker relations in the other semiskilled production areas, even though management avoided using an incentive scheme to prevent recurrence of the problems of piecework bargaining. Management lacked understanding of these new production processes and this, coupled with foremen's lack of authority, made them more reliant on the stewards to secure the co-operation of the workers, many of whom had moved from the press shops and taken with them much of the effort bargaining tradition learnt there. These workers applied the principles of mutuality to frustrate managerial efforts to achieve mobility of labour to suit the fluctuating requirements of the different product markets, particularly when the influx of additional labour threatened to erode opportunities for overtime or departmental bonuses introduced in the mid-1970s to stimulate output.

Procedural Consensus and Constitutionalism

The 'victory' of mutuality-based procedure was purchased at some cost to union independence, since the protection it offered was subject to pressures on the stewards to moderate their exercise of it. Thus, the operators and other dayworkers vigorously pursuing their job controls and sectional pay claims kept running up against the new constitutionalism of the mid-1970s, now more solidly entrenched because of the strong bargaining relations engendered by the 1971 reforms. Besides growing pressure to adhere to procedural rules, the reduced number of bargaining units and centralized bargaining structures also frustrated dayworkers' efforts to advance their relative bargaining power.

In what represented a quite striking political shift of emphasis the role of the convenor in relation to the membership and stewards turned, it seemed, full circle: from one of control 'for' to control 'over' members' activity, as envisaged in the Donovan Commission's proposals. He was seen much more regularly enforcing the procedure against sections wanting to strike, and used the weekly TGWU stewards' committee meetings to insist on section stewards' obligations to the wider interests of the organization in maintaining the joint commitment to the procedure, as this extract from the minutes of a meeting in September 1978 illustrates:

> Convenor reminded stewards that they were bound by the procedure agreement and had in this case been in breach of it. He felt, aside from the merit of the case, too many stewards are not following procedure. It is a good agreement that has protected the members' jobs in some cases, and continuity of work in others. Several stewards expressed the opinion that the company also used it to drag out arguments and not to be in any hurry to resolve them.

For the dayworkers, especially, mutuality was of less immediate relevance in protecting earnings than it had been to the operators. It was of more benefit to management in frustrating advances in earnings through fractional bargaining, and in advocating reliance on the new procedure the convenor was increasingly subject to criticism for defending the form rather than substance of union controls.

The TGWU steward leadership had long recognized the fragility of their organizational stability, and its vulnerability to the traditional strains of sectionalism. It was to deal with this problem that in the early 1970s the TGWU stewards adopted a rule that the convenor had to be allowed to meet a section before it could take industrial action and expect others to respect its strike. Still, the rule was not always obeyed, and the following extract from the TGWU stewards' committee minutes book in March 1975 points to some of the tensions behind this:

> Convenor put his personal view on what a convenor's function should be, as he felt that recently he was being used in a minor capacity and when sections were advocating strike action, he wasn't being invited to hear the pros and cons of the argument and also to put points of view in a broader context . . . After a long discussion, unanimous agreement was reached that Convenor should talk to sections before any industrial action was implemented.

Of course, the involvement of the convenor was crucial if a section in dispute needed the support of other groups. But the primary motive was defence of established controls. The strategy of the new leadership after 1970 was initially assertive. Sustained by the momentum of victory, it pushed ahead in extending the frontier of control on the presses, securing better fringe benefits and generally more relaxed employment conditions. The latter were of considerably benefit to the wider semiskilled membership whose identification with the new leadership the stewards consciously strove to consolidate. Beyond this, however, many of the traditional constraints on a more proactive strategy persisted. The commitment of the TGWU leadership to the disputes procedure became part of the process of 'sparing' the use of sanctions (Batstone *et al.*, 1977). This type of involvement in regulating conflict was premised on two main arguments, avoiding loss of wages and protecting unity within the union. Between 1972 and 1979, only 14 disputes of one or more shifts duration took place, accounting for 32 shifts in all.

Under these conditions, the TGWU stewards' committee became less a collective, as it had been from 1969 through to around 1973, and more a convenor-centred leadership again. The convenor continued to derive authority from his leadership of the press shop struggles from 1968 which, together with his new strong bargaining relations with senior management, posed major obstacles to the development among the stewards of any alternative strategy. As the economic position of the company deteriorated, the politics of survival under the convenor's leadership proved a more unifying factor than any other which the disparate associations among the different section stewards could articulate. The dayworkers never overcame their own internal rivalry based on skill and earnings to form a coherent group, nor their rivalry with the press operators whose new-found relaxation was becoming an embarrassment, nor with the craft unions who remained secure at the top of the 'pecking order'.

Nor was the TGWU stewards' committee a suitable place for them to build such an alliance. The press operators' stewards' role had changed considerably under the new regime, and the relevance of steward organization and mobilization beyond their own ranks had diminished. Indeed, there was a risk that senior management's attention would be drawn closer to their favourable conditions if they sought to include the dayworkers. At the same time the stewards had lost much of their own cohesiveness as the relaxation of bargaining narrowed their activity to their own sections again. From 1974 to 1979 press operators' stewards met together only once outside the full TGWU stewards meetings to discuss common operator issues. Inexperience and lack of credible authority with their members led stewards in three of the four operator groups to call in the convenor more frequently to sort out simple problems and enforce the procedures to discourage discontent.

The institutional reforms after 1970 clearly brought problems of identity and purpose for the semiskilled stewards' organization. As the objective conditions of regular redundancies and short-time working fostered and demanded a broader collectivism, the stewards failed to achieve this. They remained essentially responsive to events. Paradoxically, given the objectives of the reforms, the union organization was most successful in protecting job controls, which remained the priority for sections and their stewards throughout the period of study. While workers retained a (diminishing) capacity to enforce their controls, the stewards' organization was torn between following this sectionalism and challenging it. But its challenge was unconvincing because it was articulated largely in terms of management's vision of how the problems of low productivity could be resolved. There was considerable scepticism among the workforce about management's competence, and they preferred to defend what they had gained through exercizing their rights to mutuality rather than allow these to be expropriated under any new industrial relations consensus. In similar vein, the JSSC proved quite inadequate to the task of forging an alliance between the craft and semiskilled workers, with relations among the senior stewards and their committees reflecting their long-standing distrust and competitiveness. Union autonomy from each other was emphasized over union independence from management, with the result that the latter were increasingly successful in setting the agenda for bargaining.

Conclusions

What sense can be made of the origins and development of job controls among semiskilled workers, as evidenced by the experience of Presswork? How did these controls compare with those found elsewhere among craft workers? What does this tell us about the role of shop stewards and the potential for independent workplace union organization? Previous commentaries on semiskilled job controls have tended to emphasize one or more of the following factors: production technologies; craft traditions; economic or product market environments; industrial relations institutions; and shop steward organization. Analysis of the experience at Presswork has confirmed the importance of many of these factors. It has also suggested the partial nature of previous accounts, principally because of their failure to identify and explain the linkages or relations between the different factors, and to allow for the contradictory character of the economic and social organization of firms and their relations with their wider environment which open up or constrain opportunities for purposeful action and change over time.

The material basis for the pattern of control in Presswork rested largely on the company's market relation as subcontractor which made for extreme instability of demand and variability in the labour process. Under conditions of expansion in the motor industry, management had few incentives to transform the labour process. The technical division of labour and the fragmented and diverse organization of production in small batches on non-automatic machinery, together with the piecework system itself, provided opportunities for bargaining, while the more integrated work processes ('working in line') helped to generate cohesiveness among operators in order to exploit those opportunities through job controls.

However, these technical conditions of production only facilitated, and did not determine, the pattern of control. The expansion of workers' margin of discretion over the use of their labour power and the imposition of their rationality on the labour process were realized through their own conscious social activity and organization. The frontier of control was more advanced than in other similar studies (e.g. Burawoy, 1979; Roy, 1954) because effort bargaining became more firmly established once it became institutionalized in union controls. This facilitated the highly significant progression from 'making it pay' to 'getting the day in', and enabled its successful defence for so long against adverse forces from inside and outside the factory.

Whereas the craft unions' controls depended ultimately on controlling the external labour market through apprentice regulations, district standards and pre-entry closed shop, the semiskilled press operators were obliged to rely on an open recruitment policy, post-entry closed shop and 'bottom-up' organizing at the point of production. In fact, despite the substantial differences between craft control and the wider phenomenon of job control, of which the former is but a variant (Lyddon, 1983: 131), there were significant similarities in the controls over the effort bargain sought and achieved by the tinsmiths and press operators. Yet there was no evidence in Presswork of the alleged diffusion of craft controls from craft to non-craft workers.

The conventional explanation for the wide dispersal and high degree of job controls in British engineering has emphasized institutional and economic factors (Flanders, 1970; Turner *et al.* 1967; Donovan 1968). Presswork certainly illustrates what Gospel has called the 'skeletal and fragile nature of the industrial relations system' (1983: 19). Industrial relations remained heavily influenced by the company's subcontracting role and management's responsiveness to market forces throughout the 1960s. But, the rudimentary industrial relations system was more an effect than a cause of the job controls and devolved pattern of bargaining and managerial control. Under 'boom' conditions, a strategy of 'responsible autonomy' (Friedman, 1977) towards the press operators offered management certain benefits, as it did with the tinsmiths (Hyman and Elger, 1981: 135), but even then, in the press operators' case, this strategy was always more ambiguous and the frontier between it and 'direct control' much narrower and more fluid than Friedman's account allows. Nor can management weakness in face of the operators' challenge be explained simply by the lack of resources given to the industrial relations function. In the changing post-war environment, the established managerial ethos and culture rapidly became anachronistic. A failure to anticipate and accurately predict product market changes and to develop clear business strategies, investment programmes and the appropriate managerial skills and structures ensured that industrial relations policies remained incoherent and reactive, 'skeletal and fragile'.

Bargaining at Presswork resembled that in much of engineering generally, being 'largely informal, largely fragmented, and largely autonomous' (Flanders, 1970: 169). It seemed, too, to conform to the pattern of separating bargaining over 'market', for example pay-related, relations from 'managerial' relations involving less determinate issues such as discipline, redundancy and work organization (Flanders, 1970: 235). The absence of 'any substantial effort to codify' the latter in collective agreements, even after the encouragement given by Donovan, is held by Sisson and Brown (1983: 149) to have been a pervasive feature of British industrial relations. This 'basic' or 'primitive' form of collective bargaining, these authors continue, is less a process of joint regulation than of 'pressure group activity in which management and workers struggle to impose their views without any rules or agreements emerging' (p.152). For Tolliday, the stimulant to managerial initiation of institutional reform came in the 1960s from increased government intervention in the industry's deteriorating industrial relations record (1985. 132–40). Sisson and Brown, likewise, assert 'Management and government may try to institutionalize the process in order to avoid anarchy and uncertainty' whereas 'shop stewards, in particular, wish to remain free to take action which is appropriate in the circumstances' (1983: 152).

The evidence from Presswork suggests this is a somewhat unbalanced view. Before as well as after the institutional reforms in the wake of the 1970 'crisis', senior management were clearly not so coy about codifying effort and other restrictive practices when it suited them, for instance, the 'six bob' agreement and working to 197R. But it was the stewards rather than management who consciously strove to institutionalize effort bargaining as a more enduring defence against the kind of arbitrary managerial behaviour associated with the conflict surrounding that bargaining.

Management's tolerance of the semiskilled job controls over some 20 years was not due to 'weakness', in the sense of laziness or incompetence, but to a chronic incapacity, first, to make sense of their changing environment and, second, when they belatedly ventured upon more radical restructuring, to overcome the numerous obstacles, inside and outside the firm, which confronted them. With closure ruled out and 'starved' of investment from the parent company to transform the presswork technology, reform of labour relations via co-option of the senior stewards was perhaps the least costly, if not the only feasible, option for Presswork management.

The context in which these reforms were introduced was hardly conducive to coherent managerial planning. The process of institutionalization remained reactive, contradictory and spasmodic. As such it bore little resemblance in outcome to similar post-crisis industrial relations reforms identified elsewhere (e.g. Purcell, 1981; Bélanger, 1987). At Presswork, the development of 'high trust' relations between management and stewards remained flawed on account of the former's failure to transform the social organization of production on which the job controls were based. With more radical technological change management would still have encountered a confident shop floor organization, but in its absence, and by strengthening the authority of all stewards *vis-à-vis* production management, the institutional reforms only reinforced the workers' job controls and the increasingly severe problem of low productivity.

In doing so, they also helped to focus attention again on the endemic problem for workers' organizations of internal cohesion, discipline and the authority of leadership. For despite the extensive job controls and formally well-developed shop steward organization, giving credence to the latter's boast that they 'ran' the factory, it was the lack of success on the part of the steward leadership in overcoming sectional and union rivalry and in developing a more broadly based 'militant collectivism' which marks Presswork out from some other well-organized workplaces (Edwards, 1986: 226–46). As Edwards (1986) and Tolliday (1986: 217) both point out, this kind of militancy can be associated with sectional hostility. Unfortunately, both their otherwise stimulating discussions leave largely unexplored the role and scope for steward organization in overcoming this sectionalism.

The stewards' role was complex. Indeed, it is more accurate to speak of roles, since they often had to face different ways and prove themselves against different and sometimes contradictory criteria as circumstances and audiences demanded. In this sense, they were both 'lubricants' and 'irritants', and were not predisposed to any particular model of role, organization or democracy. They were bound to pursue general principles of fairness and egality (Brown, 1973), but within the constraints of their own understanding of, and the order they could impose on, the general 'anarchy' of workplace relations.

As in some other motor industry firms such as Ford (Beynon, 1973), Presswork management's long-running lack of commitment to any stable accommodation of the semiskilled job controls was clearly an important influence on the under-developed steward organization in the 1960s in both the TGWU and the JSSC. In this regard, Presswork provides an interesting comparison with the workplace studied by Batstone *et al.* (1977). The strong bargaining relations underpinning the authority of the steward leadership (or 'quasi-elite') in that plant derived in considerable measure from its traditional mode of organization in the 'gang' piecework system which accredited stewards with such a high status (Tolliday, 1986). They may also have been enhanced by a relatively favourable product market environment. But the relations seem, too, to have been sustained by the stewards' convincing management of their authority over the membership within and across the different unions. By contrast, at Presswork similar relations were frustrated not just by unstable and deteriorating demand, but by the turnover of 'leading' or senior stewards and lack of co-operation among the unions. This, in turn, seems to have reinforced in management, at 'critical' moments or crises, a lack of credence in the stewards' long-term capacity to 'deliver' a disciplined workforce, at least so long as other more coercive options seemed less costly. From this perspective, the distinction of Batstone *et al.* between 'populist' and 'leader' roles for stewards tends to exaggerate the difference between the roles and the extent of stewards' discretion in defining their own roles.

Nor was it only management who were suspicious of the stewards' pursuit of institutional reform. The press operators, too, remained highly ambivalent towards any moves to expropriate their opportunities to bargain. They regarded the job controls as their 'property', and tolerated rather than endorsed industrial relations reforms, whether proposed by their stewards or by management. This is not to suggest, as implied in notions of the 'bureaucratization' of shop stewards (Hyman, 1979), that the workers had an alternative strategy which the steward leadershop somehow colluded with management to suppress. Indeed, the operators' horizons were, perhaps inevitably, 'parochial' (Hyman and Elger, 1981: 136) and largely bounded within the immediate effort bargain. It is rather more a matter of how their social organization was constructed around a particular division of labour which fostered a narrow orientation to collectivism, namely a highly sectionalist one. Sectionalism is a widely criticized aspect of British unionism. But it is often conceived in idealist terms as a consequence of selfishness or an expression of the absence of a collectivist orientation. Presswork shows this is not necessarily the case, and that it has a definite material basis in work organization.

Workers' mistrust of institutionalism was reinforced by what they regarded as persistent evidence of managerial incompetence, and this undermined stewards' assertions of their ability to commit management to effective and sustained joint regulation. Mutuality, however, was a wholly different matter. This found favour with the workers precisely because it confirmed rather than challenged the scope for their own local or sectional deals. Under mutuality, the operators could make sense of the advances which union regulation offered over custom.

Inter-union organization remained under-developed for similar reasons. The influence of the craft unions on the TGWU was more important for the way in which their exclusivism and collusion with management helped the semiskilled stewards define their objectives in opposition to those of the craft workers, than for any support it might have fostered among the semiskilled for general union principles and a wider collectivism.

The sum of these countervailing and contradictory forces was an overbearing 'tradition' of sectional, workplace, and union autonomy which defeated the efforts of management, stewards, and the outside union to develop any coherent strategy for change. Management's belated reforms confronted the legacy of their own earlier policy of marginalizing militant semiskilled leadership and exploiting the subordination of the TGWU to the more stable craft unions. When reform was finally introduced, the TGWU leaders were uncertain about using their authority to influence the exercise of job controls. The tradition of independence from the outside union ensured a failure to articulate any wider collectivism within the plant, or with other plants owned by the parent group. The limitations of 'factory consciousness' became all too apparent as job losses called for a wider perspective. Job controls remained largely intact but parochial, while the stewards increasingly 'tailed' behind agendas set by others, either workers through their section claims or managers seeking concessions.

Note

The authors are grateful to the editors of this volume for their helpful comments on an earlier draft of this chapter and to all those workers, shop stewards and managers at 'Presswork' who so willingly co-operated with the research. Stephen Evans also takes this opportunity to acknowledge his debt and appreciation to the TGWU stewards and members for the education he received while working with them.

7

Wage Strategy, Redundancy and Shop Stewards in the Coventry Motor Industry

John Salmon

Editors' Foreword

This is the only chapter to adopt a comparative approach and investigate developments in shopfloor industrial relations in more than one factory. Doing this enables Salmon to address the first of his two central themes: the need to understand how different employer strategies influence the pattern of shopfloor union growth. The second theme retains employer behaviour as the focus and argues that a distorted view of the nature and power of shopfloor organization has emerged from a single-minded preoccupation with one aspect of employer strategy, namely wages policy. If, Salmon suggests, we look at other labour-related issues, and he singles out redundancy, we are forced to rather different conclusions about shopfloor industrial relations.

Salmon starts with wages policy in the years immediately following the war, and argues from the experiences both of the highly-organized Standard Company and of other Coventry car firms with lower levels of union organization that shopfloor bargaining by stewards was not a major contributor to wage movements, which can be better understood by considering the labour market position of the companies, and the impact of national wage bargaining on local earning levels. Shopfloor wage bargaining was not, for Coventry motor companies at least, the major spur to post-war union growth.

Nevertheless, Salmon argues, all companies experienced problems with labour costs unrelated to productivity growth and employers' most frequently-used device in seeking to control this, especially in periods of falling demand, was redundancy. Over this issue not only did employers insist on the formal retention of absolute prerogative, but it was also a matter on which shopfloor unions were able to make no progress for many years. Indeed, it was only in the small firms of Jaguar and Carbodies, with particular product market problems, that unions were able to secure any local advances before 1956. That year witnessed major struggles against redundancy at Standard, with its sophisticated shopfloor union organization, and the British Motor Corporation, with much more patchy organization. At Standard the unions lost, and this event contributed to the decline of Standard's unique features. But at BMC, despite the activities of shop steward combine committees, it was the full-time union officials who led and organized an unevenly-supported strike and who, with the assistance of some government pressure, won at least some concessions from the company. Salmon argues that it was this event that contributed to a growth of shopfloor self-confidence in BMC and paved the way for union development and an increasing militancy. His account of union growth thus downplays the importance of wage bargaining and highlights managerial behaviour, constrained by product and labour market factors; the role of full-time union officials; and, to a lesser extent, that of government.

This chapter thus corrects a number of misapprehensions in the post-war historiography of shop stewards, in particular by emphasising the lack of development in motor companies for more than a decade after 1945, and in demonstrating the vital part played by full-time officials in their eventual growth. It also demonstrates forcefully the inability of even the most sophisticated steward organization, such as at Standard, to exert any significant influence over managerial controls on hiring and firing, in contrast to the craft tradition in which such control is one of the bedrocks of union organization. In doing so it raises questions that run through several of the chapters in the book concerning the nature of shopfloor controls on the exercise of managerial prerogative.

Finally, the chapter invites speculation as to the significance of British companies' relatively unchallenged resort to redundancy as a device to control labour costs in periods of falling demand. For, it may be suggested, their ability to do so may, with the benefit of hindsight, be seen as having prevented them from adopting more innovative (and humane) approaches to solving their market problems. Not only is redundancy a bad policy on which to construct good relationships between managers and workers, but it is a policy of production that advocates reducing output to match declining demand, rather than one of seeking to stimulate demand to match output. Faced with competition from companies, especially overseas, that were adopting the latter course, companies like BMC may have lost market share. The inference that trade unions able to prevent employers from using redundancy in this way might have contributed to a more healthy domestic motor industry is intriguing (see Streeck, 1986: 12−15).

Introduction

One factor neglected in studies of workplace industrial relations in post-war engineering, and one not fully addressed in other contributions to this volume, is the part played by labour management and by the attitudes of employers towards emerging workplace organization. Attempts to do so have been hindered both by a lack of data and by a tendency to see the much-vaunted system of workplace organization at the Standard Motor Company as somehow typical of the post-war period (Lyddon, 1983).

This has meant, despite attention paid to the role of product and labour markets, a failure to investigate different employer attitudes and responses to workplace organization within market constraints on their behaviour.

This chapter will remedy this failing through an exploration of the behaviour of different employers in the Midlands motor industry in the period 1945−60. It examines employer policies in two key areas, wages and redundancies and how the development of these policies affected workplace trade unionism.

Taking two policy areas, and in particular the less common area of redundancy, enables this chapter to pursue a second set of themes, namely the strength of workplace union organization and its independence from union officialdom. It can be suggested that a narrow focus on wages may have led previous authors to a misleading understanding of both these characteristics. The account presented here begins with an analysis of employer differences in the area of wages, and argues that workplace bargaining was one, and by no means the most important, factor influencing wages. The remaining sections then look at the handling of redundancy in an effort to examine managerial control and the role of shop stewards and union officials.

Wages Strategy

Management and Wage Determination

The post-war developments in shopfloor industrial relations at the Standard Motor Company have been described in detail elsewhere (Tolliday, 1985). The wider industrial relations significance of its policy lay in its break with employer solidarity in federated engineering firms over wages policy. Its managing director, Sir John Black, was keen to avoid the protracted haggling over individual piecework wages that was going on in other Coventry car firms shortly after the war and to expand the firm rapidly through large increases in productivity. The famous gang system, with its highly sophisticated shop steward structure, was integral to that strategy.

Standard soon became the wage leader in the highest paid sector of the British motor industry, but there was no direct causal relationship between this and steward structures in that company; both flowed, in the first instance, from an underlying managerial strategy to boost production and productivity. Although the activities of stewards within the system of gang piecework had an influence on wage movements, it would be incorrect to infer a direct relationship between high levels of union organization and wages. This point can be made still more forcefully by considering what was happening to wages in other Coventry motor firms, none of them having levels of union membership or steward structures comparable with Standard.

The immediate effect of Standard Motors' leaving the Employers' Association was to contribute, along with the closure of Nuffield Mechanisations, to a decline in the Coventry toolroom rate. From a wartime peak in August 1944 until the early part of 1946, the hourly rate for skilled production workers fell by 25 per cent. However, the loss of the two highest wage plants was only part of the explanation for this decline. The rundown of war production in the period of transition reduced bargaining opportunities while redundancies dispersed established workgroups and undermined workplace organization. Despite this, the federated car companies, with the production of the first post-war car models, soon found themselves being caught in a double bind between the local price of labour in Coventry and the national changes in rates regulated by the Federation. These forces considerably influenced their labour management policies and approaches towards workplace organization and leadership.

On the one hand, pressure on wages following Standard's wage agreement of 1949 was intense. Unemployment in the industry was exceptionally low and union vacancy books in Coventry recorded negligible surplus labour. Given the acute shortages of labour, increases in wage rates were not unusual even among the less well organized plants in Coventry as they strove to attract scarce labour to meet the expansion of the industry. 'Coercive comparisons' were not the only force influencing wages rates; there was also an element of wage pull arising from competitive labour market conditions, in which Standard was setting the early pace.

On the other hand, however, the revival of national pay bargaining between the EEF and the engineering unions after 1948 placed a considerable strain upon relations between the Midland motor manufacturers and the industry-wide wage strategy adopted by the federation. The federation not only had to take account of union pressure, at national level, but also of the diffusion of interests among the differing sectors of federated engineering employers. In 1949 the EEF national wage strategy in attempting to remedy low pay in many parts of the engineering industry fell foul of skilled worker responses to the upsetting of differentials in the industry's wage structure. The national negotiators had increased the base rate for time-workers and raised the time rates for pieceworkers, from the pre-war 27.5 per cent to 45 per cent. There was little advantage in this settlement for the higher paid workers already above these rates. Faced with an outbreak of widespread local disputes, over a two year period, fought mainly in the more traditional sectors of engineering, over the restoration of differentials, the federation began to adopt an across-the-board wage policy to preserve differentials within the industry. This meant that the high-wage employer would pay a proportionate wage increase in line with the lowest paying firm. The determination of these industry-wide pay awards was not directly tied to worker effort or productivity of labour at workplace level, for the increases inevitably occurred regardless of product market conditions.

In the highly competitive Coventry labour markets, where hourly rates in 1948 were already 26.5 per cent above the federated hourly average, it was not just the national across-the-board increases which were unrelated to productivity. During recessions in trade when purchase tax changes affected consumer goods such as cars more sharply than the export-oriented capital goods sector, the weakening in workplace bargaining opportunities in the car plants was frequently balanced by increased national pay awards when sales turnover was falling. In 1948, 1951, 1952 and 1956 industry-wide agreements accounted for 40 to 50 per cent of the annual increase in the Coventry monthly rates when annual new car registrations were falling. In 1952, for example, but for the nationally agreed negotiations, wage rates at Rootes, Morris Engines, Morris Bodies, Daimler and Jaguar in Coventry, not to mention Austin in Birmingham, would have been 2d or 3d an hour *below* the rates paid in the previous, more prosperous, year.

A consequence of the combination of wage structure and local labour market competition was that by 1952 the hourly rate in Coventry was 37 per cent above the average national federated level compared to less than 25 per cent in 1948. The growing tension in the EEF between the federated motor manufacturers and the rest of the engineering industry became particularly acute in the crisis year of 1956 as new car registrations fell by 20 per cent. Federated volume car producers were hit much harder and took far longer to recover than their rivals in the United States. Pre-tax profits in BMC declined threefold while Rootes, the only federated volume car firm in Coventry, made a loss. It was over two years before either entered into modest profits. Specialist car producers such as Jaguar and Armstrong-Siddeley were less affected. But while the motor industry faced its biggest post-war crisis with sharp falls in sales and profits, wage rates elsewhere in engineering increased, largely as a result of the healthy trading conditions found in aircraft production and heavy plant, electrical equipment and locomotive construction. While workplace rates fell, nationally bargained increases placed 3/5d on the rate in the federated car plants.

Thus, in several periods it was national wage bargaining that sustained wage growth particularly in years of recession. Competitive labour market conditions in Coventry following the split in employer solidarity also played a part. The signing of the Standard agreement resulted in an increase in the firm's wage rate of 11d, the highest single post-war rise before 1956. This was followed by sharp increases of between 6d and 10d in Alvis, Jaguar, Armstrong-Siddeley, Daimler and Rootes, all in Coventry. What was distinctive about Standard, however, was that its 100 per cent bonus margin on base rates was directly related to realizing increased productivity, being an incentive towards co-operation and flexibility through gang working. This link was more tenuous among the federated plants where labour shortage was a factor in local ratefixing among small work groups and individual bargaining units.

The high burden of wage costs unrelated to production or financial performance led federated employers to try to alleviate wage costs through variations in labour content in relation to product market conditions. The recovery of managerial functions in regard to redundancy, from wartime regulations, became (as shown in detail below), an important regulator of wage costs by the federated car firms and a means by which to curb workplace bargaining and restrict the influence of shop steward leadership, particularly in periods of recession.

Wage Bargaining and Shop Steward Power

In British industrial relations it has been widely acknowledged that an important feature in the pattern of post-war wage rate increases has been the propensity for bargaining opportunities at shopfloor level (McCarthy, 1966: 4). Among British motor manufacturers, where piecework was predominant until the early 1970s, it was the frequency of domestic negotiations which appeared to be an important factor in shopfloor power and job control. Alterations in the types of materials and components being assembled, changes in working arrangements, or the reorganization of jigs and fixtures for the production of new models or for substantial face-lifts in existing cars, required regular and often fundamental adjustments in piecework prices. While these bargaining opportunities at workplace level have been closely associated with the rise of the power of shop stewards in the post war period, the payment systems themselves were viewed as being an important contributor to the fragmented, sectional nature of plant-level industrial relations, with this associated loss of managerial control.

It has been so far argued that with the notable exception of Standard Motors, the only wholly unionized plant in the industry in this early period, wage rate increases during the first post-war decade were conceded for reasons other than just the effectiveness of workplace bargaining. In Coventry, the competitive conditions in the labour market following the break in employer solidarity in the district, in addition to the outcomes of the balance of sectorial interests within the engineering national negotiations, had implications that were not entirely favourable to the interests of the affiliated membership in the motor industry.

An analysis of the monthly wage movements of the Coventry Toolroom Agreements, which itself was a weighted average based on the regular rounds of workplace bargaining with ratefixers, reveals that between 1945 and 1956, which includes the impact of national awards, there were a significant number of instances when wage rates fell. Of the 144 monthly figures, although on 78 occasions there was an increase in the rate over the previous month, in 66 months, the toolroom rate showed no change, or a decline. In a quarter of the individual months, the records show that there was a fall in the rate. What is noteworthy about this period is that in the federated sector of the UK motor industry, where there existed extensive individual and small work group bargaining units, in conditions of a sellers' market there occurred wage rate declines on several occasions.

Wage rate decline took place in every year but was most pronounced during periods of recession or when the production of existing models by individual companies was being rundown. During 1945, for example, the Coventry rate fell in ten of the monthly figures. In 1947, there was a decline in 8 months, while in 1948, 1952 and 1955 the records of the toolroom rate shows that in half of the months there were rate reductions. In the crisis year of 1956, the wage rate was down in 7 individual months. Although clearly there was still an overall increase in wage rates over the decade, the evidence of wage rate decline in the motor industry's most competitive labour market, together with the lowest level of strike frequency over wages for the whole of the 1940 to 1983 period, raises some doubts about the nature of shopfloor power and how far management had lost control to shop stewards during this first post-war decade.

The explanations which have emphasized shopfloor power have overstated the extent to which there was an erosion of managerial control. In particular, not only have they not taken sufficient account of the extent to which an influential sector of federated employers did not wholly endorse the changes which took place under wartime conditions, but they have failed to appreciate that, despite a sellers' market and non-price competitiveness among the producers, the majority of the federated firms, in addition to Standard Motors, were all manufacturing vehicles that were low in volume and had low profit margins, when compared, for example, to Ford. This had important implications with regard to the discretion which employers could exercise over labour management policies in the light of the need to control costs and improve profit margins.

Redundancy and Management Control

Ford, the most commercially successful of motor manufacturers in Britain during the 1950s and 1960s, though not without its industrial relations problems, built up a core labour force with a degree of employment security not enjoyed among the British owned sector of the industry. Under the 'continuity of employment' clauses of the Ford Blue Book agreements, fluctuations in production were to be met by regulating the hours of work of a stable labour force, rather than from regular hiring and discharges of its workers (Friedman and Meredeen, 1980: 225). Although this entailed worker co-operation in the extensive use of overtime and short time working, 'continuity of employment' as an aspect of management strategy sought to build up a degree of worker loyalty and attachment through the provision of job security, but on the basis of much greater overall management control over the day-to-day operations of the plant

(Beynon, 1973: 153). In the federated sector in Coventry, by contrast, where competitive labour market conditions contributed to high wage rates, narrow profit margins, and the operation of the guaranteed week agreements, regular labour-shedding in periods of recession or model changeover, was used to offset high wage liability.

Management control over wage costs in federated firms was far more dissipated than in Ford, owing to the incidence of individual and small workgroup bargaining with ratefixers, not to mention the determination of industry-wide negotiations. Management rights of control over redundancy, however, not only helped to adjust the total wage bill but were also a factor in labour discipline, and restriction over the development of shop steward influence within the workplace.

Federated employers jealously guarded the restoration of prerogative over the discharge of labour following the lifting of wartime regulations both nationally and at establishment level. Between 1946 and 1956 the questions of managerial control over redundancy and the issue of steward victimization were among the most serious obstacles confronting workplace organization. In the four-year period to 1950 there were 35 references from the AEU alone to Central Conference from federated establishments (Frow and Frow, 1982: 310). From 1947 until 1956 in the motor industry, despite the relatively low level of wage disputes, there were 44 strikes against redundancy which directly involved 96,598 workers and accounted for 549,000 working days lost. Of these redundancy strikes 18 were against the selection of shop stewards on redundancy lists. Although these accounted for less than 17 per cent of the total workers directly involved in strikes over redundancies, they represented 58 per cent of the working days lost.[1] The majority of these strikes before 1956, although long struggles, were often undertaken by individual unions or only sections of the workforce. Only rarely were they successful in achieving reinstatement, the main exception being a 31-day stoppage at Jaguar in 1951. The major crisis in the industry in 1956, when something of the order of 30 per cent of all manual employees in the car plants were involved in redundancy strikes, proved to be a watershed for both the handling of redundancy and management's response to shopfloor organization.

Car production had been given a high priority as a replacement for the war-time arms economy. The major West Midland manufacturers were all among the first 19 firms to be released from wartime regulations. The Interdepartmental Government Committee set up to resettle the industry found widespread concern among employers over wage costs and labour attitudes. A report compiled by the regional controller of the Ministry of Labour on 14 July 1945, based on interviews in Coventry with the managing directors of Daimler, Jaguar, Rootes and Morris Engines, found 'the most disturbing feature to be the almost unanimous view that labour was difficult, labour costs were too high, and the sooner there was a show-down with labour the better'.[2] The Coventry motor employers were advocating a period of unemployment to establish a 'more amenable and better disciplined' workforce.[3] At national level it was also clear that the employers' federation was not willing to allow steward organizations to consolidate the influence they had acquired under wartime regulations.

The EEF, for example, opposed the engineering unions' draft proposals presented on 6 August 1946 for a post-war agreement to extend the role of joint production committees. The union side advocated the creation of district production committees; the combining of works committees, under the 1922 procedure agreements with joint production, consultative and advisory committees, to handle all matters of grievance, discipline and welfare and production matters; and that workplace representation would be through annual elections from shop stewards.[4] Employer objections centred upon the influence such an agreement would provide for stewards. It was not until January 1947 that the federation, once again fearing the possibility of state intervention circulated its affiliated membership encouraging a continuation of the more limited 1942 JPC agreement.[5] Production committees were already in an advanced state of decline in the motor industry.

On the question of the post-war handling of redundancy, within weeks of the federation informing its affiliated membership of the restoration of the employers' rights of dismissal under the national agreement of 3 April 1946, a central conference reference which set out a redundancy procedure providing for steward consultation, resulted in a 'failure to agree'. The policy of the EEF was that redundancy decisions were not matters that could be shared with unions or shop stewards. They were primarily the responsibility of management. The federation did allow for individual employer discretion over how the actual redundancy decision was to be intimated. In addition, the EEF was prepared to defend employers' rights over dismissal. Between 1949 and 1951, for example, the EEF, with the considerable support from its West Midland membership, successfully led employer opposition to defeat a Private Member's Bill, which attempted to link length of notice entitlement with length of service or compensation. Although the main objective of the Security of Employment Bill was to discourage strong worker opposition to job loss, the Midland employers regarded it as a measure that would undermine worker discipline and managerial authority within the workplace by interfering with the power of dismissal.

In 1947 car production fell below the level of 1935. By March over 57,000 car workers had been laid-off, owing to shortages of steel and fuel. The Confederation of Shipbuilding and Engineering Unions received complaints from 18 union branches in Coventry of instances of victimization by employers in redundancy selection. At the Humber works the management were willing to provide section stewards with a redundancy list only after the notices had been served. In July, a redundancy of 68 NUVB members, including the chief steward and two section stewards, arose after a period of disagreement with ratefixers over piecework prices. Following a 26-day stoppage by trimmers belonging to the NUVB, management agreed at local conference with the union officials and the

Employers' Association that for future redundancies the unions would have the right to submit substitutions during the period of notice, but only after the redundancies had been served. This concession, which fell well short of the prior consultation practised under wartime regulation, became the basis for the handling of redundancy in Coventry. No guarantee, however, was given regarding re-employment of the union stewards.

Employer discretion over redundancy began to raise a number of job control matters. One example occurred in October 1947 at Rover, where owing to the shortage of trimmers a training school had been established which led to semiskilled trainees being allowed in the trim shop.[6] During the recession in trade five redundancies were declared, two of them skilled workers, while a number of trainees remained. The 60 skilled NUVB members walked out over the issue of safeguards for the skilled men in what had 'always been regarded as a skilled man's shop'.[7] After a three-day strike the dispute was put into procedure but an informal settlement provided for preference for future employment of the two skilled trimmers. Different issues arose in other companies. At Carbodies a two-day strike among engineers arose when a former employee was being reinstated while others were under redundancy notices.

Union organization itself was also involved. During January 1948 at the Armstrong-Siddeley works 2700 AEU members stopped work for two days, objecting to the placing of a non-union worker on a job formerly done by a union member who had been declared redundant. At issue in this case was a change in management approach towards the shop stewards. A recruitment campaign had been waged by the stewards to achieve complete unionization. The management had begun to restrict access to the convenor by withholding permission for stewards to leave their sections during works time. The appointment of non-unionists was seen as part of attempts to undermine workplace organization.

Although Coventry employers were not prepared to concede prior consultation they did have to face and take account of some resistance, particularly among better organized sectors such as Vehicle Builders and Engineers. Across in Birmingham, however, employers were less inclined to take account of unions. At the Rover plant in 1948 the firm declared all the joint production committee, plus 80 per cent of the production workers, together with the works convenor and the majority of stewards, redundant in the period of changeover to a new post-war model. The Rover stewards could do little except write to their MP.[8] During this same period Austin declared 600 of its labour force redundant with a week's notice. The JPC was ignored and an approach by the stewards for consultation was refused by the management who pointed to the ending of the agreement for consultations in June 1946. Mr. L.P. Lord, the Austin Chairman, was reported as saying ' . . . it is the directors and not the workers who run the factory'.[9] Although a meeting of 300 Austin workers was held, in neither of these two cases did industrial action take place. The Austin case was raised in the House of Commons on 27 January, but while the Minister of Labour was critical about the failure to consult, he only pointed to the procedure machinery for resolving differences in the engineering industry.

The insistence by the federation that redundancy decisions were a part of managerial functions did elicit some response. But this did little to undermine managerial control. The Coventry branch of the NUVB, for example, regularly circulated information on the state of employment in the city, discouraging outside labour when trade was deteriorating. Their craft practices extended to district-wide overtime bans in periods when the membership numbers signing the vacancy book began to rise. In 1946 they were taken through procedure to Central Conference for placing an advertisement in the Coventry Evening Telegraph with details of an overtime ban. Among employers there were no obligations under the guaranteed week agreements to discourage the declaring of redundancies. Car firms in Coventry appeared to prefer redundancy rather than to keeping under-utilized workers, or operating short-time working.

During 1947 it was the turn of the NUVB to take the employer, in this case Daimler, to Central Conference over a refusal to operate short-time working in place of 16 redundancies. Under the reference of the 'Principle of Short Time Working to Prevent Disturbances in the Coventry District', the NUVB discovered not only that the local employers' association defended the view that production levels should be balanced by a labour force that would give a full working week, but that Central Conference found that such a decision depended upon what was 'practical' in a particular set of circumstances. What was practical was to be determined by the employer. During February 1948 both Morris Bodies and Armstrong-Siddeley declared short-time working to be impractical, after they announced large scale redundancies.

The guaranteed week was in fact only rarely used in Coventry, in the early post-war period. It posed difficulties for both employer and shopfloor workers. For the employers it would increase wage cost liability when there was little or no work, while to the high earning car worker it meant a large drop in earnings, as it was assessed on the hourly time rate for a 34 hour week, and not the full week as under wartime regulations (Marsh, 1965: 160). Moreover the agreement disqualified unemployment claims for those working short-time. The branch secretary of the NUVB conceded that on the issue of short-time working or redundancy the 'employers take the view that they are judge and jury as to what and when it is practicable'.[10] During the 1947−8 recession in the Coventry motor industry criticism was voiced by union officials at the increasingly casual approach being adopted towards redundancy by a number of employers. Men were being taken 'back on' within a week or two of being declared redundant.[11]

This lack of workplace control over redundancy was evident even amongst the better organized sectors of the Coventry labour force, such as the sheet metal workers, the engineers, and the vehicle builders. Daimler in February 1949 provided a vivid example of the problems posed for the development of workplace organization by redundancy. A redundancy list of 28 workers in the body shop had been drawn up by the management. While the reasons for the redundancy were being explained to the stewards by the managing director the foremen were already issuing the notices on the shop floor. It was not until the stewards returned to the plant that they discovered not only who was on the list, but that it included the convenor and three NUVB stewards. A two-day stoppage by 180

NUVB members was brought to an end by the local officials in order to put the issue into procedure. The employers did not challenge the skilled status of the convenor, nor could they question his seniority in terms of service. They claimed, however, that selection was based upon individual ability and length of service was only a factor where all other factors were equal.

With the prospect of further industrial action Daimler management rejected short-time working, or assurances regarding prior consultation before redundancy, but they were prepared to consider substitutions. The whole shop volunteered. This, however, proved to be only a partial victory. During November 150 vehicle builders were declared redundant as management began to change over to a new model. Unrest had been increasing over attempts to change the piecework prices through the use of a stop watch. The vehicle builders' convenor was again on the list. The stewards were again given the reasons for the job loss but not the names. On this occasion the employer refused to accept the last six starters as substitutes. This time the Coventry branch opposed putting the issue into procedure and called upon the National Executive to call an official dispute. One-day token strikes were to be organized at Humber and Morris Bodies, while an overtime ban was in operation at Daimler. The shopfloor called for the issue to be raised at national level. The convenor had to leave Coventry to find work in Oxford. It was 59 days from the redundancy decision to the holding of the reference at Central Conference.

Thus it can be seen that before 1951 workplace organization had made few inroads into management control over redundancy. The 1947—8 recession in the industry highlighted union weakness and focused attention on the issue of victimization. Employer discretion was clearly quite widely drawn and unrestrained. Although there were different approaches proposed by individual unions at national level a common feature in union policy during the first postwar decade was the call for a return to prior consultation, before redundancy decisions were made. This was the position adopted by the TGWU in 1949. The union also called for compensation for older workers declared redundant.[12]

The NUVB, frequently at the sharp end of redundancy in the motor industry, advocated the need for agreed criteria for redundancy selection that would take account of service and skill. Their Coventry branch argued for legislation to prevent victimization.[13] By 1953 the AEU had a policy of prior consultation and overtime bans to operate at workplace and district level, but were opposed to any form of agreement or procedure that contemplated the acceptance of redundancy.[14]

Given these different approaches, which to some extent were a reflection of the different craft and skill composition of the unions in the engineering industry, the confederation was united only on the principle of prior consultation. On 10 August 1954 they agreed to propose an amendment to the 1922 procedure agreement which advocated this principle. The rights of managerial functions and the statement on trade union functions were to remain unchanged. On 8 February 1955 the General Secretary of the Confederation of Engineering Unions wrote to the EEF requesting recognition of 'the principle that joint consultation between management and worker representatives at individual firms should take place immediately redundancy is anticipated'.[15] The federation replied, 'it is not feasible for management to accept the establishment of any procedure under which they might be deemd to share their responsibility for grappling with the problem in the best interests of those who might be affected and the maintenance of employment for the greatest number'.[16] In the formal arena, and over matters of principle, the unions remained a long way from the joint consultation established under wartime regulations, a decade previously.

Redundancy and Workplace Organization

Although union policy at national level differed over the question of 'no redundancy' and support for compensation, prior consultation had been the main area for union agreement among the engineering unions. At local level, however, differences existed. The policy of the AEU had been to stop systematic overtime, either in the firm or the district. In the case of a large redundancy a special District Committee meeting would be called. The NUVB policy in both Coventry and Birmingham was to regard anyone in the trim, body and assembly shops who was not either apprenticed, or having had long service, to be regarded as 'green labour'. As dilutees, or replacements, they were to be the first to go in a redundancy.[17] Although the vehicle builders accepted a certain amount of temporary transfer to other parts of the works when redundancy threatened they took the view that all labour had to be counted on their original sections. Sheet metal workers, on the other hand, were rarely prepared to accept alternative work outside the traditional skills, and invariably left the firm, to practise their trade elsewhere.[18]

On the employers' side, too, tensions existed. For while federated employers in Coventry stood more firmly together over the issue of redundancy than over wage policy, employer discretion over the determination of redundancy lists frequently gave rise to inequities and anomalies, particularly where there existed no common criteria for redundancy selection. Although the motor employers refused to 'share the burden' of redundancy selection with shop stewards, unions could hardly be expected to ignore situations where redundancy lists included their stewards. This proved to be a particularly difficult issue to remedy within procedure. On the one hand it appeared to the federation that the unions were calling for preferential treatment for stewards. On the other hand months of delay in getting a hearing at Central Conference, which invariably upheld employer discretion over redundancy selection, made it difficult for unions to gain a satisfactory result. These factors inevitably raised the issue of workplace action against redundancy. But the tendency of the British-owned sector of the industry to respond to a decline in trade with labour reductions left shop floor organization struggling to prevent victimization at the point of weakness, where union members were being declared redundant. Without prior consultation and lacking agreed criteria for redundancy selection the redundancy issue left employers open to charges of injustice and victimization. At Morris Bodies in Coventry, for example, the NUVB were unable to stop one of their stewards with 17 years' service being declared redundant in the recession in April 1950.[19]

Workplace struggles, even though they were often long and bitter disputes, were not particularly successful in getting stewards reinstated. At the Austin plant in Longbridge a four-day stoppage by 10,400 workers failed to gain either the reinstatement of the AEU stewards Pegg and Bills, or a fulfilment of the employer policy of first preference for ex-Austin workers to future jobs (see the chapter by Jefferys in this volume). The stewards' names were included on a final list of seven redundancies in the machine shop. In 1953 a 53-day strike by 2278 of Austin's NUVB members was unable to have John McHugh, the union's chief steward, reinstated after his name appeared on the last batch of 43 names from a redundancy of over 800, not all of whom were NUVB members. This strike, fought alone by the union, had followed three attempts to resolve the issue in procedure, and began after management had not only re-engaged the majority of those declared redundant but was taking on fresh labour. The NUVB lost its case following a Court of Inquiry.[20] Although the Court was critical of Austin management's approach to industrial relations they neither recommended the reinstatement of McHugh nor requested Austin to change their approach towards redundancy.

Workplace-led strikes for the reinstatement of stewards required the employer to offer to compromise over workplace organization. Major federated companies such as BMC were not prepared to do this, particularly during a downturn in trade. It was in Coventry, however, that the first change in employer approaches towards redundancy occurred in a federated establishment. At Jaguar a 31-day strike began in March 1951 among NUVB members over the inclusion of the chief steward Holden, and the section steward Strong, on a list of nine vehicle builders declared redundant. The local branch officers refused to put the issue into procedure. Jaguar at the time was one of the smallest of the Coventry car firms and lacked the resources of the larger mass producers to withstand a long stoppage. To avert the strike the management offered alternative employment to all nine workers and agreed to discuss future arrangements for redundancy selection and to postpone the redundancy notices for 24 hours.

The refusal of the branch and the Jaguar membership to accept these terms resulted in the dispute's being put to arbitration, following the intervention of the Minister of Labour. For the EEF, 'the main purpose of the strike is to establish the right of the workers to overrule the all-time prerogative of the company management to place workers, within their sphere of trade, on whatever sections or jobs where they may be required'.[21] Despite the personal opposition of H. Halliwell, the NUVB General Secretary, the dispute was made official by the union's executive committee. It became apparent to the Ministry of Labour officials that unless Strong was re-employed in the body shop there was no hope of an early settlement. After five weeks the Chief Officer, Sir Robert Gould, set up an inquiry. It lasted less than a day. Although there were statements regarding management rights to manage, and a view of 'no special privileges for shop stewards', the inquiry also stated there should be 'no discrimination by the firm against shop stewards'. The resumption of work took place with the reinstatement of the stewards to the '*status quo*', and an immediate conference on redundancy procedure.

Arbitration had succeeded in gaining reinstatement and the discussion of a redundancy procedure where the disputes procedure in the past had failed. The problem for the company in the Jaguar case was that having initially agreed to discuss the basis of future redundancy selection it had conceded that existing arrangements were deficient. On 18 April 1951 the Coventry CSEU Secretary, Jack Jones, negotiated the Jaguar Procedure Agreement. The 10 point agreement acknowledged that redundancy would ultimately be the responsibility of the company. It set out criteria for redundancy selection based upon seniority, trade and department, to replace the former complete discretion of management. The procedure agreement finally recognized the position of the Secretary of the Joint Shop Stewards Committee and the senior stewards of the different unions in the plant, both as representatives for appeal and for communicating redundancy details one week before the termination of the period of notice. Although there was no preferential treatment for stewards, discriminating selection was erased. Ex-employees would be considered for future job applications. Management were to inform the stewards on a regular basis about employment prospects.

Although the Jaguar redundancy procedure neither removed managerial rights over the question of redundancy nor provided for prior consultations between management and stewards before redundancy decisions were taken, it did establish the senior stewards and not the JPCs as the direct channel for communication, while the details of the selection procedure removed a number of the grounds for the arbitrary inequalities and anomalies that arose from the federation's defence of managerial discretion.

The Jaguar redundancy procedure became the basis for settling a two-week strike among sheet metal workers at Carbodies where a disagreement over redundancy selection led to the union's chief steward and chairman of the joint shop stewards committee being dismissed. Although again only a small firm and largely owner-managed, Carbodies had had a history of poor relations with unions. Non-union labour had existed in the toolroom. The original redundancy issue became overtaken by an all-out strike led by the district officials of the CSEU, after 14 vehicle builders were dismissed from the shop for refusing to undertake the work of the sheet metal strikers. As with Jaguar it was the union officials who chose not to insist upon using the disputes procedure. A return to work on the basis of reinstatement and the acceptance of a redundancy procedure agreement was a significant move forward at Carbodies given its previous opposition to unions.

Both Jaguar and Carbodies, however, were small firms by motor industry standards with limited ability to withstand damaging losses. The weaknesses of the industry-wide disputes procedure and the unconstitutional action led by local union officials had resulted in a more systematic approach being formulated in those companies towards redundancy selection. Similar advances could not be made by local action in the larger firms.

The 1956 Redundancy Crisis

The Background

During 1956 the motor industry faced its most severe recession after three years in which all of the major producers had reported a period of sustained growth. The roots of the widespread strikes over redundancy developed out of the changes taking place in the industry as the Big Five manufacturers began to struggle for market share.

In the second half of 1954 both Ford and Vauxhall announced large programmes for investment which would increase the capital to labour ratio. Austin and Morris had through a defensive merger in 1952 formed BMC in an attempt to stem the growth of the American firms' control of the domestic market. Between 1954 and 1955 increased attention in the workplace began to focus upon job security. There was the fear that rationalization within BMC would result in job losses and plant closures, while the new round of investment into automation would cause widespread redundancies. To meet these fears the BMC Combine Committee had been formed immediately after the merger in order to link up the Nuffield and Austin shop steward organizations. In December 1954 a steering committee was created from the leaderships of the shop stewards' organizations at Ford, Rootes, Standard and BMC. On 8 March 1955 a conference composed of 185 delegates from 30 different factories was held in Birmingham; the main topic was automation and redundancy. On 24 September a second and even larger conference was held in Oxford which set out a policy for the conditions under which automation would be accepted. This included full consultations with the unions prior to its introduction, a shorter working week and no redundancies. In the second half of 1955, however, changes in government fiscal policy to curb consumer expenditure began to affect car sales. By the end of 1956 car sales fell by 197,000 on the previous year. Between April 1956 and February 1957 50,000 jobs went from the industry. It was inevitable that redundancy would be the major question facing the industry. The Standard automation strike and the official national dispute in BMC were to change fundamentally employer approaches towards workplace relations in the industry.

Strike at Standard

In February 1956 Standard Motors announced its investment plans which would bring automation and widespread change to its Banner Lane tractor facilities. In keeping with its established practice for consultation the plans were presented to the senior stewards at a works conference. During the period of changeover 2500 were to be made redundant. Some would be absorbed in car production, the remainder, though not specified in detail, would be re-employed as production began to expand. Though complying with management's tradition for prior consultation the policy infringed the motor industry stewards' 'no redundancy' policy. The stewards were invited to provide an alternative, which they did. It had four points: jobs common to both tractor and car production should continue during the changeover; jobs that could be changed quickly should be proceeded with immediately; three shifts should be introduced to car production; and, short-time working should be worked throughout the company. It was the last two that the Standard management could not accept. They claimed that there were insufficient chargehands and setters to operate a three shift system, while short-time working was neither efficient nor economic. The general decline in car sales began to reduce the possibility for absorbing Banner Lane workers.

Subsequent events are of great importance in grasping the relationship between the redundancy issue, workplace organization and the role of full-time officials. The Standard management had shown signs of seeking to gain a firmer control over the role of the stewards after Sir John Black left the firm at the beginning of 1954. There was a closer adherence to the provision of the procedure agreement in regard to steward facilities. Two stewards had been given dismissal notices for calling a meeting without management authorization at the beginning of 1955.[22] In the early part of 1956 the firm had already begun to consider its re-entry into the Employers' Association which would have necessitated substantial revisions of its procedure agreement with the local unions. Given its position as wage leader and the only 100 per cent unionized plant in the industry, and the influential position of its stewards both over production matters within the firm and in the wider steward network in the motor industry, Standard's handling of redundancy and automation was likely to have wide implications.

Standard's management had been able to convince the local union officials that the changeover in tractor production could not take place without redundancies. The TGWU suggested that compensation might be offered to the redundant, though it would be better if this appeared to emerge from negotiations rather than be announced. This would have been breaking new ground in the motor industry but would be firmly opposed by the EEF firms. The stewards had begun to ballot for strike action among the membership on management's refusal to accept their proposals. Like the 'Big Five' stewards conference the Standard stewards were not against automation but rather were adamant that its benefits had to be shared between shareholders, employers and workers.[23] For the management side automation was not seen as the issue but rather the stewards' demands for short-time working to avoid redundancies.[24]

The Standard stewards' organization, with its extensive facilities and day-to-day involvement in the management of the workplace, was less dependent upon the role of the local union officials for communication and negotiation with senior management than was the case in federated establishments, where the authority of senior stewards was not always recognized and where local and central conferences provided a role for officialdom. The strike which began on 26 April was called by the stewards and without the prior agreement of the local union officials. On 3 May the Prime Minister called for a special report on the strike. The Department of Science and Industrial Relations were requested to study the effects of automation on British industry. The House of Commons debated the dispute on 17 May, while in Paris it was the major topic under discussion at the International Federation of Metal Workers. At the end of the second week the handling of the dispute passed to the national union leadership under the CSEU in an attempt to break the deadlock. They agreed to pay strike pay but by one vote opposed making the dispute official. The local union officials, Harry Urwin, Secretary of the CSEU and TGWU District Secretary and Cyril Taylor, Divisional Organizer of the AEU, addressed a mass meeting to get the return to work enabling the national leaders to take over the negotiations. For Frank Cousins, the newly-appointed General Secretary of the TGWU, this was to be his first major issue.

The protracted negotiations made little progress. The national leadership proposed the working of the 34-hour guaranteed week in four out of every five weeks. Management kept to redundancy but introduced the idea of compensation. While the national negotiations stood adjourned for one week the stewards at works conference put forward a revised plan for short-time working. On 31 May Standard's management, with the national negotiations still adjourned, called a meeting of the stewards and local district officials to state its final position. While this meeting was in progress the foremen issued 1325 redundancy notices on the shopfloor, with notification of a further 1315 to follow a week later. The works management had outflanked both the national union officials and the shop stewards. Its action split the workforce between those who knew their job was being retained and those who were to be made redundant. Following pressure upon the Ministry of Labour from the national unions, Standards's management was persuaded to withhold its second round of redundancy notices to complete the process of negotiation. Already, however, the shop steward organization was in disarray. The employers' control over redundancy selection not only took no account of seniority or personal circumstances but it included the majority of stewards. Of the remaining workforce a ballot revealed that although the majority would be prepared to accept a three-day week, less than a third would support further strike action. The final round of negotiations between the national union officials and Standard's management was again adjourned to allow management to consider their response.

The next day Harry Urwin was requested to attend the Standard works to be informed that the company were issuing a statement to the press stating that they were pulling out of the negotiations with the national officials because these were being conducted under duress. The 'no redundancy' policy of the most sophisticated and unionized plant in the British motor industry had been defeated. The only compensation was that Standard's management set a new principle in British industrial relations in paying £7 compensation for those with over three years service and £10 for those with over ten years employment with the firm. The focus of attention, however, had already shifted to Birmingham, the main manufacturing base of BMC.

The BMC Strike
Clearly the British Motor Corporation had closely followed the redundancy strike at Standard. The day before the Standard workers' defeat BMC announced

6000 redundancies to take effect immediately. Although the refusal to consult with the shop stewards was not uncharacteristic of its general approach to labour management, its pre-emptive and simultaneous announcement in eight of its plants of redundancy with a week's wages in lieu of notice was specifically intended to minimize the possibility of strikes. Unlike Standard, however, in many parts of the Corporation, particularly outside its Coventry plants, unionization was weak or non-existent except in the toolrooms. At Longbridge there was no recognition of senior stewards, and the position of chief steward was the main channel of formal communication between senior management and the workplace unions. Austin management preferred, whenever possible, to deal with local union officials on important issues. The shop steward committee was therefore heavily dependent upon the position of the chief steward, Dick Etheridge, who in turn was relied upon by the local union officials. Earlier redundancies, notably the McHugh case, had undermined workplace organization, while it had been the local union officials rather than the stewards themselves who had reconstituted the shop stewards committee after 1953.

The Longbridge stewards held an influential position in the BMC Combine Committee. As the largest plant they held 50 per cent of the vote, while the dispersed plants in the Nuffield organization held the remainder. Union representation, particularly in Oxford, was exceptionally weak, moreover, the Combine was dominated not only by senior stewards but by the AEU. Before 1956 few of the Corporation's plants had had unofficial strikes, with the exception of Austin. If there was to be a response from the union side to the redundancy notices it was most likely to come from the union officials.

The BMC Combine Committee met on the Saturday immediately after the notices were issued, under the chairmanship of Dick Etheridge, with delegates from the other parts of the Big Five manufacturers in attendance. The stewards called for an official stoppage, a lobby of Parliament, local demonstrations, and an enquiry into the industry. It was the TGWU regional officials and senior stewards who sought to define the issues and demands. They called for an immediate meeting between the union National Executives and the BMC Board of Directors, and for the reinstatement of dismissed workers or payment of compensation. It was already evident that although the union leadership had been split over the question of 'no redundancy' at Standard the TGWU now accepted that redundancy had to be dealt with as an issue which might not always be avoided.

The demands put to the BMC senior management by the leadership of the four main unions, TGWU, AEU, NUVB and the NUSMW, were: re-engagement so that discussion could proceed; worksharing; compensation; procedure for future redundancies; and assurances about re-employment. The no redundancy policy had been effectively abandoned. BMC rejected all the demands, in large part because they would threaten EEF policy and create precedents which smaller firms could not fulfil. The union leaderships replied with a call for 'action in the factories'. This in fact was far from being assured. With the exception of

Nuffield Metal Products there had been no immediate stoppages as a result of the redundancy notices. In the most strongly organized sector of the Corporation, the Coventry plants, there were no redundancies. It was far from certain how far those who retained their jobs would strike in support of those who had already left.

Discontent was clear and occasional stoppages did take place, however. The selection on a 'last in first out' basis on sections gave rise to a host of grievances caused by the practice of frequent mobility, particularly in a large plant like Longbridge. Some workers with less than a year's service escaped, while others with considerable seniority, in one instance 31 years' service, were made redundant. 'Last in first out' did not, however, discriminate between union and non-union members, and therefore provided no protection to anti-union workers, particularly in the more poorly organized plants. How far such workers would join picket lines was unknown. Both management and government were prepared to ride it out in the expectation of its having little support.

In Oxford nearly 900 signatures were collected at Morris Motors opposing the strike. At Metal Products 90 NUVB members in the paint shop opposed it while at the Morris Engines plant in Coventry the AEU members in the toolroom voted against it. In the toolroom at Tractor and Transmissions in Birmingham an AEU ballot found that 60 per cent were opposed and a five to one ratio among the production workers was claimed to be against. On the first day of the strike 23,000 workers out of 43,500 in 12 factories were said to be at work. At the MG plant in Abingdon only the local NUVB secretary was on strike. Morris Radiators and Morris cars reported 90 and 85 per cent attendance respectively. Even in Longbridge where there were 3000 redundancies it was claimed that only 20 per cent were not at work. It was only in Coventry that the strike was really solid, with four out of five of those at the engine plant and nine out of ten at the bodies plant on strike.

The main obstacle on the union side was no longer the inter-union differences on redundancy, but the position of the Confederation. Shop stewards led no unofficial activity but focused upon the demands for an official dispute. It was the national leadership who called a strike before the dispute procedure had been exhausted. Although shop stewards took an active part in the running of the strike, they did so under the direction of the union officials, who not only took control of the strike organization but defined the issues and objectives. The strike began almost three weeks after the redundancies had been declared and when large stocks of unsold cars were available due to the recession in trade. Moreover, the strike call was to begin five days before the annual summer shutdown in BMC. The strike found its strongest support in the body shops, where traditionally a high proportion of NUVB, SMW and AEU membership effectively operated informal union shops, which existed as much for the defence of inter-union trade practices as for opposition to management. Morris Bodies and the two Fisher and Ludlow body plants in Birmingham and Coventry had less than 5 per cent of the labour force crossing picket lines. It was in Longbridge, however, not only the largest plant in the UK industry, but where half the redundancies had occurred, that so much was at stake for the unions. A national stoppage conducted by the union leadership, however, had recourse to a powerful sanction against the company — the blacking of BMC goods and supplies. The TGWU issued instructions to its docks and road transport sections to black all BMC work. The NUR instructed its 1670 branches not to handle BMC goods on the railways. Even Midland Red and Birmingham Corporation bus services withdrew services to the Longbridge works.

On the second day of the dispute, Morris Radiators in Oxford, with under 40 per cent unionization, came to a complete halt following a persuasive speech by Malcolm Young, the AEU Convenor, to a gathering in the canteen. Large numbers of the unorganized, semiskilled workers signed up with the TGWU who paid out immediate strike benefits. On the third day, the Pressed Steel Fisher plant stopped in sympathy, while a number of smaller companies in the components industry began to announce lay-offs and redundancies of their own. Ford, dependent on supplies from Fisher and Ludlow, uncharacteristically announced 2000 redundancies. The consequence was a strike of 12,000 of its Dagenham workforce, while Standard Motors gave notice of a further 1000 redundancies due to its reliance on the Fisher and Ludlow body plant.

Although far from being a complete stoppage within BMC, the interdependence of the motor industry caused widespread disruption within a matter of days, while the creation of secondary redundancies merely served to reinforce the significance of the main dispute. Furthermore, beyond BMC, other employers faced serious problems over how to respond to the blacking of BMC goods without generating additional strikes. There were growing fears about a national dock strike and the prospect of a complete stoppage on the railways, if disciplinary action was taken by either the port employers or BR management. At the Longbridge plant, over 1000 pickets were requiring a considerable police presence. Despite the attendance of three-quarters of the remaining workforce, production was little more than 25 per cent of normal levels. Even in Oxford, less than 40 per cent was being achieved. During the first week of the annual holiday, little of the essential plant maintenance work was carried out by engineers and electricians.

Neither Parliamentary opinion nor press coverage gave much comfort to the Corporation and there even appeared to be a division within the EEF about the wisdom of BMC's handling of mass redundancies. The Corporation came under pressure from government to reopen talks with the unions. During the first week of the works holiday, the Chief Industrial Commissioner, Sir William Neden, called on both sides for discussions on the question of consultation over redundancy. The management side were already conceding that the unions were 'pushing at an open door'. The major difficulty was compensation and particularly the position of the EEF. Harry Nicholas, the TGWU Trade Group Secretary who led the union side, stated 'the strike is against BMC not the Federation . . . We are not prepared to meet the National Federation on compensation. We do not want the question to be influenced by what the backyard foundries can pay'.[25] On Friday, 10 August, the basis of an agreement was reached with the assistance of the Chief Industrial Commissioner. A resumption of work took place in all BMC plants on 13 August. The outline of the agreement included no victimization on either side following a return to work. BMC agreed to joint re-examination at local level; ex-employees were given first opportunity of future employment when vacancies arose; compensation, with the agreement of the EEF, of one week's wages for those with three or more years service and two weeks' wages for those with ten or more years service, was to be paid at the consolidated time rate; and an agreed method was to be established for the handling of future redundancies. The 'right to work' resolutions of the AEU National Committee and the 'no redundancy' policy of the Big Five motor industry shop stewards committees had been eclipsed.

In contrast to the experience of Standard Motors, in the BMC case the leadership of the trade unions engaged in a national stoppage on the question of redundancy with one of the most powerful employers in the EEF, despite the weak and uneven state of union membership. At Standard, the elaborate shop steward structure had effectively controlled the conduct of the dispute, but at BMC this was done by union officials. Shop stewards in BMC clearly did not play a passive role in the 1956 redundancy strike, but it was the officials and not the administrative structure of the combine committees who brought co-ordination to the strike. At Longbridge, the local union officers from the TGWU and the NUVB led the mass sit-down on the picket lines that had such an adverse effect on the operations of the plant. The dispute highlighted a serious imbalance in shopfloor organization. The strike was strongest in areas such as Coventry, where despite the absence of redundancies the membership supported the union leadership. Support was visibly weaker in Oxford and Birmingham, where larger numbers of non-union workers existed, particularly among the semiskilled track workers and among the indirect labour force in the assembly plants. The strike marked the beginning of a new assertiveness within the TGWU in the engineering industry under the direction of Frank Cousins as General Secretary and Jack Jones, who moved from Coventry to be installed as Regional Secretary in Birmingham, an area with the largest recruiting potential for semiskilled labour in the motor and engineering trades.

On 26 September 1956, almost identical redundancy procedure agreements were signed by local officials of the CSEU and works management at Standard Motors and in the BMC works. The agreements, with the addition of compensatory payments, followed the principles established by the Jaguar agreements in 1951, which provided for the involvement of senior stewards in the administration of redundancy procedure. Through these agreements, works management formally recognized, for the purposes of redundancy, the position of the senior steward for individual unions. The implementation and administration of redundancies increasingly came to rely on the workplace knowledge and involvement of senior stewards. Uncertainties and disputes arose surrounding seniority, the position of those transferred between different sections in the works and queries regarding the effects of broken service or re-engagement after redundancy; all of which complicated the definition of continuous service for the purpose of redundancy selection.

Aftermath

Inevitably, the senior stewards with more intimate knowledge than local officials became the source for establishing consistent practice and the means for finding equitable solutions. At Longbridge, if only through the extension of *ad hoc* privileges and informal arrangements, works management began to develop their channels of communication through senior stewards. The rapid increase in union membership after 1956 reinforced their significance in workplace affairs, despite the failure of management formally to recognize either the position of the works committee or the joint shop stewards committee. At Longbridge, Dick Etheridge, the works chief steward, was claiming almost total unionization just over 18 months following the end of the 1956 redundancy strike and the signing of the redundancy procedure agreements. Where transfers of labour took place, section stewards were inspecting union cards to ensure they were up to date.

For the Engineering Employers' Federation, which had fought hard to prevent the principle of compensation from being established at BMC, union power in the engineering industry was further emphasized when in 1957 it backed down, though under government pressure, over the pay strike of that year (Clegg and Adams, 1957). This decision by the EEF Management Board met with much anger among the Midland motor industry employers, who were even contemplating the formation of a breakaway organization in order to gain greater control over wage policy (Wigham, 1973: 198). The impact on the self-confidence of workplace organization was dramatic.

At the workplace level management in the car firms faced an increasing tempo of industrial strife from the autumn of 1958. They began to look towards the convenors and senior stewards for immediate solutions to disruptions in production. The *de facto* recognition of the Longbridge works committee and its senior stewards was translated into official recognition by agreement between BMC management and the local CSEU officials on 7 January 1963. This conferred legitimate status on the position occupied by the chief steward and senior stewards for each union in the operation of national agreements of the dispute procedure. Under the overall constitutional authority of the CSEU, the works committee agreement tried to unify the authority of the workplace leadership in the midst of growing shopfloor dissent.

In the first six months of 1959, of the 84 stoppages reported in the industry, 13 arose at Morris Motors. Under the works committee agreements, facilities were provided for the holding of works committee meetings in works time but shopfloor discontent increased the formal contact between senior works management. During 1958, at Longbridge, there was a meeting each week with management, but between 1965 and 1966 this rose from two to three. In Morris Motors at Oxford, three meetings a fortnight became four meetings a week in 1965. In the old Morris and Austin assembly plants, the high incidence of individual and small workgroup bargaining units overwhelmed the capacity of senior stewards to contain discontent within constitutional boundaries. Of the 100 unofficial stoppages in BMC in 1960, 67 took place in Longbridge where the senior stewards had a reputation for close adherence to procedure. During 1965, there were 115 unofficial disputes at Longbridge and 142 strikes at Morris

Motors in the first six months of 1966. In 1965, of the 297 strikes in the Cowley assembly plant, 256 broke out before the senior steward arrived in the shop.[26]

At Standard, employer responses were rather different. Having dismissed almost half the stewards through redundancy in 1956, management broke up the gang system and undermined the function of the joint works committee. These changes were intended to reduce steward discretion and to establish a more direct relationship between incentive payments and individual effort. In their new role, senior stewards became increasingly confined to grievance resolution, especially over piecework disputes. In several ways, therefore, the aftermath of the redundancy strikes witnessed a collapse of Standard's unique qualities and a convergence between it and the other car firms in their approach to steward organization.

Conclusions

This chapter, along with recent comments by Lyddon (1983) and Tolliday (1985), has questioned the extent to which shop steward organization made significant inroads into management prerogative in the British-owned sector of the motor industry before 1960. Whereas Lyddon has cast doubt on Zeitlin's (1980) thesis that the growth of shop steward organization among the lesser skilled car workers was dependant upon a prior model of craft unionism, Tolliday has emphasized the actions of government as being decisive in the 'emergence, shaping and consolidation of workplace organization'. However, both have ignored the contribution of employer behaviour. It has been argued here that weaknesses in employer solidarity over wage strategy were the key to union growth at Standard, while in other companies redundancies were crucial issues in the development of workplace organization and the character of job control, to which both union officialdom and arbitration contributed much.

Lewchuk (1983) has suggested that British employers in the motor industry had already rejected direct control strategies such as Fordism for the patterning of work organization, as it entailed a high day rated payment system and close supervision because of the antagonistic nature of British labour. Instead, domestic manufacturers looked for alternative managerial strategies and regarded piecework, in which productivity was a major factor in the determination of the level of the weekly wage, as a mechanism for reforming the attitudes of the workforce. The attraction of individual or small workgroup incentive payments lay in penalizing the unproductive worker through low earnings. In the post-war period, however, although all motor manufacturers had come to terms with the changes that had taken place in the war period, the importance of the break from employer strategy by Standard Motors in Coventry arose, not merely from the attitude of labour, but from a restructuring of the gang system. As Tolliday's account makes clear (Tolliday, 1985: 210–13) this was intended not only to guarantee the supply of labour but, through a more egalitarian system of bonus distribution, to gain the support of shop stewards for a more co-operative and flexible labour force that would accept new investment and mobility within the plant and thereby achieve high output and productivity. Standard was thus a vivid illustration of how far the influence of steward organizations was also contingent on the complicity of a particularly personalized employer strategy, which itself was vulnerable to the limited achievement of high volume production. The limitation of the product market and a change in senior management saw a dramatic change in direction, whereby Standard were able to exercise their control over redundancy selection to remove a substantial number of stewards and pave the way towards a rekindling of employer solidarity through a reapplication to the EEF, as the British sector of the industry came under increased competition from the advances of both Ford and Vauxhall.

The factors shaping management approaches to workplace organization, rather than the common political allegiances of the leading stewards, were probably of more importance in explaining differences of workplace organization in the early years. At Austin, for example, the greater dependance of the chief steward on the local union officials as a channel to senior management clearly weakened the influence of workplace organization before 1956. Moreover, the inability of both shopfloor organization and the NUVB to defend stewards dismissed through redundancy, led to a volatile pattern of membership growth and influence. At Jaguar, on the other hand, a smaller firm less able to endure a long dispute if it badly disrupted production, had to concede a more rational approach to redundancy selection. Although this did not provide for prior consultation, it did reduce grounds for the victimization of stewards through redundancy and increased the role of senior stewards in the affairs of the workplace.

Elsewhere, however, managerial policies had continued to frustrate the advances of shopfloor union organization, and local officials played a crucial role. Before 1959 union officials exercised an important influence over workplace relations. On the question of redundancy, despite the policy of the motor industry shop stewards, it was the union officials who led the crucial disputes and who set the agenda. Although the stewards continued to maintain their policy of 'no redundancy' it was the leadership of the TGWU, organizing among the lesser skilled, rather than the policy of the skilled unions with their craft controls, which paved the way for the principle of compensation for job loss. It was only in the wake of the 1956 redundancy struggles and the co-ordination provided by union officials that shopfloor organization began to develop and extend its role. In this process too, full-time officials played an important part (Jones, 1986: 145−7).

There have certainly been subsequent advances, notably the 1965 Redundancy Payments Act and the 1975 Employment Protection Act. The latter included (at section 99) a requirement that employers discuss with unions the timing and method of redundancy. But it remained management's right to decide whether there should be redundancies in the first place. The issue has remained one over which unions have been able to exercise little control.

In terms of labour management, although the domestic producers have faced considerable rigidity over deployment of labour within the firm, British employers, perhaps more than other overseas firms, have experienced far fewer restrictions over the recruitment and discharge of labour. State provision, as well as union agreements, has placed few obstacles in the way of management control over redundancy. Shop steward organizations have found it particularly difficult to sustain a policy of 'no redundancy'. Despite stewards' increased involvement in the administration of redundancy, they have continued to find it hard to control: their administrative involvement made them useful to management, but not influential on this issue. The handling of redundancy has thus been a profound influence on the character of shopfloor trade unionism in British-owned car firms.

Notes

This chapter is based on a wide variety of primary documentary material, supplemented by interviews with several of the principal participants in the events of the period. These include national and local union officials, convenors, senior stewards, and industrial relations managers. The documentary material includes the archives of the Engineering Employers' Federation; the Coventry and District Engineering Employers' Association; the Ministry of Labour (at the Public Records Office); the Transport and General Workers' Union; the Coventry District Committee of the Amalgamated Engineering Union; the National Union of Vehicle Builders; the Coventry branch of the National Union of Sheet Metal Workers and Braziers; the Confederation of Shipbuilding and Engineering Unions. Also consulted were the Dick Etheridge and Les Gurl shop steward collections and the Richard Stynes and Sir Jack Scamp papers at the Modern Records Centre, University of Warwick; and the minutes of the Coventry Toolroom Agreement. The author is grateful to all the people and organizations who have assisted his research.

1. These figures are based upon DE Disputes Record Books, 1940–60, for MLH 381. Public Record Ofice LAB 34, 55–77.
2. PRO LAB 8/1–11.
3. *Ibid.*
4. Central Conference, 6 August 1946.
5. EEF CL 73.
6. Local Conference, 3 November 1947.
7. *Ibid.*
8. *Metal Worker*, February 1948.
9. *Daily Telegraph*, 17 January 1947.
10. Local Conference, 11 March 1949.
11. *Coventry Evening Telegraph*, 14 February 1949.
12. Minutes of the Biennial Delegate Conference, TGWU, 1949, minute No. 31.
13. Minutes of NUVB EC, 2 July 1949.
14. Report of Proceedings, CSEU, August 1953.
15. Report of Proceedings, CSEU, August 1954.
16. EEF CL 221.
17. NUVB Branch Committee, Coventry, 26 June 1950.
18. Etheridge Papers, Modern Records Centre, University of Warwick.

19. Works Conference, April 1950.
20. Cmd 8839.
21. EEF Correspondence, 16 March 1951.
22. Frow and Frow (1982: 156); R.J. Stynes Papers, Modern Records Centre, University of Warwick.
23. Stynes, *Ibid.*
24. *Coventry Evening Telegraph*, 3 May 1956.
25. *The Times*, 27 July 1956.
26. The Scamp Papers, Modern Records Centre.

8

Conclusions: Another Way Forward?

P. K. Edwards and Michael Terry

Introduction

In this chapter some of the themes arising from the foregoing studies are addressed. We offer no general assessment of British workplace unions, but concentrate on matters that stem directly from the case studies. In doing so, we make frequent reference to Tolliday's (1985, 1986) pioneering work, for this has established an important framework of ideas not only through its empirical analysis but also in its assessment of the origins, operation, and outcomes of shopfloor bargaining.

The chapter has four main parts. The first two examine the operation of workplace relations. We begin by looking at the origins of job controls and how they operated: what light do the case studies throw on when and why job controls emerged and on the dynamics of shopfloor industrial relations? In the second section we turn to specifically trade union issues by considering the process of unionization and union organization and democracy. The last two sections broaden the discussion by looking at the implications of the processes analysed earlier. The third outlines the light which the case studies throw on the much-debated issue of the impact of job controls on productivity. The final section is more speculative. Many of the case studies contribute to the picture of British workplace industrial relations as revolving around battles over narrow issues: a form of trench warfare which neither side could win and which made change very difficult. Was this inevitable, or were there aspects of workplace relations which permitted other developments? Can a possible alternative route be identified? We think that it can, and that it offers lessons not only for the assessment of the past but also for the understanding of contemporary developments.

Origin and Operation of Job Controls

Origins

As argued in chapter 1, it is a great mistake to see the job controls of the post-1945 era as self-contained processes. They are a product of a focus on the point of production which has characterized British unions from at least the nineteenth century. But, apart from cases such as the Craft Union in the Premier Metals case, where a craft tradition rooted directly in the past continued to operate, it would also be wrong to see contemporary job controls as part of an unbroken tradition stretching back into the mists of time. We recognize the important continuities between recent job controls and those of the past (Price, 1982), together with the need to relate them to the long-standing emphasis on bargaining at the point of production (Fox, 1985). However, we concentrate here on the specific question of why controls emerged in the post-war period.

Job controls and union organization are intimately related, and the conditions promoting them are likely to be similar, but they can emerge and vary independently. The steward organization at Herbert's, for example, with its long-established recognition from management, was in some ways more developed than the organizations at Longbridge or Presswork, where employer hostility was evident much longer, even though the power of *workers* to challenge managerial authority appears to have been greater in the latter two cases. As Bélanger and Evans show, moreover, established union influence on effort bargaining has a different character from job controls at workgroup level, which tend to be covert and fragile. They also stress that stewards' power had an intimate and complex relationship with workers' controls and could not be reduced to them or treated as though they were entirely free-standing. In this section we refer to shopfloor organization either when the conditions promoting it also affected job controls or when discussing the work of other writers who, though referring to steward organizations, are plainly talking about the general balance of power between workers and employers. We discuss union organization in the strict sense of institutional developments and internal democracy in the following section

Wartime conditions, notably the tight labour market, legal controls on dismissal, and the encouragement of joint production committees, facilitated shopfloor effort bargaining (see Jones, 1986: 91–116). There also seems to be little doubt that product market conditions after the war provided fertile conditions. 'The district conditions of Coventry clearly provided a favourable environment for union development, especially the pressing demand for labour, the drive for high output and the relatively slack cost constraints on products before the 1960s' (Tolliday, 1986: 227–8). Other conditions that might be mentioned include a heavy reliance on piecework, with its well-attested opportunities for bargaining (Brown, 1973).

As Tolliday goes on to note, however, such conditions did not necessarily lead to developed job controls. Herbert's is the most obvious example, but several of our other studies, notably those by Jefferys and Salmon, point to difficulties and setbacks in attempts to shift the frontier of control. Although favourable external conditions were necessary for shopfloor controls to emerge, the process by which they did so was long and difficult. Some existing periodizations appear to be questionable. Friedman (1977: 212) argues that 'during the 1940s and early 1950s the shop stewards' movement in Coventry's engineering industry became very powerful'. The studes in this volume and elsewhere present a different picture in which managements continued to resist the development of steward organization and to victimize shop stewards until well into the 1950s, and workers' control of the labour process remained patchy. For the car firms, Salmon sees the struggles over redundancy in 1956 as marking a turning point, and other studies point to the late 1950s and early 1960s as a key period during which shopfloor organization and job controls became more established.

Our studies add some evidence to existing arguments about structural conditions. Bélanger and Evans, for example, demonstrate the impact of piecework, with its constant haggling between workers and ratefixers, on shopfloor bargaining. Scullion and Edwards show that slack cost constraints meant that management at Premier Metals had few incentives to resist the entrenchment of the Craft Union's job controls or the rise of the General Union. But the particular lesson to emerge concerns the role of managements and workers.

On the question of management, it is at first sight tempting to array firms according to the intensity of their opposition to shopfloor job controls, with Premier towards one end and Herbert's at the other. Yet, as Cressey *et al.* (1985: 133), having identified four different patterns of organizational politics, note, 'we would expect to find many mixed situations in which fragments of more than one orientation could be located in an enterprise'. Herbert's management, for example, was insistent on the right to manage but it also permitted the stewards' committee to operate, and the system of shopfloor order seems to have involved an implicit balance of low wages combined with low effort levels and an absence of change.

Two popular models of management were identified in chapter 1: the vacuum theory in which job controls are presented as filling a gap left by management, and the view that firms had clear-cut strategies of labour control. The latter has been much criticized recently (Littler and Salaman, 1982), and the criticisms do not need repeating here, save to note that deliberate schemes of labour management were conspicuous by their absence.[1] The former is more interesting, for it recognizes that job controls could move into areas where managerial control had been weak. But it would be wrong to see management as entirely passive. All our firms were actively engaged in trying to manage the shopfloor; even at Premier Metals the frontier of control was contested. Issues that came to be resolved through custom and practice and open bargaining were not newly invented. Prior to the growth of job controls managerial rights had been either taken for granted or asserted uncompromisingly, for example in the strict application of discipline to which Jefferys, Salmon, and Bélanger and Evans all draw attention.

As Lewchuk (1986) argues, the Midlands car firms never adopted the policy of close supervision, rationalization, and high wages associated with Ford. Their approach can be seen as a lengthy accommodation with job controls and 'weak managerial control over labour' (p. 136). In this general sense, managerial policy, which can in turn be related to a wider approach to business management in which a short-run view and a lack of long-term investment predominated, was central to the growth of job controls. Lewchuk (1986: 139) also makes the important point that a shopfloor accommodation need not be predicated on developed steward bodies. Writers such as Tolliday (1985: 108) use the weakness of unions until the 1950s to imply that job control issues were largely absent before then. Lewchuk argues that what he terms 'labour independence' could impose constraints on management even though the workers were unorganized. His analysis is, however, limited by its picture of accommodation as more or less permanent. As just noted, the frequency and extent of attacks on steward organizations is a feature of the present studies which has often been neglected. With the exception of firms such as Premier and Coventry Precision, where there was a developed accommodation, managements appear to have oscillated between vigorous actions when they felt that the right to manage was under threat and an acceptance of shopfloor arrangements based on custom and practice. The term 'accommodation' does not really capture the latter, since it implies a conscious decision and an unchanging order. The situation was in fact one in which managers were willing to follow the same principles of imprecise arrangements and long-standing tradition but in which these principles were applied differently at different times. There was a continuity in firms' approaches, but how these were applied in detail varied according to product market conditions and the state of shopfloor relations.

At Austin, for example, a traditionally autocratic employer attempted to preserve the right to manage on the shopfloor. But labour and product market pressures such as the need to introduce new models and to produce them in volume made the firm vulnerable to stoppages. It was gradually forced into an accommodation with the unions, part of which was a loss of unilateral control of the work process. The stable market conditions facing Herbert's during the 1950s, by contrast, enabled the firm to continue its highly personalized style of management. It did not need to be aggressively anti-union. Presswork was different again, with management apparently being less ideologically opposed to unions than Austin had traditionally been but having had no alternative style of labour management. Both here and at Austin management could oscillate between an accommodation with shopfloor organization and attempts to resist it, as when discipline was imposed harshly. It was not a matter of a firm's having a labour policy which was then amended in the light of external circumstances and internal challenges. There was, instead, a search for solutions in which existing assumptions were blended with reactions to specific events.

Although responding to similar external conditions, managements behaved in different ways. It is probably the case that the approaches at Longbridge and Presswork represented an 'average' in that shopfloor job controls emerged through a long process of struggle. Herbert's represented one distinct alternative, as did Premier Metals. A third exception was Standard Motors, with its deliberate policy of paying high wages and ceding control of the details of work operations to gangs of workers. Apart from such clear cases, it would be inappropriate to identify coherent approaches. To the question, 'what was the role of management in the growth of job controls?' it is not possible to say that they resisted or promoted the controls. One management could well do both. But there was a development to wider acceptance of them as managements wrestled with problems of production and marketing and, in view of external conditions, had to reach some kind of accommodation on the shopfloor.

The role of shop stewards was also complex. Our studies underline the ways in which stewards could challenge or help to reproduce a given system of order. On the latter, Grainger's particular contribution is to show how the 'corporatist' politics of the senior stewards at Herbert's reflected and reproduced managerial authority. The stewards were not just the passive recipients of managerial decisions and product market circumstances but were active agents in shaping shopfloor relations. The hierarchy of skill and the exclusion of black workers, for example, were promoted by the stewards' approach. And, crucially, their politics meant that workers' job controls remained limited, covert, and private. At Presswork, by contrast, stewards played a more active role in articulating and generalizing controls, albeit with problems of unity being ever-present. As noted in the introduction to Bélanger and Evans's chapter, this study is one of the few which explores how shopfloor activists operated and relates their activities to the material conditions of the production process.

In short, the case studies underline the role of workers' and managers' relations in the development of job controls. External conditions were important, but they did not impose outcomes: their effects had to be interpreted in the light of existing arrangements and assumptions.

Operation

The contradictory nature of job controls is now well-established. Not only are they ways for workers to challenge managerial authority, but also they are often modes of accommodation with that authority, and they can actively assist the production process (Hyman and Elger, 1981). Furthermore, they can encourage a narrow view of workers' interests, in so far as they stimulate a focus on the immediate issues of the effort bargain and not wider questions of production strategy, and can be divisive, because workers adopt a sectional view of their position and are often led into conflict with other workers. Our case studies illustrate many aspects of these processes, but the points that they make are often familiar and require no special comment. There are, however, some less obvious themes that merit attention.

In an important passage, Tolliday (1986: 230) comments on the difficulty that stewards had in developing broad strategic goals. Their strength lay in the manipulation of custom and practice, which reflected not unilateral workers' control but the random growth of arrangements in situations where managerial decisions had been largely absent. The two sides were each liable to give ground to the other because the consequences of particular decisions could be obscure. The random nature of the gains made by stewards meant that it was impossible to push in any planned direction or to generalize the gains.

Our studies are particularly useful in showing in detail the processes involved. As the Presswork case shows most clearly, controls were assembled from a variety of elements and reflected the exigencies of specific issues and the circumstances in which these arose. The 'six bob' agreement, for example, was not an elegant conclusion to a careful campaign but was a compromise nailed together from various components to meet perceived problems. At Premier Metals, materials handlers invented the idea of covering for absentees and sharing the wages of the absentees among the rest of the gang. This practice, originally an informal arrangement, became more permanent and was eventually subject to managerial control in the shape of rules governing what proportion of the wages saved could be paid to the gang. Such rules became important parts of the operation of factories, and workers could become strongly attached to them even though their purpose was not always clear. Premier Metals also illustrates why workers could cling to apparently irrational and outmoded practices. The division between 'press operators' and 'press assistants', for example, came to express inter-union hostility, claims to job rights, and the very occupational identities of the workers concerned. Attempts to end the distinction met deep suspicion, even though the workers were perfectly friendly on a personal basis and even though the skills involved were almost entirely social constructs.

As new circumstances arose, job controls had to be reshaped to meet them. Thus even the long-established Craft Union at Premier Metals had to alter old controls and introduce new ones in the face of the product market uncertainties of the 1960s. The unplanned nature of developments is readily apparent, as is the way in which arrangements arose whose results were far from clear to the participants at the time. There is, however, a danger in placing too much weight on randomness, for it can imply that development in any direction was possible. Particular rules certainly emerged in unpredictable ways. But how they took hold, and indeed whether they were allowed to survive, depended on the existing pattern of relationships. The types of control developed at Premier, in particular their centralized nature, would have been unthinkable in other factories. At the opposite extreme, Armstrong *et al.* (1981) have shown how, in poorly organized factories, concessions and informal practices do not grow into custom and practice rules. Management can deny the practices any legitimacy, and workers lack the language and traditions to develop alternatives. Given a starting-point, the next 'mutation' of job controls might be unpredictable, but different mutations were more likely in some environments that others, and some were also more likely than others to survive and to mature into custom and practice rules.

This point leads into the role of management in the operation of shopfloor bargaining. Their great differences in the conduct of industrial relations nothwithstanding, the companies considered here have a considerable similarity in this respect. This is most apparent in the efforts at reform made by several of them during the late 1960s and early 1970s. These all had parallels with the approach advocated by the Donovan Commission: altering payments systems, in particular by moving away from chaotic and decaying piecework systems; increasing the authority of supervisors; and centralizing bargaining at plant or company level. Presswork provides a classic instance of such reform in the context of an established shop steward organization and a severe product market crisis. Yet reform failed to secure its promised end of increased productivity and greater predictability on the shopfloor (see also Bélanger, 1987, for detailed discussion). At Herbert's, despite the much weaker position of the stewards, similar product market pressures and perceived problems of productivity led to very similar reform efforts. Their failure was, of course, bound up with wider changes affecting the company which ended in bankruptcy in 1974 and the intervention of the National Enterprise Board. But the logic of hurried reform in the context of a production crisis was the same. And at Longbridge the well-known attempts by BL management to introduce Measured Day Work met limited success. The 'influence of shop steward organization was [not] markedly reduced' and the structure of collective bargaining 'remained fragmented and conflict-prone' (Willman and Winch, 1985: 69).

Our case studies help to show the conditions under which reform affects the amount of conflict. At Presswork there was a steep rise in the incidence of strikes, but at Premier Metals there was little change. The latter result was due to two factors. The plant's internal wages structure was barely disturbed, and in contrast to other plants, where opposition to reform reflected a fear among section stewards that their power would be lost to union officials and committees operating at plant level, the centralization of the stewards' authority removed the fear of a loss of influence.

More subtly, the dynamics of managerial failure are highlighted. Several of the case studies suggest that managers did not really understand the shopfloor organizations with which they had to deal. There seems to have been a belief that the logic of reform would be accepted on the shopfloor by stewards and members alike. In some abstract sense stewards may well have believed that reform was necessary and desirable, but in their political circumstances they were, in view of the obvious reaction of the membership, often unable to endorse managerial logics even had they been willing to do so; and it is unlikely that much willingness was present, given that they themselves were suspicious both of managerial motives and managerial competence.

This point emerges particularly clearly in the Presswork and Premier Metals cases. In the former, managers had presided over a labour process governed more by the unpredictable exercise of power than by a regulated order. The history of shopfloor struggles did not predispose stewards to take managerial demands and promises very seriously. At Premier Metals, managerial efforts to respond to product market pressures by altering the nature of this order provoked a cycle of increasing distrust. Similar processes were at work in the very different environment of Herbert's. Management found it impossible to generate commitment to reform. The hurried nature of the reform process, together with increasingly obvious failures to invest in new products and to deal with competition from other firms, undermined managerial legitimacy.

This suggests that there were some common dynamics in the operation of job controls even though the actual circumstances differed greatly. There was a similarity of managerial response with Herbert's having problems with achieving reform and increasing productivity that were similar to those at Longbridge or Presswork. Some qualification to the picture of Herbert's presented by Tolliday (1986: 225) is thus needed. He writes of the absence of control and organization within the management structure and contrasts this with the workplace, 'the one area where Herbert's did keep firm control'. But what does this mean? For Tolliday it signifies an absence of challenges to management. But this should not be equated with control in the sense that managers were able to run the production process effectively. Two considerations enter here. First, when they came to reform the pay system they found that existing assumptions and traditions had a massive inertia, so that new systems could not be imposed by managerial *fiat*. Second, the managerial skills of co-ordinating production were lacking. Managers may have had control of the immediate effort bargain, but this did not mean that they were able to change the social organization of production as they wished, still less that they were in control of the technical aspects of workplace operation.

In general, then, job controls were not established against determined managerial opposition. They grew out of situations in which no one was 'in control'. They reflected and reinforced traditional unplanned ways of doing things. Managements were implicated in their origins and operation. Managerial efforts at reform did, however, affect the role of unions in the workplace, as the following section shows.

Unionization

The case studies provide ample confirmation of Tolliday's assertion that, by the end of the war, unionization in Midlands engineering, though certainly more developed than it had been in 1939, was still patchy and, in some cases, virtually non-existent. The 'shadow factories', such as the 'Aero' at Longbridge, stand out as exceptions, as does the craft union organization at Premier Metals, a union that had preserved its organization and discipline throughout the harsh years of the 1920s and early 1930s.

Two indices may be used to estimate 'unionization': union density and union organization. Regarding the former it is clear that developments were uneven and incomplete. None of the factories studied here had anything approaching 100 per cent membership by 1945; in some cases it was another 15 years before that figure was reached. However, it is on the second index that more substantial progress may be discerned. The war years had given the opportunity to most shopfloor unions in Midlands engineering to develop at least the basis of a shop steward structure. The wartime legal framework, the encouragement of collective bargaining and, perhaps most important, the Joint Production Committees, provided a clear and distinct shopfloor role for trade unions quite different from much that had gone before, even in the traditionally well-organized craft unions. The wartime period thus witnessed the emergence of a framework and rationale for union activity that was not necessarily dependent on high levels of union density and the exercise of direct collective worker pressure. The recognition of shopfloor trade unions, often only grudgingly extracted from hostile employers and managers, was a critical factor in the wartime development of union structures.

If the war imposed a degree of uniformity on managerial behaviour and thus encouraged broad similiarities in the patterns of workplace unionism, that was quickly to change after the war, as managements confronted the transition to peacetime production and a new set of market situations. For some companies, such as Austin, this meant a return to pre-war hostility to unionism as the company sought to recapture greater control over the processes of production and greater discretion in their handling of labour relations. In the case of the Standard Motor Company it meant a radically different approach, encouraging both union membership and steward organization as elements in a novel approach to production. Other companies, by contrast, not as hostile as Austin, nor as bold as Standard, were uncertain how to respond to the new environment. Reluctant to attack unions directly, managers in such companies responded to steward organizations either with a mix of uncertainty and ambiguity, or by pretending that they did not exist.

In the case of Standard a direct link can be established between the company's production and industrial relations priorities. Nearly two decades later the management at Presswork appear to have behaved similarly, at least in so far as they perceived (wrongly) that an enhancement of steward authority might ease the production problems. Other cases suggest caution in inferring that policies towards stewards are necessarily rooted in the production strategies of the company. In the cases of Austin and Herbert's, for example, company policy appears to have been informed more by a deep-rooted ideological dislike among senior managers of semiskilled trade unions. Indeed, we suggest towards the end of this chapter that a more explicit consideration of production priorities in the case of companies like Austin might have led them to rather different industrial relations policies. In yet other cases, such as Coventry Precision, with long-standing commitments to 'good personnel practice', there does appear to be some validity to the suggestion that industrial relations policies were developed independently of other considerations, to conform to some notion of 'good industrial relations' — although of course in a context where there was no managerial perception of any union-based hindrances to production. Thus, while the processes of production and managerial policies across a range of issues necessarily provide an environment that informs the development of union organization, it was only rarely that the relationships were explicit. In most cases there was considerable scope for workers to influence the nature of the organizations they were creating.

In all cases except Standard, however, the ending of the war led to fresh problems for steward organizations. Paramount among these was the need to build and strengthen membership as the protection provided by wartime controls was lost. Key to this process in many factories were a handful of activists and, for the TGWU at least, a full-time official, Jack Jones. It now appears that the role of these officials was crucial to shopfloor organization in many of the car companies, at least until the late 1950s (see also Jones, 1986: 128—47). The case studies support an 'activist' approach to union organization, while at the same time refuting an 'agitator' analysis of industrial action. The need to restate this point, self-evident to many practitioners, is testimony to the extent that in a desire to refute Cold War allegations of Communist agitation, academic analyses for many years shrank from acknowledging the importance of activists. Our case studies give no indication of Communist Party influence; Jefferys acknowledges its wartime importance but mentions it no further, thus indirectly supporting Hinton's contention (based on experiences in Coventry) that CP influence fell sharply after 1944 (Hinton, 1980: 106).

Many of the activists were neither skilled nor craft workers. It was not only some employers who wished to return to pre-war practices in 1945; several of the established craft unions showed, at most, scant enthusiasm for, and occasionally outright hostility towards, the continued organization of semi and unskilled workers. In its most extreme form the tradition of craft exclusivity can be seen at Premier, but that was in many ways a rarity. More common appears to have been the pattern of indifference towards an extension of union organization among minority groups of skilled and craft workers. Short-sighted as this might now appear, and whatever its damaging consequences for union unity, it was almost inevitable. For, as Scullion and Edwards make clear, the strength of those unions was based on controlling the craft and entry to it; to have opened the doors to non-craft workers would have weakened this control — and the shopfloor discipline it engendered.

For the craft unions as for employers a return to the *status quo ante* was impracticable. Not only had workers and stewards built new forms of organization; they had also come to believe that union membership should be the norm for all workers, not just the elite. In this context, craft union indifference acted as a stimulus to other activists, at Coventry Precision in the late 1940s, and at Herbert as much as two decades later. Several of the case studies identify a moment at which action (or inaction) by craft unions goaded their less skilled colleagues into action. But, as Scullion and Edwards argue (p. 144 this volume), such workers only rarely sought to emulate craft practices; more often, as the case studies here demonstrate 'semiskilled workers operated without reference to craftsmen and developed their own forms of . . . union organization'. This is not to say that efforts were not made to ape craft structures. One clear parallel would be the development of the closed shop and attempts to control recruitment by semiskilled workers. There is no evidence of general success in controlling the labour market in this way, although there is clear evidence of successful union pressure in at least three of the cases to block the recruitment of black workers, women and young workers, although these moves appear, regrettably, to owe more to the prejudices of the white male workforce than to any obvious trade union logic.

Union activists worked to obtain and maintain organization in an environment reflecting managerial attitudes ranging from indifference to hostility, and craft union antipathy. Assets included market conditions that at least occasionally put such workers in a relatively strong bargaining position (e.g. Tolliday, 1986:

227—8), a drive for production that forced supervisory-level managers to make concessions, and, what cannot be quantified but emerges from several of the studies, a general workforce predisposition to join a trade union if the opportunity was available. In this context it is worth noting that both Salmon, and Scullion and Edwards reject a simple association between the existence of strong steward organization and high wages. As the former notes, at least for Coventry, wage increases owed more to labour market conditions and employer policy than to union activity. It is difficult to sustain a view, popular in more recent years, that a key component in workers' predisposition to join trade unions was a perception of short-term wage increases.

Problems in building up organization were reinforced by having to live in an environment complicated by managerial ambivalence towards trade unions. This was shown, for example, in an ability to combine accommodation with craft organization with outright hostility to other unions, as at Herbert's, or a total hostility to unions at employer and top management levels combined with a pragmatic acceptance of their existence among supervisors, as at Longbridge. While in some cases, such as Coventry Precision, a degree of consistency in managerial approaches to trade unions over a long period could be discerned, in other companies this was reached only during the period of reform in the late 1960s and early 1970s.

But during the 1950s and 1960s, within a general, albeit uneven, trend to growth, the organizational forms adopted by shopfloor unions, especially those of semi and unskilled workers, showed wide variations. In factories where managements were hostile, unions tended to grow 'from below', almost clandestinely, and their growth reflected variations in sectional responses. In such cases, and Presswork is a clear example, the resultant structure gave sovereignty to the sections. In Coventry Precision, by contrast, a combination of early circumstances led the stewards and members to adopt a formal constitution that emphasized convenor authority and diminished sectional autonomy. In all cases the particular mixture of central steward authority, tight membership discipline and practice of direct democracy that was part of the craft tradition was absent, largely because the mechanism for such discpline — control of the craft through the pre-entry closed shop — was missing. For the non-craft unions that particular mix was unavailable; for them the choice was between direct democracy, which implied sectional autonomy, and central (convenor) authority and reduced membership participation in union affairs. The membership homogeneity tied up in the notion of 'craft' and the egalitarian union structures and objectives that resulted, were unlikely to be freely created by a more heterogeneous membership with strong sectional loyalties. Even in allegedly multi-union joint shop stewards' committees, such as that at Presswork, craft unions insisted on their autonomy of action. It might be concluded that 'direct democray' is difficult to put into practice at any level of organization of semiskilled workers higher than that of the section. A combination of factors including size, occupational heterogeneity and related competing interests, and the lack of a material basis of internal union discipline, all mitigate against it. Some

form of representative democracy is therefore likely to be espoused by semiskilled stewards looking to build organization across the plant or the company.

The ability of union activists to impose a degree of centralized control under
these circumstances was related to two sets of factors: the resources available
to convenors to underpin their central authority, and the interest shown by
managers in assisting the development of such centralization, usually for reasons
connected with dominant production priorities.[2] Clearly these two were inter-
related, with certain convenor resources (time off, office facilities, etc.) often
provided by management, while others (tenure in office, political ability and,
crucially, the preparedness of workers to offset stewards' loss of earnings)
reflected stewards' individual or collective talents and choices and the
preferences of the membership.

Convenors and senior stewards frequently worked towards the development
of plant- and company-wide organizations, for which there were strong
arguments within the logic of trade unionism. But it is clear that some senior
activists, especially those at Presswork, were frustrated in their attempts to build
such organization in the face of sectional autonomy and managerial indifference.
Semiskilled unions at the workplace appeared to find it difficult to overcome
such obstacles without at least some external intervention; they lacked the
internal disciplinary sanctions available to craft unions. But the trade union interest of such activists could combine with managerial interests of securing
greater order and productive stability into a consensus on the need for more centralized shop steward structures. Such appears to have been the case during the
post-Donovan period of reform. As Bélanger and Evans make clear, the reforms
were greeted more keenly by stewards, and especially the senior stewards and
convenors, than by managers, since the changes appeared to open the way to
factory-wide organization long denied by sectional autonomy.

This last finding combines with others to refute apparently naive statements
of the thesis of shop steward 'bureaucratization', if by this we mean the development of central authority, the growth of formalization and the disappearance of
'direct democracy'. First, as is clear from both Coventry Precision and
Standard, the existence of formal steward structures with centralized convenor
and steward authority was by no means an invention of the 1960s. Second, as
has been suggested above, there is a clear trade union logic pushing in such a
direction. Comparisons with the 'direct democracy' of craft trade unions are
misleading, as they understate the degree of formalization within such structures
and they misunderstand the different material bases of organization in non-craft,
heterogeneous groups.

The few accounts that take us beyond the period of reform confirm previous
analyses in suggesting that stewards' gains from the process through an enhancement of their authority were often partial or short-lived. At Presswork they
strengthened the convenor's central authority, but even then the dayworkers and
craft groups remained on the outside. At BL the reforms appear to have contributed to the isolation of the senior stewards and their consequent weakening,
although, arguably, that owed more to developments in the wider political arena.

As both accounts make clear, managerial interest was in using convenor authority to restore order on the shopfloor in a period of production crises. Their failure
owes at least something to a misunderstanding of the relationship between convenor and steward authority, and the development of job controls on the
shopfloor. As Bélanger and Evans argue forcefully, there is a highly ambiguous
relationship between work groups and shop stewards, and this ambiguity is more
pronounced for semiskilled workers than for craft workers, for whom job control is a central aspect of their craft tradition. In a situation where convenors
have little or nothing to do with the formation of job controls it is not surprising
that attempts to weaken shopfloor job controls by enhancing convenor authority
rarely worked. It is equally noteworthy that in factories such as Coventry Precision, with long-established traditions of central convenor authority, and structures that anticipated Donovan norms of formalization by several decades,
shopfloor job controls were rarely an issue.

Job Controls and Productivity

The previous section developed the argument of the first section concerning
management, to suggest that attempts to reform shopfloor relations and thus to
raise productivity were often insufficiently developed to have the desired effect.
We can now go further by looking directly at productivity.

It is widely argued that the importance of strikes and restrictive practices has
been grossly exaggerated (Hyman and Elger, 1981; Williams *et al.*, 1983).
Tolliday (1986: 232) concludes that

> It is becoming increasingly apparent that the long-run decline of the British
> motor industry was due not to strike-proneness, excessive earnings and
> low productivity, but a failure to produce the right models for the right
> markets at the right time. . . . Broader managerial failures outweighed the
> rather overstated adverse effects of shop floor bargaining.

Those case studies that contain information on productivity, or permit reasonable inferences about it, support much of this argument. At Herbert's, restrictive
practices were conspicuous by their absence. Even at Premier Metals extensive
craft controls did not lead to rigid or static 'restrictive practices' and could contribute to productivity, both through their restraining of 'disorder' and through
the self-discipline and standards of workmanship that a craft tradition promoted.
There is also information on managerial behaviour away from the shopfloor.
Herbert's, as Tolliday makes clear, is again a particularly clear case, with a very
conservative approach to produce design and marketing, making the firm less
and less able to compete with foreign competitiors. Similar forces seem to have
been at work at 'Presswork', with efforts to develop new product lines founder-
ing and with the firm staggering from crisis to crisis.

It is less clear, however, that shopfloor relations escape all responsibility. By
shopfloor relations we do not mean specific constraints on management: the

evidence that such arrangements cannot, in and of themselves, have significantly restrained productivity is overwhelming. We mean, rather, the whole way of conducting the work process: the understandings, assumptions, and customs that create expectations about how work should be performed. The above case studies, and other evidence, suggest that British managements have tended to adopt a piecemeal approach, with little by way of strategic thinking. When reforms have been attempted, they have come too late, have lacked the managerial resources to make them effective, and have often worsened the lack of trust that they have tried to remedy. As Elbaum and Lazonick (1986: 2) argue, Britain's industrial development has been constrained by 'entrenched institutional structures' embracing enterprise and market relations and links between the state and business as well as industrial relations. These structures should be seen as connected and mutually reinforcing. It was not job controls as such but the wider system of regulation of which they were part which was important.

A similar point stems from the comparison of British and US shopfloor relations. The conventional wisdom argues that shop steward organization in Britain constrained managerial freedom much more than did the system of formal contracts in the United States. Tolliday and Zeitlin (1982) question this, and suggest that in many respects US firms were more limited in their powers than were British ones over much of the post-war period. This argument has been assessed in detail elsewhere (Edwards, 1986: 185–92). For present purposes all that needs stressing is that the authors tend to see shopfloor relations in stark terms, as though there was or was not control of everything. Yet they remark at one point that the situation in Britain in the 1950s was not one in which 'management exercised effective control over the workplace' (p. 11), for foremen made concessions to workers in order to secure continuity of production. This pattern could characterize plants with weak steward organizations as well as strongly-organized factories. It may be suggested that, although detailed written contracts limited the freedom of managements in the United States to act autocratically, they did not interfere with, and often assisted, the pursuit of production by specifying workers' obligations. They were part of a clear policy of establishing shopfloor order and managerial rights. In Britain, by contrast, the 1950s was a period of drift. Shop steward organizations may not have been very powerful, but this does not mean that managers were firmly in command of the production process.

It is, then, unsatisfactory to conclude that relations within the workplace had nothing to do with a firm's competitive position. A managerial approach of relying on past methods and taking a short time-horizon arguably characterized shopfloor relations as much as commercial policy. As time went on, moreover, the consequences of this approach became more and more difficult to escape. Shopfloor organizations either became confirmed in their traditions, as at Premier, or grew up to exploit the weaknesses of managerial control of piecework, as in the (probably more common) case of Presswork. The result was that managements found it very hard to institute reforms just when these became most pressing. Shopfloor relations may not have caused their crisis but they certainly made it difficult to manage a way out of the crisis successfully.

This is not, of course, to argue that only the shopfloor workers were to blame. If blame is to be attached it is to the system of shopfloor relations that had grown up. This was not the deliberate creation of either party but was the unintended consequence of their past relationships. Shopfloor relations have played a part in Britain's poor productivity record, but their role has been complex. It may not even be possible to establish their importance relative to other factors for, apart from formidable problems of evidence, they and managerial behaviour elsewhere are intimately connected and are not independent influences.

As argued above, the distinctive forms of job control which emerged in the post-war period had parallels with earlier traditions and developed logics which were hard to change. They were, however, the product of a long series of decisions. Was the eventual result of the collapse of many firms inevitable, or can an alternative path of development be identified?

Alternative Possibilities

Numerous historical studies show that British firms have, in contrast to their US counterparts, failed to institute new technologies and new forms of control, in part at least because of workers' shopfloor power (Lazonick, 1979, 1981; Elbaum and Wilkinson, 1979). But there is the danger of implying that decline was inevitable. Thus Elbaum and Lazonick (1986: 2, 14) 'attribute the decline of the British economy in the twentieth century to rigidities in the economic and social institutions that developed during the nineteenth century' and argue that the post-1945 economy 'inherited a legacy of major industries too troubled to survive the renewed onslaught of international competition'. Lewchuk (1986), focusing on the car industry, sees Fordism as the model which British firms failed to emulate and at one point speaks of a 'belated' transition to Fordism which was 'necessary' to reduce workers' control of the pace of work (p. 150).

This approach has three difficulties. First, use of the term 'rigidity' can suggest that the solution is to remove the sources of rigidity so that markets can work. This would be to run counter to other arguments presented by Elbaum and Lazonick, namely that Britain has been dominated by short-term market approaches compared with the longer-term institutional planning of Western Germany or Japan. On this argument, it is not institutional rigidity that is the problem but the wrong kind of institution. Second, the roots of industrial decline are located deep in the past, as though there could be no escape from historical legacies; yet surely the car industry in 1945 was not pre-ordained to develop as it did. Finally, the argument approaches to the model of the ideal capitalist and of one set of changes that were necessary: if only British capitalists had been determined and foresighted they could have been like their counterparts in the United States.

What British capitalists needed was not a model based on what was being done under quite different circumstances in the United States or Western Germany but a practical means of building on existing traditions. We cannot comment on all aspects of this, but can offer some speculation on the role of craft traditions in the workplace. Although such a tradition in the strict sense has been rare, the assumptions on which it is based, namely the independence of workers and a reliance on custom, has been widespread.

The 'positive' aspects of craft controls are well known. They include the provision of a skilled labour force at little cost, a commitment to standards of craftsmanship, and the promotion of self-discipline among groups of workers (see Allen, 1984). Some of these have important similarities with currently fashionable ideas of autonomous workgroups and giving workers responsiblity for quality control. There are equally obvious differences. Craft controls are not managerially inspired devices. Workers' loyalty is to the craft and not to the firm. And the whole climate is different: craft workers retain their pride and independence, whereas workers given autonomy by firms are often enmeshed in a structure in which business needs are paramount and they have little or no discretion in the deployment of their abilities. They are, in short, more fully subordinate to the demands of managers.

But the similarities are worth stressing. Analytically, both situations are forms of what Friedman (1977) calls 'responsible autonomy' wherein management tries to use the creative potential of workers instead of constraining and controlling them, using what he calls a direct control strategy. It is possible to argue that what British management needed was not a model of deskilling and rationalization but a means of developing the potentials of responsible autonomy that existed within the craft tradition. As it in fact developed, the tradition came to reflect an increasingly conflictual mode of shopfloor relations.

At Premier, even when the craft system was in place, workers were treated simply as people hired to do a job: they entered the factory in the morning and left at night, and that was that. There was no attempt to treat them as a part of the firm or to build on their traditions of workmanship by involving them in the design of products or other aspects of the firm's activities. Attempts to reform industrial relations led to a cycle of distrust that heightened perceptions of distance between managers and workers.

What would have been required to develop the rather limited 'relative autonomy' of craft production into a system that permitted flexibility instead of encouraging a defence of tradition? At least four major changes would have been needed in the managerial conduct of industrial relations, and there were two other issues, relating to the wider operation of the business and to the role of the state, that would also have needed attention. We begin with the industrial relations issues, then turn briefly to what would have been needed from the union, before looking at the wider questions and considering whether the changes we identify had any prospect of success.

Management would, first, need to have looked at payment systems. Piecework encouraged a focus on the price of the immediate job and led to sectionalism and frequent effort bargaining. Some form of bonus related to the production of a whole factory might have preserved incentives while encouraging a broader identification with the ends of the business as a whole. Second, the stewards' informal role in production organization needed recognition and formalization. The model of wartime joint production committees could have been useful in building on workers' productivist concerns to enable firms to develop joint approaches not only to day-to-day matters but also on the planning of future labour needs and investment policy. As the Premier case study indicates, stewards could have a deep interest in these matters, and some influence over labour needs developed as the earnings ceiling and overtime were manipulated. But this was part of a conflictual relationship with mangement, as stewards tried to assert their own interests, and not a joint planning arrangement. This issue is closely linked with the third, namely job security. As Salmon points out, Ford, in contast to the Midlands car firms, was making some effort to reduce workers' vulnerability to market fluctuations. To have developed any sense of trust among their workers, the Midlands firms would have needed to move even further in this direction. Finally, the role of foremen needed attention. At Premier, their authority was negligible and their ability to organize production correspondingly weak. Considerable training and reorganization would have been needed.

These four areas are closely connected. Giving workers more job security, for example, might have made them more willing to participate in labour planning, which would in turn have assisted the performance of the firm, thereby further enhancing job security. In his analysis of the West German car industry Streeck (1986) has argued that something very similar to this had emerged there. West German firms are in many ways more constrained than their British counterparts in that they cannot, for example, declare redundancies or lay off workers at will; and, despite the common view that unions are weak at shopfloor level, unions, together with the works councils, have several ways of making life difficult for managers. High productivity and an acceptance of change have been created not by untrammelled managerial power but by managements' treating constraints as opportunities. Because, for example, they have not been able to rely on a hire and fire policy they have had to plan labour requirements and also to develop appropriate production strategies, notably by shifting to high value-added products. Gaining secure markets has further contributed to the ability to plan industrial relations on a long-term basis. There are obviously unique features of the West German case, but they should not be used as an excuse for British failures. In the 1950s British manufacturing had many strengths, and it was not until 1958 that Western Germany's share of world exports of manufactures overtook that of Britain (Williams *et al.*, 1983: 116). A British route to a high productivity system of industrial relations was in principle feasible.

Change would have been required from the unions too. Mobility between trades would have had to be granted permanently instead of being a concession that the unions could withdraw, and flexibility across the inter-union demarcation line would have been needed. Since it was generally recognized that this demarcation was illogical, there was nothing in principle to prevent unions from agreeing to its dismantling. What in fact prevented them from doing so was a profound distrust of management, and not a belief in the demarcation for its own sake. Recruitment through union offices could have been retained, although the right of unions unilaterally to ban recruitment would have had to be ceded. It could have been replaced with a planning system in which managers and stewards jointly assessed likely demand, and consequent labour needs, and developed a manpower plan accordingly. The earnings ceiling could have been replaced with guarantees of job security and bonuses linked to company performance.

Some rather different issues would have been raised in areas where the craft system was not entrenched. But the principles are similar. Managements needed to abandon their insistence on the right to manage and their reliance on a philosophy of hire-and-fire. There were alternatives available, but, apart from the need for a radical transformation in approaches to industrial relations, wider issues also discouraged the search for a new model.

One of these was the internal organization of the firms. As Williams *et al.* (1983) and Lewchuk (1986) demonstrate, British car firms were small and fragmented, and the merger of Austin and Morris in 1952 failed to produce any real rationalization of production. Short-term approaches were thus encouraged. Added to this was a reliance on a low level of investment. In the short run it was possible to make adequate profits, but firms were sowing the seeds of their own downfall as they became increasingly unable to respond to new innovations. As Armstrong (1984: 102–5) has noted, moreover, accountants have had a particularly important role in British firms, and this has heightened a short-term focus; the contrast with the greater role of engineers in West Germany, for example, is striking and often remarked. This is not the place to speculate on the consequences of such facts. But they underline the point that change on the shopfloor would have required a wider change in managerial organization. Once the process was under way, it would have been self-reinforcing as new policies on marketing, investment, and production organization interacted with new labour policies.

Firms themselves had little incentive to make such change. Perhaps crucial was the second external influence, the state. As Tolliday (1985: 109–21) shows, during the war and under the Labour Government of 1945–51 the state powerfully influenced labour relations in the car firms. But this had more to do with seeking a workable compromise given the exigencies of the war and subsequent attempts to boost exports than with thorough-going rationalization. No significant pressure seems to have been placed on firms to modify their anti-unionism, for example. The changes outlined above were, in principle, feasible. For these changes to have had any chance of success some external pressures on employers would have been required. As Salmon in particular shows, the Midlands car firms were resolute in insisting on the sole right to determine redundancy issues. This approach, which laid much of the basis of the subsequent highly conflictual nature of workplace relations, was plainly not undermined by shop stewards. It needed authoritative pressure from the state.

Perhaps there was a period during the 1940s when a radical, modernizing Labour Government could have pressed through some of these changes. On the shopfloor, traditions of wartime planning must have retained some salience. As several contributions in this volume suggest, there was no massive loyalty to monolithic restrictive practices. Certainly, reform effects during the 1960s met with suspicion strengthened by twenty years of consolidation of job controls. Certain habits of mind had become deeply entrenched. It is also true that, even though lacking union organization, many workers had a deep-rooted tradition of independence from the employer. But the tradition was not immune to change, and it was not pre-ordained that sectionalism and narrow disputes over the effort bargain should follow. The possibility existed that a different path of development could have been followed.

A 'historical moment' in 1945 should not be idealized. As Croucher (1982: 325–56) has shown, there were many problems in translating wartime planning into a peacetime environment. On the key issues of keeping the 'shadow factories' in public ownership and resisting redundancies, it was hard for shop stewards to develop campaigns, since it was difficult for them to challenge a government with a set policy, and since they could claim to speak for only their members' interests and not the national interest. Added to this was the great difficulty of mobilizing members, many of whom wanted to leave war factories as rapidly as possible. The managerial interest in 'returning to normality' and the absence of a government policy which challenged this interest on such crucial issues as the future of the shadow factories have been noted above.

A modernized craft system was not, then, a strong possibility. But an objection might be that, even in its own terms, it is incoherent. Did not Standard try something similar and fail? Melman (1958) saw Standard's policy of high wages and ceding a large degree of control to the stewards as a prototype for joint regulation and positive sum industrial relations. The many subsequent criticisms fall into two types. First, the firm was unable to gain a large enough market share to survive in an increasingly competitive environment: the labour peace of the late 1940s and early 1950s was an exceptional interlude. Second, the firm may have been buying industrial peace; as Turner et al. (1967: 98) comment acidly, there was evidence of 'management's abdication from control of shopfloor working arrangements'. This meant that stewards were not really brought into the running of the firm: as Salmon demonstrates, the firm adopted a tough line on redundancy, and the stewards' much-vaunted power was unable to do anything about this.

On the first point about market conditions, the weakness of the Standard approach is plain. The present model assumes, instead, a developed marketing strategy. It is not really a model for an individual firm in isolation but is instead a picture of how engineering as a whole might have progressed. As for the internal operation of industrial relations, the present model does not propose an abdication of authority. It suggests, instead, that firms could have tried to foster joint responsibility. This has two ramifications: taking a view of shopfloor relations and refusing to abdicate responsibility, but also the involvement of stewards in planning and trying to develop long-term labour and production policies. Instead of allowing stewards to look only to their own gangs, firms would have had to involve stewards in the firm, and stewards would have had to accept the responsibility as well as the benefits that this brought.

Finally, we should stress that we do not equate this 'alternative model' with current proposals for resurrecting craft ideas. Piore (1986) has argued that a reformulated craft model is necessary in the United States, citing as illustrations the textile and building industries where unions and employers have co-operated in introducing technical change and economic planning. This argument draws on his wider suggestions that new forms of work organization permit 'flexible specialization', involving small production units and workers with craft-like skills; the historical model used as a basis here is the small workshop using craft workers (Piore and Sabel, 1984).

As we will suggest below, our reading of current developments is that there is certainly pressure for flexibility but that this stems not from small firms but from large and increasingly internationalized bodies of capital; and the nature of flexibility is not the autonomous exercise of workers' skills but involves the deployment of specific task abilities under the overall direction of management: genuine autonomy has decreased (Shaiken *et al*. 1986). As Turnbull (1988: 14) argues in his study of the introduction of Japanese management techniques,

> the function of teamworking, job flexibility and the like has been to re-define the level of work effort and customary levels of active co-operation on the job. These practices not only complement attempts to intensify work by encouraging workers to internalise the company goals of efficiency and quality, they also help to marginalise the role of union representatives at the workplace.

A craft-based model of development is not an expression of flexibility within a work organization planned by managerial *diktat* under the coercive pressures of market competition but is a statement of how this result might have been avoided.

Although not a realistic possibility, the 'alternative' suggested here indicates what a workable model of shopfloor industrial relations might have looked like. Of course it would have been difficult to use, and it would not doubt have produced problems of its own, but there is no reason to assume that the destruction of craft and non-craft jobs that has taken place over the past few years was inevitable. British workers' traditions had strong elements of a productivist ethos. The tragedy is not that 'restrictive practices' have prevented an otherwise vigorous management from modernizing the workplace but that managements and workers alike have been locked into narrow struggles and perspectives. Other possibilities existed. These are as important in assessing the present as they are in analysing the past.

The Past and Future of Shopfloor Bargaining

One reading of this book is that it is of merely historical interest: the massive changes that have taken place during the 1980s have surely rendered obsolete many of the practices that we have considered. Over and above any defence of historical analysis in its own right, this argument is open to criticism. It is always tempting to view current developments as radical departures from everything that has gone before. Yet, as noted above, British workplace industrial relations have been shaped, perhaps more powerfully than those of any other country, by the past. It would be surprising if the tradition of effort bargaining at the point of production were to be eradicated. Circumstances plainly change, and it would be as incorrect to see the future as a repeat of the past as to assume that there are no connections with it. The problem is to try to assess the impact of some complex changes on the pattern of bargaining.

On the one hand, it is now well-established that direct atttacks on shop steward organizations have been rare (Batstone, 1984; Millward and Stevens, 1986). Stewards continue to be present in much of British industry. On the other hand, many changes seem to have reduced their role. Most obviously, plants with strong organizations have closed. Others have experienced sharp falls in employment, and the state of the labour and product markets has reduced the bargaining power of stewards. Internal changes have also reduced the significance of traditional bargaining practices. Several firms have tried to eliminate demarcation lines between trades, thus reducing shopfloor control of job allocation. Attempts have also been made to reassert managerial authority more generally. Although some reform efforts of the 1970s were partial and met with little success, it is widely argued that in the harsher climate of the 1980s managements have pressed through changes in working practices and that workers have had little alternative to going along with them, the alternative being the loss of jobs.

Some writers are confident that shop stewards continue to play an important role. Batstone and Gourlay (1986: 149) conclude from their survey of shop stewards that 'the range of bargaining remains remarkably high' and that the 'majority of respondents believed that the union continued to have a significant degree of influence over management'. Against this must be set Millward and Stevens's (1986: 251) analysis of the views of managerial respondents to the 1984 Workplace Industrial Relations Survey on the range of negotiation: 'so far as manual workers were concerned, there appeared to be substantially less negotiation over non-pay issues in 1984 [than in 1980] and the contrast was particularly marked at the workplace level'. Tolliday (1986: 238) argues that sectional bargaining has been replaced not by the destruction of steward organizations but by the institutionalization of powerful convenors. The 'scope of bargaining has often widened', although at the cost of the responsiveness of steward organizations to the members. On such a view, the range of issues bargained may have stayed the same or even increased, but its nature has changed.

As argued elsewhere (Terry, 1986), there is much to commend the latter view. Observable characteristics such as the number of stewards or the frequency of strikes do not bear directly on questions of power. There is a great deal of evidence that managements have made significant changes in work organization and that shop stewards are less assertive and autonomous than they once were.

Case studies of three companies, two of which were not in engineering, support this argument (Terry, forthcoming).

The position of some of the factories considered above is clear. The closure of Herbert's and Premier Metals and the sale of Presswork meant that the steward organizations had no continuity. Longbridge has been the subject of a barrage of comment about alleged productivity miracles and the destruction of shop steward power, as symbolized by the sacking of the convenor, Derek Robinson, in 1979. From their study of Longbridge, Willman and Winch (1985: 181) conclude that 'shop stewards in BL have lost almost all of the control they once possessed over the effort bargain'. But they also point out that the company has been seeking very high levels of productivity without the job security that accompanies it, in Japan, for example. It is thus possible that, although currently weakened, stewards will have sufficient institutional resources to challenge management, particularly if grievances about job security and similar issues begin to develop on the shopfloor and if growing profitability gives workers enough confidence to begin to assert their demands.

Changes in payment systems and the technical organization of work mean that old forms of custom and practice have been squeezed. In those companies which have taken the language of motivation and commitment seriously, it may even be that a system of order is created in which managerial logics are accepted and an individualized attachment is generated. Two major questions remain, however: how committed are British managements to such development, and how far-reaching are they? Those firms which adopt the language of 'human resource management' half-heartedly may well leave spaces in which discontents grow and in which steward organizations can find a continued rationale. It would be a naive management which neglected the lessons of the past analysed above.

Three lessons in particular stand out. First, managerial approaches to labour relations can often be *ad hoc* and inconsistent, the result being a failure to develop an integrated approach to shopfloor management. In this environment of uncertainty and, sometimes, overt threat, workers have had good reason to turn to shop stewards. To the extent that distrust, uncertainty, and differences of interest continue to shape the shopfloor, the material basis for independent worker organizations remains. Second, the craft tradition contained some powerful productivist elements. Third, initiating new forms of commitment is an expensive task, as resources have to be devoted to communication and training programmes, and also raises the problem of creating resentment and distrust. Although disinclined to do so, British managements might well gain by considering the sources of shopfloor order and pride in workmanship to be found in long-established traditions.

Steward organizations, whatever their weaknesses and limitations, were means of articulating members' interests and of promoting democracy on the shopfloor, not in the narrow sense of holding ballots but by giving workers some say in the decisions that affected their daily lives. The need for bodies to perform this function is as pressing now as it ever was.

Notes

1. Friedman (1977) has attracted particularly heavy criticism. Although it is true that he tends to simplify the history of post-war workplace relations and to interpret managerial behaviour too directly from product market conditions, his analytical framework has been dismissed too readily. The idea that there are two basic control strategies, direct control and responsible autonomy, and that firms can combine elements of both is a valuable insight. As Friedman (1987a, 1987b) has argued in defending his position, concrete management policy is likely to contain aspects of the two strategies, which were never intended to be seen as opposites.
2. A third, not really dealt with in this volume, concerns the narrowing of the 'skill gap' between skilled and other workers. It could be argued that at Coventry Precision, perhaps the best case of co-operation between skilled and others, workers performed jobs considered to be skilled regardless of their official classification. In other cases, a coming together of unions might have reflected a reduction in the autonomy of craft unions as their craft-based bargaining power was eroded by the introduction of new technology.

Bibliography

Aldcroft, D.H. 1966, 'The Performance of the Machine Tool Industry in the Inter-war Years'. *Business History Review*. 11, Autumn, 281–96.

Alexander, K.J.W., and C.L. Jenkins. 1970. *Fairfields*. London: Allen Lane.

Allen, S.G. 1984. 'Unionized Construction Workers are More Productive'. *Quarterly Journal of Economics*, 99, May, 251–74.

Armstrong, P. 1984. 'Competition between Organizational Professions and the Evolution of Management Control Strategies'. In Kenneth Thompson (ed.), *Work, Employment and Unemployment*. Milton Keynes: Open University Press.

____ and J. Goodman. 1979. 'Managerial and Supervisory Custom and Practice'. *Industrial Relations Journal*, 10, Autumn, 12–24.

____, J.F.B. Goodman, and J.D. Hyman. 1981. *Ideology and Shop Floor Industrial Relations*. London: Croom Helm.

Bain, G.S., and R.J. Price. 1983. 'Union Growth, Dimensions, Determinants and Destiny'. In G.S. Bain (ed.), *Industrial Relations in Britain*. Oxford: Blackwell.

Barou, N. 1947. *British Trade Unions*. London: Gollancz.

Batstone, E. 1984. *Working Order*. Oxford: Blackwell.

____ and S. Gourlay. 1986. *Unions, Unemployment and Innovation*. Oxford: Blackwell.

____, I. Boraston, and S. Frenkel. 1977. *Shop Stewards in Action*. Oxford: Blackwell.

____, I. Boraston, and S. Frenkel. 1978. *The Social Organization of Strikes*. Oxford: Blackwell.

Bélanger, J. 1985. 'Job Control and the Institutionalisation of Labour Relations in the Workplace: a Study of Two Engineering Firms in England'. PhD thesis, University of Warwick.

____. 1987. 'Job Control and Institutional Reform: a Case Study in British Engineering'. *Industrial Relations Journal*, 18, Spring, 50–62.

Beynon, H. 1973. *Working for Ford*. Harmondsworth: Penguin.

Brooks, D., and K. Singh. 1979. 'Pivots and Presents: Asian Brokers in a British Foundry'. In S. Wallman (ed.), *Ethnicity at Work*. London: Macmillan.

Brown, W. 1973. *Piecework Bargaining*. London: Heinemann.

____ (ed.). 1981. *The Changing Contours of British Industrial Relations*. Oxford: Blackwell.

Burawoy, M. 1979. *Manufacturing Consent: Changes in the Labor Process Under Monopoly Captialism*. Chicago: University of Chicago Press.

Burgess, R.G. 1984. *In the Field*. London: Allen & Unwin.

Chamberlain, N.W. 1948. *The Union Challenge to Management Control*. New York: Harper.

Clack, G. 1967. *Industrial Relations in a British Car Factory*. Cambridge: Cambridge University Press.

Clegg, H.A. 1972. *The System of Industrial Relations in Great Britain*. Oxford: Blackwell.

——, and R. Adams. 1957. *The Employers' Challenge*. Oxford: Blackwell.

——, A.J. Killick, and R. Adams. 1961. *Trade Union Officers*. Oxford: Blackwell.

Cliff, T. 1970. *The Employers' Offensive*. London: Pluto.

——, and C. Barker. 1966. *Incomes Policy, Legislation and Shop Stewards*. Harrow: London Industrial Shop Stewards Defence Committee.

Cockburn, C. 1983. *Brothers: Male Dominance and Technological Change*. London: Pluto.

Collins, H. 1950. *Trade Unions Today*. London: Frederick Muller.

Commission on Industrial Relations. 1970. *First General Report*. Report No 9, Cmnd. 4417. London: HMSO.

Coventry Workshop Institute for Workers' Control. 1979. *Crisis in Engineering*. Nottingham: IWA.

Cressey, P., J. Eldridge, and J. MacInnes. 1985. *Just Managing*. Milton Keynes: Open University Press.

Crossley, J.R. 1968. 'The Donovan Report: a Case Study in the Poverty of Historicism'. *British Journal of Industrial Relations*. November, 296–302.

Croucher, R. 1982. *Engineers at War, 1939–1945*. London: Merlin.

Daniel, W.W., and N. Millward. 1983. *Workplace Industrial Relations in Britain*. London: Heinemann.

Davies, J.M. 1986. 'A Twentieth Century Paternalist: Alfred Herbert and the Skilled Coventry Workman'. In B. Lancaster, and T. Mason (eds.), *Life and Labour in a Twentieth Century City: the Experience of Coventry*. Coventry: Cryfield Press.

Derber, M. 1955. *Labor-Management Relations at the Plant Level under Industry-wide Bargaining*. Illinois: University of Illinois.

Donovan, 1968. Royal Commission on Trade Unions and Employers' Associations. *Report*. Cmnd. 3623. London: HMSO.

Dubois, P. 1980. 'Niveaux de main-d'oeuvre et organisation du travail: étude de cas français et anglais'. *Sociologie du Travail*, Vol. 3, No. 3, 257–75.

Dunn, S., and J. Gennard. 1984. *The Closed Shop in British Industry*. London: Macmillan.

Dunnet, P.J. 1980. *The Decline of the British Motor Industry*. London: Croom Helm.

Edwardes, M. 1983. *Back from the Brink*. London: Pan.

Edwards, C., and E. Heery. 1985. 'The Incorporation of Workplace Trade Unionism? Evidence from the Coal Mining Industry'. *Sociology*, 19, August, 345–63.

Edwards, P.K. 1983a. 'The Pattern of Collective Industrial Action'. In G.S. Bain (ed.), *Industrial Relations in Britain*. Oxford: Blackwell.

——. 1983b. 'The Political Economy of Industrial Conflict: Britain and the United States'. *Economic and Industrial Democracy*, 4, November, 461–500.

——. 1986. *Conflict at Work*. Oxford: Blackwell.

____, and H. Scullion, 1982. *The Social Organization of Industrial Conflict: Control and Resistance in the Workplace*. Oxford: Blackwell.

Elbaum, B., and W. Lazonick. 1986. 'An Institutional Perspective on British Decline'. In B. Elbaum, and W. Lazonick (eds), *The Decline of the British Economy*. Oxford: Clarendon.

____, and F. Wilkinson. 1979. 'Industrial Relations and Uneven Development: A Comparative Study of the American and British Steel Industries'. *Cambridge Journal of Economics*, 3, September, 275—303.

England, B. 1950. *Trade Union Problems*. London: Labour Research Department.

England, J. 1981. 'Shop Stewards in Transport House: a Comment on the Incorporation of the Rank and File'. *Industrial Relations Journal*, 12, November, 16—29.

Evans, S. 1980. 'The Impact of Formalisation on Management Strategy and Worker Resistance: a Case Study'. MA thesis (Industrial Relations), University of Warwick.

Flanders, A. 1952. *Trade Unions*. London: Hutchinson.

____. 1964. *The Fawley Productivity Agreements*. London: Faber.

____. 1970. *Management and Unions*. London: Faber.

____, and H.A. Clegg (eds.). 1954. *The System of Industrial Relations in Great Britain*. Oxford: Blackwell.

Floud, R. 1976. *The British Machine Tool Industry, 1850—1914*. Cambridge: Cambridge University Press.

Fox, A. 1985. *History and Heritage*. London: Allen & Unwin.

____, and A. Flanders. 1970. 'Collective Bargaining: From Donovan to Durkheim'. In A. Flanders, *Management and Unions*. London: Faber.

Friedman, A.L. 1977. *Industry and Labour*. London: Macmillan.

____. 1987a. 'The Means of Management Control and Labour Process Theory: a Critical Note on Storey'. *Sociology*, 21, May, 287—94.

____. 1987b. 'Managerial Strategies, Activities, Techniques and Technology: Towards a Complex Theory of the Labour Process'. In D. Knights, and H. Willmott (eds.), *Labour Process Theory*. London: Macmillan.

Friedman, H., and S. Meredeen. 1980. *The Dynamics of Industrial Conflict*. London: Croom Helm.

Frow, E., and R. Frow. 1982. *Engineering Struggles*. Manchester: Working Class Movement Library.

Gallie, D. 1978. *In Search of the New Working Class*. Cambridge: Cambridge University Press.

Gardner, J. 1960. *Key Questions for Trade Unionists*. London: Lawrence & Wishart.

Glyn, A., and R. Sutcliffe. 1972. *British Capitalism, Workers and the Profits Squeeze*. Harmondsworth: Penguin.

Goodman, J.F.B., and T.G. Whittingham. 1973. *Shop Stewards*. London: Pan.

____, E.G.A. Armstrong, J.E. Davis, and A. Wagner. 1977. *Rule-Making and Industrial Peace*. London: Croom Helm.

Gospel, H. 1983. 'Managerial Strategies and Industrial Relations: an Introduction'. In H.F. Gospel, and C.R. Littler (eds.), *Managerial Strategies and Industrial Relations*. London: Heinemann.

Gouldner, A.W. 1955. *Wildcat Strike*. London: Routledge & Kegan Paul.

Government Social Survey. 1968. *Workplace Industrial Relations*. London: HMSO

Hannah, L. 1983. *The Rise of the Corporate Economy* (2nd edn). London: Methuen.

Hart, M. 1979. 'Why Bosses Love the Closed Shop'. *New Society*, 15 February, 352—4.

Hinton, J. 1980. 'Coventry Communism: a Study of Factory Politics in the Second World War'. *History Workshop*, 10, Autumn, 90–118.

Hyman, R. 1971. *Marxism and the Sociology of Trade Unionism*. London: Pluto.

——. 1972. *Disputes Procedures in Action*. London: Heinemann.

——. 1977. *Strikes*. 2nd edn. London: Fontana-Collins.

——. 1979. 'The Politics of Workplace Trade Unionism: Recent Tendencies and Some Problems for Theory'. *Capital and Class*, 8, Summer, 54–67.

——, and T. Elger. 1981. 'Job Controls, the Employers' Offensive and Alternative Strategies'. *Capital and Class*, 15, Autumn, 115–49.

Jackson, R.M. 1984. *The Formation of Craft Labor Markets*. Orlando: Academic Press.

Jefferys, S. 1986. *Management and Managed: Fifty Years of Crisis at Chrysler*. Cambridge: Cambridge University Press.

Jones, J. 1986. *Union Man*. London: Collins.

Kahn-Freund, O. 1979. *Labour Relations: Heritage and Adjustment*. Oxford: Oxford University Press.

Kilpatrick, A., and T. Lawson. 1980. 'On the Nature of Industrial Decline in the UK'. *Cambirdge Journal of Economics*, 4, March, 85–102.

Kuhn, J.W. 1961. *Bargaining in Grievance Settlement*. New York: Columbia University Press.

Lane, T. 1974. *The Union Makes Us Strong*. London: Arrow.

Lazonick, W.H. 1979. 'Industrial Relations and Technical Change: the Case of the Self-Acting Mule'. *Cambridge Journal of Economics*, 3, September, 231–62.

——. 1981. 'Production Relations, Labor Productivity and Choice of Technique: British and US Cotton Spinning'. *Journal of Economic History*, 41, September, 491–516.

Lewchuk, W. 1983. 'Fordism and British Motor Car Employers, 1896–1932'. In H.F. Gospel, and C.R. Littler (eds.), *Managerial Strategies and Industrial Relations*. London: Heinemann.

——. 1986. 'The Motor Vehicle Industry'. In B. Elbaum, and W. Lazonick (eds.), *The Decline of the British Economy*. Oxford: Clarendon.

Littler, C.R. 1982. *The Development of the Labour Process in Capitalist Societies*. London: Heinemann.

——, and G. Salaman. 1982. 'Bravermania and Beyond: Recent Theories of the Labour Process'. *Sociology*, 16, May, 251–69.

Lupton, T. 1963. *On the Shop Floor*. Oxford: Pergamon.

Lyddon, D. 1983 'Workplace Organisation in the British Car Industry'. *History Workshop*, 15, Spring, 129–40.

McCarthy, W.E.J. 1962. 'The Future of the Unions'. *Fabian Tract*, No 339. London: The Fabian Society.

——. 1964. *The Closed Shop in Britain*. Oxford: Blackwell.

——. 1966. *The Role of Shop Stewards in British Industrial Relations*. Research Paper 1, Royal Commission on Trade Unions and Employers' Associations. London: HMSO.

——, and S.R. Parker. 1968. *Shop Stewards and Workshop Relations*. Research Paper 10. Royal Commission on Trade Unions and Employers' Associations. London: HMSO.

Mann, M. 1973. *Consciousness and Action among the Western Working Class*. London: Macmillan.

Marsden, D., T. Morris, P. Willman, and S. Wood. 1985. *The Car Industry: Labour Relations and Industrial Adjustment*. London: Tavistock.

Marsh, A.I. 1963. *Managers and Shop Stewards*. London: IPM.

____. 1965. *Industrial Relations in Engineering*. Oxford: Pergamon.

____, and E.E. Coker, 1963. 'Shop Steward Organisation in the Engineering Industry'. *British Journal of Industrial Relations*, 1, June, 170–90.

Mathewson, S.B. 1969. *Restriction of Output among Unorganized Workers*. Carbondale: Southern Illinois University Press (original edition 1931).

Melman, S. 1958. *Decision-making and Productivity*. Oxford: Blackwell.

Millward, N., and M. Stevens. 1986. *British Workplace Industrial Relations 1980–1984*. Aldershot: Gower.

Monk. S. 1969. 'Communications in the Transport and General Workers' Union'. MA thesis (Industrial Relations), University of Warwick.

National Board for Prices and Incomes. 1968. *Payment by Results Systems*. Report 65, Cmnd. 3627. London: HMSO.

Parker, P.A.L., W.R. Hawes, and A.L. Lumb. 1971. *The Reform of Collective Bargaining at Plant and Company Level*. Department of Employment, Manpower Papers, No 5, London: HMSO.

Parker, S. 1974. *Workplace Industrial Relations, 1972*. London: HMSO.

____. 1975. *Workplace Industrial Relations, 1973*. London: HMSO.

Paulden, S., and W. Hawkins. 1969. *Whatever Happened at Fairfields?* London: Gower.

Piore, M. 1986. 'The Decline of Mass Production and Union Survival in the USA'. *Industrial Relations Journal*, 17, Autumn, 207–13.

____, and C.F. Sabel. 1984. *The Second Industrial Divide: Possibilities for Prosperity*. New York: Basic.

Price, R. 1982. 'Rethinking Labour History: the Importance of Work'. In J.E. Cronin, and R. Schneer (eds.), *Social Conflict and the Political Order in Modern Britain*. London: Croom Helm.

Purcell, J. 1981. *Good Industrial Relations: Theory and Practice*. London: Macmillan.

Rimmer, M. 1972. *Race and Industrial Conflict*. London: Heinemann.

Roberts, B.C. 1956. *Trade Union Government and Administration in Great Britain*. Cambridge, Mass.: Harvard University Press.

Rolt, L.T.C. 1962. *The Dowty Story*. London: Newman Neame.

Rose, M., and B. Jones. 1985. 'Managerial Strategy and Trade Union Responses in Work Reorganisation Schemes at Establishment Level'. In D. Knights, H. Willmott and D. Collinson (eds.), *Job Redesign*. Aldershot: Gower.

Roy, D. 1952. 'Quota Restriction and Goldbricking in a Machine Shop'. *American Journal of Sociology*, 57, March, 427–42.

____. 1954. 'Efficiency and "The Fix": Informal Intergroup Relations in a Piecework Machine Shop'. *American Journal of Sociology*, 60, November, 255–66.

____. 1970. 'The Study of Southern Labor Union Organizing Campaigns'. In R.W. Habenstein (ed.), *Pathways to Data*. Chicago: Aldine.

Royal Commission. 1967. *Restrictive Labour Practices*. Research Paper 4, Royal Commission on Trade Unions and Employers' Associations. London: HMSO.

Sayles, L.R. 1958. *Behaviour of Industrial Work Groups*. New York: Wiley.

Scarborough, H. 1986. 'The Politics of Technological Change at British Leyland'. In O. Jacobi, B. Jessop, H. Kastendiek, and M. Regini (eds.), *Technological Change, Rationalisation and Industrial Relations*. London: Croom Helm.

Schloss, D.F. 1892. *Methods of Industrial Remuneration*. London: Williams and Norgate.

Scullion, H. 1981. 'The Skilled Revolt Against General Unionism: the Case of the BL Toolroom Committee'. *Industrial Relations Journal*, 12, May, 15–17.

Shaiken, H., S. Herzenberg, and S. Kuhn. 1986. 'The Work Process under More Flexible Production'. *Industrial Relations*, 25, Spring, 167–83.

Shanks, M. 1961. *The Stagnant Society*. Harmondsworth: Penguin.

Sisson, K., and W. Brown. 1983. 'Industrial Relations in the Private Sector: Donovan Re-visited'. In G.S. Bain (ed.), *Industrial Relations in Britain*. Oxford: Blackwell.

Slichter, S.H., J.J. Healy, and E.R. Livernash. 1960. *The Impact of Collective Bargaining on Management*. Washington D.C.: The Brookings Institute.

Soffer, B. 1960. 'A Theory of Trade Union Development: the Role of the "Autonomous" Workman'. *Labor History*, 1, Winter, 141–63.

Stinchcombe, A.L. 1959. 'Bureaucratic and Craft Administration of Production: a Comparative Study'. *Administrative Science Quarterly*, 4, September, 168–87.

Streeck, W. 1986. 'Industrial Relations and Industrial Change in the Motor Industry: An International View'. Text of a Public Lecture at the University of Warwick, Coventry: Industrial Relations Research Unit.

Terry, M. 1977. 'The Inevitable Growth of Informality'. *British Journal of Industrial Relations*, 25, March, 76–90.

____. 1983. 'Shop Steward Development and Managerial Strategies'. In G.S. Bain (ed.), *Industrial Relations in Britain*. Oxford: Blackwell.

____. 1985. 'Combine Committees: Developments of the 1970s'. *British Journal of Industrial Relations*, 23, November, 359–78.

____. 1986. 'How Do We Know if Shop Stewards are Getting Weaker?'. *British Journal of Industrial Relations*, 24, July, 169–80.

____. forthcoming. 'Recontextualizing Shopfloor Industrial Relations: Some Case Study Evidence'. In S. Tailby, and C. Whitston (eds.), *Manufacturing Change*. Oxford: Blackwell.

Thompson, P., and E. Bannon. 1985. *Working the System*. London: Pluto.

Thoms, D.W., and T. Donnelly. 1986. 'Coventry's Industrial Economy, 1880–1980'. In B. Lancaster and T. Mason (eds.), *Life and Labour in a Twentieth Century City: the Experience of Coventry*. Coventry: Cryfield Press.

Tolliday, S. 1983. 'Trade Unions and Shopfloor Organization in the British Motor Industry. 1910–1939'. *Bulletin of the Society for the Study of Labour History*, 46, Spring, 8–9.

____. 1985. 'Government, Employers and Shop Floor Organisation in the British Motor Car Industry, 1939–1969'. In S. Tolliday, and J. Zeitlin (eds.), *Shop Floor Bargaining and the State*. Cambridge: Cambridge University Press.

____. 1986. 'High Tide and After: Coventry's Engineering Workers and Shopfloor Bargaining 1945–80'. In B. Lancaster, and T. Mason (eds.), *Life and Labour in a 20th Century City: the Experience of Coventry*. Coventry: Cryfield Press.

____, and J. Zeitlin. 1982. 'Shop Floor Bargaining, Contract Unionism, and Job Control: An Anglo-American Comparison'. Paper presented to the American Historical Association Convention, Washington D.C., December.

____, and J. Zeitlin (eds.). 1986. *The Automobile Industry and its Workers, Between Fordism and Flexibility*. Oxford: Polity. Blackwell.

TUC. 1960. *Annual Report 1960*. London: TUC.

Turnbull, P.J. 1988. 'The Limits of "Japanisation" – Just-in-Time, Labour Relations and the UK Automotive Industry'. *New Technology, Work and Employment*, 3, Spring, 7–20.

Turner, H.A. 1962. *Trade Union Growth, Structure and Policy*. London: Allen & Unwin.

____. 1968. 'The Royal Commission's Research Papers'. *British Journal of Industrial Relations*, 6, November, 346−359.

____, G. Clack, and G. Roberts. 1967. *Labour Relations in the Motor Industry*. London: Allen & Unwin.

Ulman, L. 1955. *The Rise of the National Trade Union*. Cambridge, Mass.: Harvard University Press.

Wigham, E. 1961. *What's Wrong with the Unions?* Harmondsworth: Penguin.

____. 1973. *The Power to Manage*. London: Macmillan.

Wilkinson, B. 1983. *The Shopfloor Politics of New Technology*. London: Heinemann.

Williams, K., D. Williams, and D. Thomas. 1983. *Why Are the British Bad at Manufacturing?* London: Routledge & Kegan Paul.

Williams, R. 1968. 'Payment by Results Reference, Case Study 6'. Unpublished mimeo, National Board for Prices and Incomes. January.

Willman, P. 1981. 'The Growth of Combined Committees: A Reconsideration'. *British Journal of Industrial Relations*, 19, March, 1−13.

____. 1984. 'The Reform of Collective Bargaining and Strike Activity at BL Cars'. *Industrial Relations Journal*, 15, Summer, 1−12.

____, and G. Winch. 1985. *Innovation and Management Control*. Cambridge: Cambridge University Press.

Zeitlin, J. 1980. 'The Emergence of Shop Steward Organization and Job Control in the British Car Industry: a Review Essay'. *History Workshop Journal*, 10, Autumn, 119−37.

____. 1983. 'Workplace Militancy: a Rejoinder'. *History Workshop Journal*, 16, Autumn, 131−6.

Zweig, F. 1951. *Productivity and Trade Unions*. Oxford: Blackwell.

Index

Adams, R., 207
'agitator theory' of shop stewards, 12, 22
Aldcroft, D.H., 89
Allen, S., 129, 227
Armstrong, P., 217, 229
Armstrong-Siddeley company, 194
Austin car company, 194, 198, 215
   see also British Motor Corporation
Austin, Herbert, 57–8

Bain, G.S., 56
Barou, N., 8
Batstone, E., 48, 136, 178, 183, 232
Bélanger, J., 154, 157, 165, 182, 218
Beynon, H., 145, 146, 192
black workers, 96–7, 133, 221
British Motor Corporation, 200, 202–8
Brooks, D., 97
Brown, W., 181, 182, 213
Burgess, R., 154

Cameron Inquiry, 11
Carbodies company, 194, 199
Clack, G., 152
Clegg, H.A., 118, 207
Cliff, T., 18
closed shop, 33, 63

Cockburn, C., 118
collective bargaining, reform of, 78, 109–11, 153, 156, 167–8, 175–6, 181, 182, 217–18
Collins, H., 9
Commission on Industrial Relations, 16
Communist Party, 11–12, 54, 60, 66, 70, 82, 221
Confederation of Shipbuilding and Engineering Unions, 34, 196, 202
convenor, authority of, 41–6, 51, 92–3, 107, 127, 177–9, 223–4
Coventry Toolroom Agreement, 104
Coventry Workshop, 89
craft unionism,
   general unions and, 20–1, 104–5, 123, 131–4, 144, 221
   job controls and, 20, 122, 125–7, 135–6, 137–9, 158–9
   nature of, 117–19, 145–6
   productivity and, 146–8
custom and practice, 29
Crossley, J.R., 2
Croucher, R., 25–6, 122, 230

Daimler car company, 195
Davies, J., 84
demarcations, 123, 132, 140, 147, 161

Department of Trade and Industry, 114
Derber, M., 13
Donovan Commission, 1–2, 26, 152, 153
Dowty Group, 30
Dubois, P., 173
Dunn, S., 33

Edwardes, M., 54, 80–1
Edwards, P.K. 144, 173, 182, 225
effort bargaining, 164–7
Elbaum, B., 56, 225, 226
Elger, T., 129, 152, 181, 183
Engineering Employers' Federation, 188, 193, 207
engineering industry, 5–6, 56
  comparison with USA, 55, 225, 226
engineering procedure, 49, 67
England, B., 28
England, J., 29
Etheridge, Dick, 59–60, 63–4, 66–7
Evans, S., 154

Flanders, A., 9–10, 11, 152, 181
Floud, R., 89
Ford Motor Company, 191
Fox, A., 3, 117, 213
Friedman, A., 18, 131, 181, 214, 227
Friedman, H., 191
Frow, E. and R., 27, 192
full-time officials, *see* trade union officials

Gallie, D., 144
Gardner, J., 11
Goodman, J., 38
Gospel, H., 181

Harley, Sir Harry, 30, 35
Hart, M., 34
Hinton, J., 54, 221
hiring policy, 191–2, 195
Humber car company, 193
Hyman, R., 28, 49, 129, 152, 181, 183

inter-union rivalry, 32–3, 79
  see also demarcations

Jackson, R.M., 159
Jaguar car company, 198–9
job controls, 17–21

consolidation, 75, 132–3, 135, 167, 170, 217
diffusion, 144, 160–1
origins, 122, 159–60, 213–16
semiskilled workers and, 131–4, 162–71
shop stewards and, 19–20, 75, 135–6, 153, 160, 163–6, 168, 176, 213
see also craft unionism
Jones, Jack, 32, 35, 77, 199, 206, 209, 213, 220

Kahn-Freund, O., 28
Kilpatrick, A., 145

labour market, importance of, 14
labour mobility, 126, 135, 146, 163–4
Lawson, T., 145
Lazonick, W., 56, 225, 226
Lewchuk, W., 208, 214–15, 226, 229
Littler, C., 102, 214
Lupton, T., 18, 118
Lyddon, D., 180, 187

McCarthy, W.E.J., 10, 11, 12, 190
management,
  job controls and, 129–31, 147, 152, 162, 181–2
  reassertion of control, 134, 140, 155–7, 214
  reform of bargaining, 78, 109–11, 153, 156, 167–8, 175–6, 181, 182, 217–18
  strategy control, 130, 140, 147–8, 157, 181, 186–7, 208, 215, 225
  union organization and, 33, 48–9, 57, 63, 68, 90–1, 107, 132, 175–7, 219–22
  wages policy, 187–91
  see also redundancy
Marsh, A.I., 14, 195
Mathewson, S., 118
measured day work, 76–7, 139, 152
Melman, S., 13, 230
Meredeen, S., 191
Midlands, industrial relations and, 1, 15, 35
Millward, N., 232

National Board for Prices and Incomes, 16, 49

piecework bargaining, 43—5, 65, 93,
    101, 124, 125, 137, 159, 164—7,
    168, 170, 227—8
Piore, M., 231
Price, R., 3, 152, 213
product market, importance of, 62, 66,
    71, 73, 76, 88—9, 130, 135,
    155—7, 180, 213
productivity, 18—19, 146—8, 170—1,
    217—18, 220—1, 224—6,
Purcell, J., 182

recruitment, control of, 122, 126, 158
redundancy, 72, 112
    employer control of, 191—2, 196
    shop stewards and, 195—6, 200—2
    strikes over, 192, 193—4, 195—6,
        198, 200—8
    trade union policy on, 128, 197, 200,
        209
Rimmer, M., 95
Roberts, B.C., 10, 11—12
Rolt, L., 50
Rover car company, 194
Roy, D., 118, 154, 165—6

Salaman, G., 214
Schloss, D.F., 102
Scullion, H., 120, 126, 129, 138, 144,
    146
Second World War, legacy of, 5—6,
    9—10, 57, 58—61, 219—21, 228,
    230
Shaiken, H., 231
Shanks, M., 18
shop steward committees, 127, 153, 161,
    175, 176, 182, 200, 203, 207,
    222—3
shop stewards,
    bureaucratization of, 25—30, 39, 46,
        50, 183, 223
    external union of, 28, 46—8, 138—9,
        201
    financing of, 42
    job controls and, 135—6, 153, 160,
        163—6, 168, 176, 213
    organization of, 39—40, 171—7,
        182—3, 207—8, 219—22
    turnover of, 38, 172
    union democracy and, 7, 9—12, 36—9,
        51, 127—8, 173, 177—9, 183, 222

    victimization of, 66—7, 70, 73,
        172—3, 198, 214
    wage bargaining and, 43—6, 96—7,
        190—1
    see also shop steward committees
Sisson, K., 181
skill, skilled workers, 119
    and semiskilled workers, 91—2, 126,
        132, 221
    see also craft unionism
Soffer, B., 119
Standard car company, 187—9, 220—2,
    208—9, 230
Streeck, W., 187, 228
Stynes, Dick, 31—2, 34
supervisors, role of, 64, 72

Terry, M., 49, 232—3
Thompson, P., 20
Tolliday, S., 7, 26, 27
    on Anglo-American comparisons, 225
    on gang system, 208—9
    on Herbert's, 84—5, 100—4
    on job controls, 152, 213
    on productivity, 224
    on reform of bargaining, 181
    on shop stewards, 151, 153, 174, 182,
        216
    on state and industrial relations, 229
    on union organization, 122, 219, 232
trade union officials,
    local, 128—9, 168—70, 201
    national, 202, 204—6
    see also shop stewards, external union
        and
transfer pricing, 138
trust, absence of, 134, 136, 176, 183,
    218, 224—5, 227—9
Turnbull, P., 231
Turner, H.A., 1, 14, 15, 118, 133n,
    145, 152, 230

Ulman, L., 161
union membership, development of,
    32—5, 59, 66, 74
United States of America, 55, 225, 226
Urwin, H., 202

wage differentials, 126, 132—3
wage levels, 141—3, 222
Whittingham, T., 38

Wigham, E., 18, 207
Wilkinson, F., 226
Williams, K., 148, 229
Williams, R., 97, 98–9, 101, 102, 107
Willman, P., 218, 233
Winch, G., 218, 233

women workers, 106, 133, 221
work organization, 124, 157–9, 164, 180

Zeitlin, J., 118, 144, 152, 160, 225
Zweig, F., 18

- Redoendreade et chelmi soy anny
  cotr

- Um strategies unde sense.